P9-DMG-628

KF
4119
.H8

LAW AND EDUCATION: CONTEMPORARY ISSUES AND COURT DECISIONS

By

H. C. HUDGINS, JR.

PROFESSOR OF EDUCATIONAL ADMINISTRATION
TEMPLE UNIVERSITY

and

RICHARD S. VACCA

PROFESSOR OF EDUCATION
VIRGINIA COMMONWEALTH UNIVERSITY

THE MICHIE COMPANY
Law Publishers
CHARLOTTESVILLE, VIRGINIA

Tennessee Tech. Library
Cookeville, Tenn.
293686

COPYRIGHT 1979
BY
THE MICHIE COMPANY
Library of Congress Catalog Card No. 79-63438
ISBN 0-87215-228-6

This book is lovingly dedicated to Hazel Bolmeier and to the memory of her husband, E. C. Bolmeier

CONTENTS

CONTENTS

CONTENTS

INTRODUCTION

Day-to-day decisions made in and for the public schools frequently have their genesis in law; consequently, people in decision-making positions should have some knowledge of basic educational law. Such knowledge is needed, whether it comes from an attorney or an educator who has studied school law. This book is written for that purpose. It is designed to aid professional educators — teachers and administrators — and school board members in their understanding of law as it applies to education. Administrators, teachers, and specialists may find it useful for clarifying the state of law on given topics with which they are confronted; school board members may find it useful for a clarification of their roles and in guiding them in enacting policy.

This book is written also for the purpose of keeping one up-to-date with developments in law. Its emphasis is on current legal issues and court decisions. The authors identify legal principles growing out of recent court decisions as they interface with day-to-day decision-making in education. At the same time, older cases are treated insofar as they have precedential value.

This book identifies, from time to time, a number of guidelines that should aid persons involved in education. The authors believe that knowledge and acceptance of current legal decisions prevent litigation and lead to better administration and boardsmanship. When teachers operate within acceptable legal boundaries, they are demonstrating a respect for law.

This book is written as a general treatise, and it has value for educators in all fifty states. We recognize that, in its narrowest sense, a court decision applies only to a specific jurisdiction but general principles emanating from these decisions are often persuasive in other courts. Similarly, each state has its own school code, but there are commonalities among the fifty states. These are pointed out from time to time and, when general principles are not so evident, examples of differences among states are given.

Educators who teach and study school law fall in two categories: those who have access to a law library and those who do not. In recognizing this, we have attempted to write a text to accommodate both groups. For the former group, coverage is given to over 500 court decisions, and an interested scholar can then read an opinion in its entirety in a law library. For the latter group, we have sufficiently treated court decisions so as to provide an understanding of the state of the law on specific issues.

This book is also designed for individuals who may experience difficulty in understanding complex legal materials. The text is written in non-technical language so as to be understandable. Terms are defined in the text.

We have also added a unique chapter to a school law text: an explanation of basic legal tools and how to use them. This chapter is designed to aid the uninitiated legal scholar in education who experiences difficulty in learning how to undertake legal research.

On a more personal level, this book is a result of our involvement for a number of years in school law. We first became interested in this field while pursuing doctoral study at Duke University with E. C. Bolmeier. It was because of his teaching and influence that our interest mushroomed and each of us concentrated in and wrote dissertations on education law. Since receiving our degrees over a decade ago, we have been actively involved in teaching, publishing, and consulting on the subject.

We acknowledge, with grateful appreciation, the cooperation of our respective institutions which helped make the researching and writing of this manuscript possible. Professor Hudgins completed his manuscript while working under a study leave from Temple University for the spring semester, 1978. While on leave he used the facilities of the nearby Villanova University School of Law, to which he expresses appreciation, and, in particular, to Professor William Valente. Professor Vacca is also indebted to the School of Education, Virginia Commonwealth University, for its cooperation and understanding during the writing of the manuscript. He also thanks his beloved wife, Nancy, and their children, Richard Steven, Lynn Marie, and John Joseph, whose love, faith and encouragement helped bring this book to fruition.

PART I

LAW AND EDUCATION

Chapter 1

SOURCES OF EDUCATION LAW

§ 1.0. The American Legal System.

The American legal system is not a monolithic structure. Born of the United States Constitution and bound by a common set of principles, this nation's legal system is nevertheless very complex and multifaceted. As one observer commented,

> The legal systems of the United States baffle most foreign visitors. And not a few American citizens stand in awe of them. There is such a multiplicity of courts, laws and jurisdictions that even the perceptive observer frequently becomes lost in the legal maze. . . .[1]

Basically, our nation is organized into one federal legal system and fifty separate state legal systems. Each of the latter is unique, in that each one is created by individual state constitutional and legislative enactment. Subsequent sections of this Chapter will discuss the federal and state legal systems in more detail.

---

1. A.A. MORRIS, THE CONSTITUTION AND AMERICAN EDUCATION 46 (St. Paul, Minnesota: West Publishing Company, 1974).

§ 1.1. Sources of Law.

Law may be defined as a body of principles, standards, and rules that govern human behavior by creating obligations as well as rights, and by imposing penalties. Law in our nation is made up of constitutional provisions, legislative enactments, court precedents, lawyer's opinions, and evolving custom.[2]

Our current, complex Anglo-American system of law (its concepts, principles, and procedures) is the result of over eight-hundred years of development.[3] In our present society, elements of law can be found in every aspect of our daily lives. One writer has said that law

> . . . guides our relations with each other. It tells us how we may be punished for our crimes; it makes us pay when, by our fault, we injure others; it says what we must do if we want our promises to be endorsed as contracts; it makes us pay our taxes; it requires us to take out licenses in order to engage in business, to get married, and even to practice such a pastoral pastime as the art of angling.[4]

Suffice it to say, public school systems are not immune from the law; in fact, they are actually creatures of the law. Created by state constitutional and legislative mandate, most of what is done in carrying out the daily affairs of a public school possesses a legal dimension.

§ 1.2. Forms of American Law.

This nation's body of law (federal and state), manifests itself in three forms or types. These forms of law are statutory law, common law, and administrative law.

Statutory law is written law and includes formal acts of a legally constituted body. Examples of statutory law are the federal and state constitutions, acts of the United States Congress, state codes, and city ordinances.

---

2. For a more complete and formal definition of law, *see* BLACK'S LAW DICTIONARY, at 1075.

3. F.G. KEMPLIN, HISTORICAL INTRODUCTION TO ANGLO-AMERICAN LAW IN A NUTSHELL 2 (St. Paul, Minnesota: West Publishing Company, 1973).

4. *Id.*

Common law is unwritten law and emerges from custom (the ways that things are done over a period of time), and from the decrees and judgments of courts of law. Some legal experts refer to common law as "judge-made law." Examples of common law are the body of precedents set by court decisions, the body of opinions rendered by attorneys general (federal and state), and the decisions of various Chief State School Officers (*e.g.,* the State Commissioners of New Jersey and New York).

Administrative law is comprised of the formal regulations and decisions of various governmental agencies. For example, the regulations and decisions of the Interstate Commerce Commission, the Federal Communications Commission, and the Federal Securities and Exchange Commission.

With the exception of the State of Louisiana (where the historical development of that State's legal system stemmed from the French legal system of the European Continent), our nation's legal system is a common law system (growing out of the legal system of England).

As a legal system dependent upon decided (precedent) cases, it is imperative that students of the law seek out and examine the opinions of courts of record interpreting the written law. Generally, constitutional provisions, federal or state statutes, and city ordinances lack practical meaning and remain legal abstractions until they are interpreted by a court of law, and are made to apply in a given situation. To put it another way, even though statutes control all situations legally contested, the interpretations of statutes by judges in courts of law are what give meaning and force to written legislative pronouncements.[5]

§ 1.3. The Adjudication Process and Conflict Resolution.

At the very core of the American legal system is the principle that for every *wrong* (violation of a right), done to an individual by government or by any other individual, there should be a *remedy* (some form of compensation or relief), provided. A citizen must be protected from injustice and must also have some place to go (when all else fails), to seek justice. In our social structure the courts of this nation exist for such purposes.

---

5. *Id.,* at 12-16.

In our system of justice there are acts or failures to act enumerated in statutes (federal and state). These violations of statutory law are known technically as *crimes,* the commission of which will result in government prosecution and in government-imposed punishments. In *criminal* courts, the government (federal or state) is always the plaintiff. On the other hand, our system of justice also includes a mechanism for allowing one person to seek remedy when wronged by another individual. The *civil* courts exist for this purpose, and do not involve matters of government-imposed sanctions.

In our country there are several formal, rational means available to citizens to settle disputes. For example, *arbitration* (the settlement of a dispute through the intercession of an impartial third party) has brought many disputes to a final determination, as has the process of *mediation.* In recent years, however, individuals and groups of citizens have increasingly resorted to *adjudication* for settling disputes. Complaining parties have taken their conflicts to courts of law for the application of pre-existing rules and precedents to their conflict in search of a just settlement.

Bound by strict rules of procedure, courts do not solicit their business, petitioners must seek their help. As such, courts of law

> ... do not act on their own initiative. They assume jurisdiction only of controversies and other legal matters referred to them for decision. Once a controversy is before the courts, they are relatively free to effectuate complete justice as they deem it to be.[6]

Individuals seeking redress of their grievances must make certain that their matter is taken to the appropriate court. A formal petition must be filed, and the matter must be accepted for adjudication (a decision that is the court's alone to make).

Generally, school controversies do not result in petitions for redress filed in a court of law. Mechanisms to resolve conflicts exist at all administrative levels within state education systems. Generally, grievance and appeals channels are available to professional employees, parents, and students. What is more, state statutes often provide vehicles of grievance and appeal from the

---

6. E.E. REUTTER, JR., AND R.R. HAMILTON, THE LAW OF PUBLIC EDUCATION 10 (2d ed. Mineola, New York: The Foundation Press, 1976).

lowest administrative level within a school building up through the highest level in the educational system (*e.g.,* the state board of education and chief state school officer). There are occasions, however, when someone alleges that the actions of a school board, an administrator, or a teacher are in some way a violation of constitutional or statutory law and that such actions go beyond the channels available. Such matters more often than not culminate in adjudication.

§ 1.4. Federal Government and Public Education.

Historically, the absence of specific language in the United States Constitution regarding education and schools, coupled with the application of the Tenth Amendment, placed the direct responsibility for establishing and maintaining public school systems in the hands of state governments. Each state assumed complete control of education within its boundaries. Thus, in this country today, there is no single, national public school system; rather, public education exists in fifty, different, state public school systems. To fully understand the legal aspects of public education the researcher must study the school codes and related court decisions from each state.

In the past and up to the present, however, the federal government has exercised growing influence in educational matters, primarily through congressional enactment, agency regulations and guidelines, and federal court decree.

All three branches of the federal government exercise significant influence on the day-to-day operation of public school systems. Matters of finance, curriculum, personnel, and student control have each felt the influence of Congress, the President, and federal judges.

a. *Congress and the Schools.* Article I, section 1, of the United States Constitution provides: "All legislative powers herein granted shall be vested in a Congress of the United States. . . ." [7] Over the years, Congress has passed numerous laws having direct impact on public education. From the early years of this nation the national government has taken steps to ensure an important place

---

7. UNITED STATES CONSTITUTION, Art. I. § 1, ratified 1789.

for education in our society, and to stimulate the growth of education in the states. For example, as early as 1787, Congress (in establishing the Northwest Territory) expressed the following belief:

> Religion, morality, and knowledge being necessary to good government and the happiness of mankind, schools and the means of education shall be forever encouraged.[8]

Article I, section 8 of the United States Constitution, grants Congress the power to tax and to "provide for the common defense and general welfare of the United States." This constitutional provision has served as a legal foundation for the passage of specific education laws, each of which has funneled billions of federal tax dollars into school programs within the states. Federal laws have provided extensive programs in such areas as adult education, vocational and technical education, multicultural education, special education, science education, foreign language education, and others. Congressional actions have even made it possible to reimburse public school systems for providing their children with milk, with breakfasts, and with lunches served at school.

A recent act of Congress having direct impact on the day-to-day operation of public schools is Public Law 94-142 (P.L. 94-142), The Education for All Handicapped Children Act. Referred to as a "Bill of Rights for the Handicapped Children," P.L. 94-142 (a revision to Part B, Education for All Handicapped Act), was enacted in November, 1976.

Public Law 94-142 mandates that states provide a free public education for all handicapped children between the ages of three years and eighteen years. Penalty for failure to comply with this mandate is loss of all current federal funding, and disqualification from eligibility to receive future federal funding.

Among other things, P.L. 94-142 requires that an individualized educational program (IEP) be written for each handicapped child. Moreover, that all handicapped children be placed in classes with nonhandicapped children to the "maximum extent" possible.[9]

---

8. N. Edwards and H.G. Richey, The School in the American Social Order 216 (Boston, Massachusetts: Houghton Mifflin Company, 1963).

9. For a detailed summary of the provisions of P.L. 94-142, see L.V. Goodman, "A Bill of Rights for the Handicapped." American Education (July, 1976).

The above law, coupled with section 504 of the Rehabilitation Act of 1973,[10] will undoubtedly cause public school systems and public higher educational institutions to take immediate action to remove all forms of exclusion and discrimination involving handicapped students.

b. *The Executive Branch and Schools.* Of the three branches of our national government (legislative, executive, and judicial) it is difficult to see, at first glance, just where and how the President of the United States has an effect on public education.[11] Unlike Congress and the federal courts, the President's involvements in public school matters tend to be more indirect; yet, several responsibilities of our nation's Chief Executive do impact directly on school matters.

The President, through public pronouncements, messages to Congress, and interagency communications voices his opinions and beliefs on education and school-related matters. Generally, these oral and written remarks help set a level of "national priority" for education.

Another point of impact on education is found in the President's *veto* power. Federal programs and ultimate funding (after passing Congress), must have the President's signature in order to be implemented.

The power of appointment also represents a significant source of executive involvement in matters of education and schools, especially as it concerns appointments of certain cabinet officers and the appointment of federal judges. The two most significant cabinet positions affecting schools are the Secretary of Health, Education, and Welfare (HEW), and the Attorney General (United States Department of Justice).

HEW is responsible for administering most federal education projects. Guidelines written by HEW staff members for the implementation and administration of federal funds and federal projects are published in the *Federal Register.* These published guidelines set forth procedures for school officials to follow

---

10. P.L. 93-112, 29 U.S.C. 794. This law mandates that "... no otherwise handicapped individual ... shall, solely by reason of his handicap, be excluded from participation, be denied the benefits of, or be subjected to discrimination under any program or activity receiving federal financial assistance."

11. UNITED STATES CONSTITUTION, Art. II, ratified 1789.

7

regarding the application for, the receipt of, and the expenditure of federal funding through a particular federal law.

The Department of Justice (the Attorney General's responsibility) often gets involved in public school matters when claims of discrimination and other injustices are brought by parties against public school systems and institutions of higher education. In recent years the Department of Justice and its attorneys have investigated several such complaints from citizens in all sections of the country.

The U.S. Office of Education and the newly organized National Institute of Education are also vitally important federal governmental agencies. The U.S. Commissioner of Education, who administers the U.S. Office of Education, and the Director of the National Institute of Education are both appointed by the President.

Established by Public Law 92-318 (1972), as a component of HEW, the National Institute of Education (NIE) was originally charged with the responsibility to focus federal research efforts on the study and alleviation of educational problems confronting public school systems. In recent years Congress has added several specific responsibilities for the NIE. For example, the improvement of student achievement and basic skills, the resolution of educational finance problems facing states, the improvement of school programs for non-English speaking students, and the dissemination of educational research findings to school systems and other educational institutions.

Federal judges are appointed by the President. As will be shown in subsection c. below, and in subsequent sections of this book, much of what is done and can't be done in American public schools (and to a more limited degree in private schools), in matters of finance, governance, curriculum, personnel, parent involvement, and student control is a direct result of federal court decree.

c. *The Federal Courts and Schools.* Article III, section 1, of the United States Constitution provides that "[t]he judicial power of the United States shall be vested in one Supreme Court, and in such inferior courts as the Congress may from time to time ordain and establish." [12] These courts have authority to adjudicate all cases

---

12. UNITED STATES CONSTITUTION, Art. III, § 1, ratified 1789.

in law and equity arising out of the Constitution, Acts of Congress, and United States treaties and, among other things, to decide controversies to which the United States shall be a party, or which are between one State and citizens of another State.[13]

The United States Supreme Court, in addition to having original jurisdiction in certain matters, has jurisdiction to review: "(1) all cases in lower federal courts, and (2) all cases in state courts in which there is involved a question of the meaning or effect of a federal statute or a constitutional provision. . . ." [14]

While state courts have *general jurisdiction* (the presumption is that they have authority to hear all cases that involve the state's constitution and state law, unless a showing is made to the contrary), federal courts have *limited* jurisdiction. The presumption is that the federal court lacks jurisdiction unless a plaintiff can show the court that the problem presented for judicial review involves a federal question (the United States Constitution or federal law.)[15]

The federal court system is structured into three levels. The United States Supreme Court is at the highest level. The *eleven* United States Courts of Appeals are intermediate courts of appeal and function at the next level down from the Supreme Court. The third level, below the Courts of Appeals, houses the ninety-four United States District Courts, the trial courts of the federal structure. Additionally, there are some specialized courts to hear such matters as customs, patents, and taxes. The chart below outlines the current federal court structure.

---

13. *Id.,* § 2.

14. E.C. BOLMEIER, SCHOOL IN THE LEGAL STRUCTURE 55, 56 (2d ed. Cincinnati, Ohio 1973).

15. C.A. WRIGHT, LAW OF FEDERAL COURTS 15 (2d ed. St. Paul, Minnesota: West Publishing Company, 1970).

Chart 1 [16]

THE UNITED STATES COURT SYSTEM

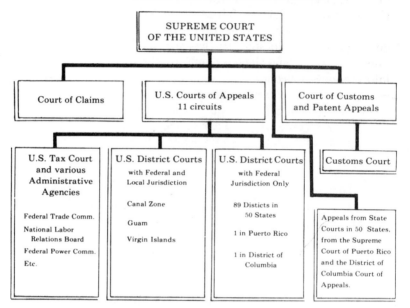

As shown above, the federal court structure contains ninety-four United States District Courts (federal trial courts). Each State has at least one such court, with large states like California, New York, and Texas having as many as four.[17]

Each possessing a life-time Presidential appointment, there are more than three-hundred United States District Court judges, with each district having from one to twenty-seven judges.[18] Generally, *one* judge sits (presides) in a United States District Court. However, special situations often warrant that a panel of district court judges sit to hear a case. A trial may be by jury or by the judge (or judges) hearing the case.

---

16. This chart is taken directly from *The United States Courts,* Report of the Committee on the Judiciary, House of Representatives (Washington, D.C., 1975), at 3.

17. *Id.,* at 7.

18. *Id.*

One receiving an adverse decision in a United States District Court has an automatic right to appeal to the Federal Circuit Court of Appeals, for the circuit wherein that trial court is located.[19] The United States is divided up into eleven *circuits* for the purpose of hearing these appeals. More often than not a public school case does not go beyond this intermediate level to the United States Supreme Court. The chart below shows the division of the nation into the eleven circuits.

19. *Id.,* at 5.

Chart 2[20]

Mainly possessing appellate jurisdiction, the United States Courts of Appeals for the Circuits also have jurisdiction to review orders issued by federal administrative agencies.

Federal Circuit Court judges are appointed by the President (with advice and consent of the Senate), and serve life-time terms. The number of judges on each circuit court varies from *three* (in the First Circuit) to *fifteen* (in the Fifth Circuit). The chart below shows the names of the circuit courts of appeals, their geographical jurisdictions, and the number of authorized judgeships in each circuit court.

---

20. *Id.,* at 6.

Chart 3[21]

FEDERAL CIRCUIT COURTS OF APPEALS

Courts of Appeals	Number of authorized judgeships	Location and postal address
District of Columbia Circuit (District of Columbia)	9	Washington, D.C. 20001.
1st Circuit (Maine, Massachusetts, New Hampshire, Rhode Island, and Puerto Rico)	3	Boston, Mass. 02109.
2d Circuit (Connecticut, New York, and Vermont)	9	New York, N.Y. 10007.
3d Circuit (Delaware, New Jersey, Pennsylvania, and the Virgin Islands)	9	Philadelphia, Pa. 19107.
4th Circuit (Maryland, North Carolina, South Carolina, Virginia, and West Virginia)	7	Richmond, Va. 23219.
5th Circuit (Alabama, Florida, Georgia, Louisiana, Mississippi, Texas and the Canal Zone) .	15	New Orleans, La. 70130.
6th Circuit (Kentucky, Michigan, Ohio, and Tennessee)	9	Cincinnati, Ohio 45202.
7th Circuit (Illinois, Indiana, and Wisconsin)	8	Chicago, Ill. 60604.
8th Circuit (Arkansas, Iowa, Minnesota, Missouri, Nebraska, North Dakota, and South Dakota)	8	St. Louis, Mo. 63101.
9th Circuit (Alaska, Arizona, California, Hawaii, Idaho, Montana, Nevada, Oregon, Washington and Guam)	13	San Francisco, Calif. 94101.
10th Circuit (Colorado, Kansas, New Mexico, Oklahoma, Utah, and Wyoming)	7	Denver, Colo. 80202.

---

21. *Id.*, at 5.

Of the few school-related conflicts heard by federal courts, only a small percentage ever reach the Supreme Court. When school cases are heard, however, certain provisions of the United States Constitution are involved more than others and might be regarded as foundations for seeking relief in federal court. These provisions are the First, Fourth, Sixth, Eighth, and Eleventh Amendments, with the primary vehicle for taking school cases into federal court being the provisions of the Fourteenth Amendment; both the Due Process Clause and the Equal Protection Clause.

In the recent past, the number of education-related issues going beyond the eleven circuits to be finally decided by the Supreme Court has increased. In most of these cases petitioners claimed that a state's legislation or the policies of a local school board have in some way violated their constitutional rights or some provisions of federal statutory law (for example, recent cases involving the application of 42 U.S.C., section 1983, a provision of the Civil Rights Act of 1871).

Even though the Supreme Court maintains a reluctant attitude toward hearing school cases, it has nevertheless rendered several decisions altering the daily operation of public school systems across the country. Such issues as school integration, student rights, religion in schools, school finance, and teachers' rights offer excellent examples of this phenomenon and are discussed in subsequent sections of this book.

§ 1.5. State Government and Public Education.

The silence of the federal Constitution, coupled with the language of the Tenth Amendment ("... powers not delegated to the United States by the Constitution, nor prohibited by it to the States, are reserved to the States respectively, or to the people"), bestowed upon state government the legal responsibility for the establishment of public school systems. Thus, as the nation grew, and our population increased, individual states assumed complete authority to provide public education for their children, only restricted in action by the provisions of the United States Constitution and by subsequent acts of that state's legislature.[22]

a. *State Legislatures and Schools.* Generally, the constitution of each state contains a mandate for the establishment of public

---

22. REUTTER AND HAMILTON, *supra.,* at 73.

education.[23] Typically, this constitutional mandate places the legal authority to establish and to maintain a public school system directly in the hands of the state legislature. The following provision from the Constitution of the Commonwealth of Virginia offers an excellent example of such a mandate:

> The General Assembly shall provide for a system of free public elementary and secondary schools for all children of school age throughout the Commonwealth, and shall seek to ensure that an educational program of high quality is established and continually maintained.[24]

Not every state constitution includes such a detailed mandate as does Virginia's. For example, the Pennsylvania Constitution states very simply that:

> The General Assembly shall provide for maintenance and support of a thorough and efficient system of public schools to serve the needs of the Commonwealth.[25]

Despite the fact that legislatures generally have constitutional authority to construct a state's system of education through statutory enactment, their authority is not without legal boundaries. Historically, federal courts, through their application of Fourteenth Amendment guarantees and through their interpretations of federal statutes have conditioned the exercise of state authority over educational matters. As early as 1923, in deciding the first case to reach it in which state authority over public school curriculum was involved, the United States Supreme Court suggested: ... "That the State may do much, go very far, indeed, in order to improve the quality of its citizens, physically, mentally, and morally, is clear; but the individual has certain fundamental rights." [26] Two years later, the high court went one step further in an Oregon case and made it clear that children are not mere "creatures of the State." [27]

Down through the years federal courts have consistently limited

---

23. BOLMEIER, *supra.*, at 88-99.

24. CONSTITUTION OF VIRGINIA, Art. VIII, § 1, effective July 1, 1971.

25. CONSTITUTION OF THE COMMONWEALTH OF PENNSYLVANIA, Art. III, § 14, enacted.

26. Meyer v. Nebraska, 262 U.S. 390, 43 S. Ct. 625, 67 L. Ed. 1042 (1923).

27. Pierce v. Society of Sisters, 268 U.S. 510, 45 S. Ct. 510, 69 L. Ed. 1070 (1925).

state authority over education as cases were decided challenging several aspects of public school operation. Decisions on such state matters as compulsory attendance, compulsory flag salutes, prayer and Bible reading in schools, teachers' rights, and others all placed state authority over public school matters under a federal constitutional overlay.

Over the past twenty years a child's chance to become involved in public education provided by a state has (primarily through court action) become a matter of legal *entitlement.* This judicial trend began with the United States Supreme Court's benchmark decision in *Brown v. Board of Education.*[28] In that decision the high court established the notion that "[t]oday, education is perhaps the most important function of state and local governments. . . . Such an opportunity, where the State has undertaken to provide it, is a right which must be made available to all on equal terms." The judicial mold was thus set for a series of landmark decisions to follow. Through such cases as *Tinker v. Des Moines,*[29] *P.A.R.C. v. Commonwealth of Pennsylvania,*[30] *Mills v. Board of Education,*[31] *Goss v. Lopez,*[32] and others the legal *entitlement* of children to be included in public schools became a reality.

State courts themselves have rendered decisions limiting the educational authority of legislatures. As early as 1926, for example, the State Supreme Court of Appeals for Virginia said, in *Flory v. Smith,* that

> The legislature . . . has the power to enact any legislation in regard to the conduct, control, and regulation of the public free schools, which does not deny to the citizen the constitutional right to enjoy life and liberty, to pursue happiness and to acquire property.[33]

Contemporary state courts have continued to check and balance the educational authority of state legislatures.

Since State legislators themselves can't possibly assume actual

---

28. 347 U.S. 483, 74 S. Ct. 686, 98 L. Ed. 873 (1954).

29. 393 U.S. 503, 89 S. Ct. 733, 21 L. Ed. 2d 731 (1969).

30. 334 F. Supp. 1257 (E.D. Pa. 1971), final consent agreement at 343 F. Supp. 279 (E.D. Pa. 1972).

31. 348 F. Supp. 866 (D.C. D.C. 1972).

32. 419 U.S. 565, 95 S. Ct. 729, 42 L. Ed. 2d 725 (1975).

33. 145 Va. 164, 134 S.E.2d 360 (1926).

supervisory responsibility for public schools, the general supervision and administrative control over a state's public school system is generally placed in the hands of a state board of education. As Bolmeier pointed out:

> Although the legislature is usually charged with the responsibility of organizing, providing for, and administering a state system of education, it is obvious that the legislature cannot perform these functions directly by itself ... accordingly most state legislatures have delegated a good share of the responsibility of policy making, as well as other school matters, to state boards of education.[34]

Thus, whether they be called State Regents or State Boards, these high level policy-makers exercise considerable regulatory authority over all public school matters in a state.

To completely understand the legal nature of a state school board of education, one must examine the specific constitutional and statutory provisions of each state. Subsequent chapters of this book will delve more deeply into issues related to state board action in matters of public education.

b. *The Governor and Schools.* Much like the President of the United States, each state's governor has more of an *indirect* impact on education and schools. Limited in authority by state constitutional and statutory law, governors nevertheless have a substantial impact on public education and schools within their state's boundaries.

Governors, as their state's chief executive, through official messages to the legislature and through other public pronouncements, help chart the state's course for education. In the past, some governors gained a reputation as "education governors" because of the high priority they placed on education during their terms of office. In recent history several states have experienced significant growth and development in post-secondary education through the efforts of a particular governor. Whole, statewide community college systems have developed, in states where no community college system existed, because of a governor's efforts.

In some states the governor appoints all state-level education officials. For example, in Virginia all high level state education

---

34. BOLMEIER, *supra.*, at 115.

17

officials are appointed by the governor, with approval of the General Assembly. Members of the State Board of Education, the State Superintendent of Public Instruction, the State Secretary of Education (in the Governor's cabinet), the State Community College Board, the State Council of Higher Education, the Boards of Visitors over each four-year state college and university, and several other high officials are appointed by the Governor of Virginia.

A state governor, as chief executive, also exercises the power of *veto* over all legislation. North Carolina is the only state whose Governor does not have veto power. Thus, statewide programs and program funding for education and schools in most states are effected by a stroke of the governor's pen.

Some state statutes grant to a governor the authority to appoint local and state level judges to courts. Suffice it to say, the kind and caliber of judicial appointee may have an effect on the conduct of the schools and the quality of education produced as school cases are adjudicated in state court.

c. *The State Judiciary and Schools.* As emphasized in previous sections of this chapter, public education is an entity of state law. Thus, what a particular state's courts say about education and schools is most important. One cannot possibly understand the legalities of public education by simply reading a state's education code, or by studying the regulations of a state board of education. State court decisions must be analyzed and interpreted if meaning and understanding are to be found.

Given that similarities exist among the fifty state judicial systems, each state does, however, have its own unique court structure. The more populous states (*e.g.,* California, New York, and Texas), tend to have complicated court structures with several levels of trial court, intermediate court, and appellate courts while the less crowded states tend to have very simple court structures (*e.g.,* Virginia). Additionally, the names for courts with similar jurisdictions often change from state to state. The researcher must, therefore, examine the court structure of particular states to understand the route taken by a school-related issue in litigation. Examples of different state court systems follow.

In Maryland, the state's highest court is called the Court of Appeals. An intermediate court of appeals, called the Court of

Special Appeals, sits between the Court of Appeals and the Circuit Courts of the various counties (having original jurisdiction over all civil and criminal cases). The Maryland court structure also contains District Courts, People's Courts (in some counties and cities), Orphan's Courts, and there is a Superior Court and a Court of Common Pleas for the City of Baltimore.

The highest court in the State of Illinois is the Supreme Court of Illinois. There are District Appellate Courts (intermediate appellate courts), and Circuit Courts (possessing original jurisdiction) that exist in the various counties and cities of the State. Cook County has a Superior Court functioning as its Circuit Court.

The Supreme Court of Pennsylvania is that Commonwealth's highest court. The Superior Court of Pennsylvania is an intermediate-level appellate court and beneath it is a new, statewide court (Commonwealth Court) with original and appellate jurisdiction in criminal and civil cases. The lower-level courts are called Courts of Common Pleas, while the City of Philadelphia has Municipal and Traffic Courts.

Generally, State courts assume the same attitude of "non-intervention in school matters" as is evident among the federal judiciary. School matters heard by state courts are usually settled at the trial court level, with the state courts of appeals (intermediate or supreme court level) functioning as the courts of last resort.

d. *State Attorneys General and Schools.* The state attorney general may also become involved in public school matters. The school law student may neglect searching the opinions of state attorneys general for material concerning the legal aspects of public school operation; yet, such opinions are vitally important sources to explore when looking for the interpretations of state statutes.

Typically, a state's attorney general will issue an official opinion only to another state or local official (for example, a local school board chairman can request an opinion, but not a local school principal). The request for an attorney general's opinion must be made on the official stationery of the individual or the governmental organization requesting the opinion, and the request must state a specific legal question to be answered. After

19

researching the question by drawing upon statutory law, case law precedents (state and federal), and state board policy, the attorney general will send his official answer back, on letterhead paper, to the individual who requested it. The opinion-letter will bear the signature of the attorney general.

Not all experts in school law agree to the importance of formal opinions from state attorneys general. Basically, there are two schools of thought regarding their impact on legal matters. One school of thought sees the opinion of an attorney general as having the same weight of importance as a court decision. A second group sees the opinion of an attorney general as no more important than is the opinion of any other attorney. These latter individuals will most probably challenge the attorney general if and when an opinion, adverse to their cause, is written and published.

Whatever their true importance, opinions of a state's attorney general do, from time-to-time, interpret state education law, school board policy, and the pronouncements and actions of school administrators and teachers. Thus, these official pronouncements of the state's chief legal counsel represent another vital area to explore when searching for sources of school law.

§ 1.6. Summary.

Public education is a function of federal, state and local government. Public school systems are creations of state law. Thus, students of educational law must constantly strive to gain a more thorough understanding of the American legal system and the position of public education and schools in that complex setting.

Additionally, a need has grown in recent years for professionals in public schools to become more knowledgeable about the interplay of courts with the day-to-day operation of schools and school systems. Once thought to be the sole concern of school board attorneys, school board members, and school administrators, education-related legal problems have, in recent years, become problems of supervisors, counselors, and teachers, as well.

To comprehend the impact and ramifications of emerging court decrees and legislative enactments effecting public education, the student of school law must study the complex legal nature of public school problems. The remaining chapters of this book are planned to help the reader accomplish that objective.

Chapter 2

TOOLS OF LEGAL RESEARCH

§ 2.0. Law Libraries.

Increasingly, educators are involved in problems that have their resolution in law. For example, a teacher debates whether law and academic freedom clash in teaching a controversial short story in literature class. A principal studies whether law applies equally in searching a student's locker for stolen library books and narcotics. A superintendent reviews "due process" procedures when he rates a teacher as being unsatisfactory and subject to dismissal. A school board member reminds himself that he may now be sued for damages under a statute over 100 years old if he violates a constitutional right of one employed in the school district.

Not only have educators become more aware of law, but law itself has become more complex. Problems that were previously resolved easily and without a challenge from the affected party may well now get to court. This is particularly true when decisions are made without an understanding and application of what current law is.

Why should one study law? The superintendent who, ten years

ago, only occasionally called on his board attorney for advice, may today hold daily discussions with him. Today's educator is also dealing with an electorate better informed than ever. The public at large is more likely to challenge an educator's decision. Further, courts have increasingly entertained legal suits, and, as a result of judges' decisions, people have been encouraged to challenge school authority in court. If one is familiar with law, not only is he more likely to behave legally, he is also better prepared for preventing problems.

How does one become familiar with law? That is the basic question of this chapter. One becomes familiar with law by studying it — by mastering basic legal principles from which specific issues are more readily resolved. In order to achieve this purpose, one must first become familiar with techniques and tools of legal research. This study should be done systematically rather than haphazardly.

An educator who has become familiar with a general education library, and made frequent use of it, soon finds himself comfortable in being able to locate and isolate materials appropriate for a research topic. That same educator, in being introduced to a law library, may initially find the experience to be confusing. Legal materials are assimilated and organized differently from educational materials. In law, constitutions, statutes, and court decisions comprise much of basic research, and the way these materials are organized, so that one can get at them, means that the neophyte researcher must learn a new research system. Although learning to do legal research may appear at first to be overwhelming, one learns by familiarizing himself step by step while spending a number of sessions in a law library.

Legal research of statutes may be undertaken by one of three methods. They include the descriptive word method or relying on terms in an index to point out a statute covering the topic; a second method, called the topic method, refers to the topics listed in the contents section. The third method is use of the popular name of the statute which will then give information about the act's official name.

Legal research in other reference works which lead to court decisions may also begin in one of three ways, two of which correspond to research of statutes. They are the descriptive word method and the topic method. The third way to undertake a study of court decisions is through the table of cases method. If one has a case citation, he can proceed to locate it in the law library. Each of the above methods will be treated more fully in subsequent sections.

This chapter introduces the reader to materials that are basic to law libraries and useful to one researching in education law. By necessity, the legal tools identified here are selective rather than exhaustive; there are others that a more advanced legal scholar will become familiar with. Those that are identified in this chapter will, however, provide the reader with a comprehensive, basic knowledge of legal tools.

§ 2.1. Statutes.

a. *In General.* A statute refers to a legislative law; it is derived from the action of a legislature. It may refer to a state or a federal law. The law of a local legislative body is referred to as an ordinance. In engaging in legal research, one should examine first the statutes that may govern the legal issue before proceeding to other sources, including case law or the decisions of judges. Either a state or a federal statute, or both, may bear on the topic.

The official designation of federal laws is *Statutes at Large.* After a term of Congress or a state legislature is concluded, the laws are then published in bound form. They become a chronological arrangement of laws on the various subjects with which a legislative body has dealt.

The terms "codes," "compilations" and "revisions" are used interchangeably. They designate topical breakdowns of legislative acts, as, for example, the laws treating education are organized into a school code. Codes are organized further by specific subject.

A code may or may not reflect the elimination of laws that have been superseded or become obsolete. Since organizing and publishing a code is often by a commercial body not otherwise authorized by the legislature, it is viewed as not having official sanction. Nonetheless, the use of it is authoritative in legal research.

Many codes are published in annotated editions. Accompanying each section of law is a statement of the legislative history as well

23

as citations to court decisions treating that section. These annotations are a very valuable service to legal researchers.

One may locate a statute by using one of three methods: the descriptive word method, the topic method, and the popular name method.

The Descriptive Word Method. This method involves using the index of a code similarly to the way one would use an index to a textbook. In classifying sections of the code, editors select significant words or phrases that identify the subject of the specific law. These words and phrases are then arranged alphabetically. In the index to codes, one may find not only the appropriate word or phrase, but also the section number of the law from which it was derived, and the title or chapter of the law. From that information, one can then proceed directly to the appropriate statute.

The Topic Method. This method involves use of the classified subject or title arrangement of the code similar to the way one would use the contents page of a textbook. For the novice researcher, this method may be more difficult than the descriptive word method, for it presumes familiarity with the organization and topics of the code. A more experienced researcher may go directly to the title or chapter of a code and study the outline of topics. He would then identify his specific subject by the appropriate section of the code and proceed to locate it in the text.

The Popular Name Method. If a researcher knows a statute only by its popular name, he may find its official name and citation. Federal statutes may be identified in one of several sources, among them the following: *United States Code Annotated, United States Supreme Court Digest,* and *Federal Code Annotated Popular Name Table for Acts of Congress.* Popular names for state statutes may be located through *Shepard's Citations* for the states or through the State Codes and their Popular Names of State Acts.

b. *Federal.* Supreme over any federal statute, state constitution, or state law is the Constitution of the United States. Not only is the text of the Constitution significant in legal research, but also of particular importance is its construction as determined by court decisions. The Constitution, as construed by court decisions, is available in several sources, among them the following: *United States Code Annotated, Federal Code Annotated, United States*

Supreme Court Reports Digest, and *United States Supreme Court Digest.*

Prior to their publication in bound volumes, Congressional laws are referred to as "slip laws." As each law is enacted, it is printed on a separate piece of paper (a slip of paper, hence the name). Later, the "slip laws" are cited according to the number of the Congress enacting them and the order of enactment. For example, Public Law 94-142 was enacted by the 94th Congress, and it was the 142nd law passed by that Congress and signed by the President. One may cite a slip law by its number until the bound volumes appear, at which point one then cites from the Statutes at Large.

Statutes at Large is the designation of the permanent form of federal statutes. Its 74 titles are the official source for laws of Congress. They are now published after each session of Congress. The volumes are numbered consecutively as they are published from session to session. Each volume contains a numerical and chronological list of the laws contained within it as well as a subject index.

A different publication from the Statutes at Large is the United States Code (U.S.C.). This work grew out of a perceived need of Congress to accumulate and bring up-to-date the permanent laws of Congress. It was felt that instead of having to go through each session of the Statutes at Large to find appropriate statutes on a topic, one should be able to go to a source in which the statutes were organized cumulatively around subjects. For this monumental work, Congress sought the assistance of a commercial publisher who initially classified the subject matter into 50 general subjects called "Titles," number 20 being Education. The titles, in turn, were divided into sections. There were gaps in the numbering of sections to provide for future expansion.

The editors made some minor modifications in the wording of the statutes without attempting to change the meaning or intent of them.

The task of compiling the federal statutes was first begun in 1925, and editions have appeared since then at approximate six-year intervals. After each session of Congress, a cumulative supplement is issued. Each code has an index as does each supplement. In addition, there are a number of tables, including a parallel reference table to the United States Statutes at Large, acts which have been repealed, and a table of statutes by popular name.

The *United States Code Annotated* is organized like the *United States Code* with one valuable added feature. It contains annotations of various court decisions which have construed sections of the Code, historical notes, cross references, and other editorial aids. It is kept current by both temporary and annual cumulative supplements. A subject index of several volumes, individual title indexes, and a table of acts by popular names are also features.

A competing work of the *United States Code Annotated* is the *Federal Code Annotated.* It is organized similarly to the U.S.C.A. and provides the same kind of information.

Two loose leaf services may aid the researcher with statutory research. *United States Law Week,* treated elsewhere in this chapter, publishes the text of significant federal legislation. *Commerce Clearing House, Congressional Index,* gives current references to pending and new legislation. It is a useful guide to the status of pending legislation as well as that already enacted.

c. *State.* Just as the federal Constitution is supreme over any federal law, so is the constitution of a given state supreme over any of its laws. When researching a topic peculiar to any state, it is necessary to examine the state's constitution to determine if it has a provision applicable to that law. It may or may not have a provision on a given topic, but since some state constitutions contain very specific provisions one should check its content. Next, one should also examine the state statutes applicable to that topic.

Although laws of states differ considerably, the classification of those laws is similar. Thus, if one is able to research statutory law in one state, he should also be able to do it in another.

Like federal laws, the laws of a state legislature are synonymously known as "codes," "compilations," or "revisions." Their subdivisions are called either "titles," "chapters," or "subdivisions." Pennsylvania's school code is organized by titles, number 24 being Education. These titles are further divided into 15 chapters and then into sections. For example, under Title 24, section 15-1512 refers to "Courses of study adapted to age, etc., of pupils." The codes are broken down by subject matter, contain annotations about their legislative history, and have court decisions construing the law. Annual pocket-part supplements keep the codes current.

If one wished to research the laws of the fifty states on a given topic, he might try one of two sources. The Law Digest volume of the *Martindale-Hubbell Law Directory,* published annually, contains a brief digest of the laws of the fifty states. Its classification plan allows for all laws on a given topic to be organized around the same general topic. After building a bibliography of case law, one must then go to the statutes of the various states that have a law on that subject.

A similar publication is *The Lawyers Directory,* also published annually, that is arranged like the *Martindale-Hubbell Law Directory.*

Shepard's Citations covers statutes for every state. The citator indicates whether a given statute has been amended or repealed, and it gives references to state and federal court decisions which cited that statute. In order to use *Shepard's* for legislative research, one must know the title and section number of a given statute. (See discussion of *Shepard's,* § **2.6**).

§ 2.2. Legal Digests.

a. *In General.* Digests are indexes to case law, the law growing out of court decisions. They provide the researcher with a system for identifying case law on a given problem. These works contain, in a systematic fashion, a concise summary of the facts and the court decision in a case. They identify the point or points of law in which a case is classified and give the case citation. One uses the digests to build a bibliography of court citations from which he can proceed directly to a study of the cases themselves.

Digests serve a variety of courts. They may appear for courts for a single state, a group of states, a single court, or court systems. The best known and most comprehensive is the American Digest System, to be treated later in this chapter.

The material in a digest is classified according to topics. Analytical notes in both the American Digest System and the National Reporter System are identical.

One may begin his preliminary research in the digests by using one of three methods: the descriptive word method, the topic method, and the table of cases method. These three methods do not have to be used in isolation but may complement each other as a need arises. As in the previous section, each method will be treated here briefly.

The Descriptive Word Method. One would use this method just as he would an index in any textbook. He would select a word or term that is descriptive of his problem and locate it in the index. The descriptive words in the index come from actual court opinions that help describe the facts of the case. These descriptions are arranged in volumes of the American Digest System called the *Descriptive Word Index.* These indexes contain, not only the words describing the points of law, but also refer the researcher, in bold type, to the topic and a key number. The topic is the classification of the subject matter; the key number denotes the more specific point of law around which the case is decided. Having this information, the researcher can then refer to the specific volume in the digest that contains his topic and key number.

The Topic Method. A second method of beginning legal research in the digest is through the topic method. The American Digest System contains over 400 major topics, and one cannot possibly readily master all of them. Further, legal problems can usually be classified under more than one topic. Since it would be unwieldly to classify each problem under every conceivable topic, the editors instead resolved this matter by placing a problem under one topic and then cross-referencing it. If one begins research through this method, he should survey the total topical classification in order to become familiar with it. From the Law Chart of over 400 topics, one would be likely to find his appropriate topic. When he has identified the topic, he is referred to a key number, which he uses in seeking an analysis of that topic. Preceding the actual analysis are scope notes which alert the reader as to whether the subject matter digested is within the ambit of his topic.

The Table of Cases Method. A third method of engaging in legal research is through the table of cases method. In order to use this method, one must first have the name of a case treating his topic. In locating the case, one identifies the key number for that topic and then proceeds to find other citations appropriate for that topic. One can locate a key number from the table of cases in both the state digests and the regional reporters.

A table of cases serves several functions. It gives the correct title of the cases. It gives parallel citations to the National Reporter System, the State Reports, and the Annotated Reports. It gives the history of the case. It also gives the topics and key numbers under which the points of law have been classified. With this resource, after one has a case citation and has located it in the table of cases, he can identify his topic, key number, and then proceed in locating other relevant case citations on the subject.

b. *State Digests.* There is also a state digest for reported decisions for all courts of record of a given state. Many of these state digests use the key number system. They are constructed in the same manner and are identical in organization so that a point of law, having been searched in a local digest, does not need to be researched in the American Digest System for that same jurisdiction.

The names of the state digests often follow the name of the state, as, for example, *The New Jersey Digest.* Some digests may serve more than one state as does *The Virginia and West Virginia Digest.* The digest for Pennsylvania is known as *Vale's Pennsylvania Digest.*

Some state and local digests have classification systems of their own. However, their use as well as their special features are similar to the organization of the American Digest System. They have a topical arrangement with a fact index to all cases.

§ 2.3. The American Digest System.

The American Digest System is the most comprehensive and most used of the digests. It contains digests of court decisions that may be found in the National Reporter System, discussed more fully in § 2.5 of this chapter. It is so organized that one can locate relatively easily any court decision, provided one has even limited information.

The American Digest System has over 400 major topics. The number may change in that, as new issues arise, new topics are added. A complete list of topics is found in the front of every volume of the *Decennial Digest.* The major topic in which educators should begin is "Schools and School Districts." It contains 178 subtopics. Under the subsection of "Pupils, and Conduct and Discipline of Schools," the following partial list appears:

(H.) Pupils, and Conduct and Discipline of Schools.
148. Nature of right to instruction in general.
148½. Aid to indigent children.
149. Eligibility.
150. —— In general.
151. —— Race or color.
152. —— Age.
153. —— Residence.
154. —— Assignment or admission to particular schools.[1]

Each decennial digest also has a table of cases. These digests contain the full citation to the official reports and the key number for the case. These cases are arranged alphabetically. The following is an example of a citation: *Deutsch v. Teel,* 400 F. Supp. 598 (E. D. Wis. 1975). The citation reveals that Deutsch was the plaintiff or the one who initiated the suit; Teel was the defendant. The case is reported in volume 400 of the *Federal Supplement,* the case begins on page 598, and it was decided in 1975 by the federal court for the Eastern District in Wisconsin.

Its indexes contain decisions of American courts of record, beginning in 1658 and continuing to the present. A court of record is viewed as being the first-level appellate court and all other appeals courts at the state level. Included at the federal level are cases heard by the district courts, circuit courts, and the Supreme Court.

Within the digests, the cases are arranged according to ten-year periods. An exception is the *Century Digest* which contains in its 50 volumes the decisions of courts from 1658 to 1896.

The digests for the ten-year periods are referred to as decennial digests. They cover the following time periods:

First Decennial Digest	*1897-1906*
Second Decennial Digest	*1907-1916*

---

1. The American Digest System is published by the West Publishing Company, St. Paul, Minnesota. The example here was taken from Vol. 27 of the *Seventh Decennial Digest,* page 461.

Third Decennial Digest	*1917-1926*
Fourth Decennial Digest	*1927-1936*
Fifth Decennial Digest	*1937-1946*
Sixth Decennial Digest	*1947-1956*
Seventh Decennial Digest	*1957-1966*
Eighth Decennial Digest	*1967-1976*

In addition to the above digests, a general digest keeps the decennial digests current. It includes, after the latest decennial digest, a pamphlet issued once a month and a bound volume every four months. For one to locate a complete list of all relevant court citations since the issuance of the latest decennial digest, it is necessary to go through each of the general digests. Each of these general digests is complete within itself; each has a table of cases. A separate *Descriptive Word Index* is issued for each volume. It contains all the topics arranged alphabetically and the key number under which that topic is digested.

a. *The Key Number System.* The standard plan of legal classification of subject matter is the key number system. Developed by West Publishing Company, it is a system of classification of all sections of topics in the American Digest System. It is organized so that all cases that refer to a point of law are classified according to the key number system. The following are examples of three key numbers under the subsection of "Teachers."

145. —— Actions.
146. Pensions.
147. Duties and liabilities.[2]

The value of the key number is that all past, present, and future legal authority is classified according to the key number. Once one has located a topic and a key number, he then has access to all the cases decided in American courts of record on this issue. The key number system is thus, in effect, a system for indexing case law.

The key number system treats seven major categories: persons, property, contracts, torts, crimes, remedies, and government. These seven categories, in turn, are divided into over 400 topics. One of the topics under the category of government, "Schools and

---

2. *Id.* at 461.

School Districts," is the one in which educators do most of their legal research. Those searching in higher education would begin their research in "Colleges and Universities."

Each of the subtopics is numbered separately, beginning with 1 and continuing as far as necessary. Under "Schools and School Districts," the subtopics run from 1 to 178. If new legal points are added since the original listing of subtopics, decimals or fractions are used to divide a numbered subtopic further. This preserves consistency in the numbering of subtopics as well as in grouping them according to subject matter. Under subtopic 133, "Employment (of teachers) in General," fifteen other subtopics have been added. "Transportation of pupils" became subtopic 159½ after it was separated from 159, "Payment for tuition."

Each point of law in each court decision is digested under one of the key numbers. A specific key number refers to only one point of law, but one case may include several key numbers since it may contain more than one point of law. The *Century Digest* does not contain key numbers since the use of the key number system antedates that digest. However, if one knows the key number of his topic and wishes to research it in the *Century Digest*, he may look up the key number in either the First or Second *Decennial Digests* where a reference is made to the corresponding classification of the *Century Digest*.

b. *The National Reporter System.* The National Reporter System is a set of hundreds of volumes containing all cases from all courts of record, including all state and all federal courts. It also gives the actual court opinion in each case.

For ease in finding court opinions in appropriate volumes, a numbering system has been devised. Each of the reporters began with a first series and continued until 200 volumes appeared, as in the following reporters: Atlantic, North Eastern, South Eastern, and Southern. The numbering then began anew and the series was designated as a second series with the abbreviation "2d." The following reporters in the first series ran from 1 to 300: South Western, Pacific, and North Western. As of mid-1978, the numbered volumes in the second series varied from 241 (2d) in the South Eastern Reporter to 574 (2d) in the Pacific Reporter, an indication of the amount of business in the two regions.

Several bound volumes of the reporters appear each year. The number of volumes vary according to the workload of the various courts and the length of the judges' opinions. Bound volumes appear on the shelf of a law library several months after a decision has been handed down. Prior to publication of each bound volume, preliminary reports are issued. These preliminary reports contain several court opinions, bound in paper. Slip sheets are also issued. These are single opinions and are generally available within one week of the decision.

Each volume of the reporters contains, in addition to the court opinion, information of assistance to the researcher. At the front of each volume is a list of judges for the courts in the region reported within the volume. A contents page identifies the cases reported, and they are organized by states. Each volume also contains a digest of the cases in the volume. A table of cases lists citations to all decisions in the volume. That table includes references to statutes, constitutions, court rules, municipal ordinances and session laws. A section on words and phrases contains terms judicially defined in the volume. In addition to regional reporters which contain state court opinions, many, but not all, states also have reporters which contain opinions that are covered in the regional reporters. Thus, the same court opinion may be found in two places. For example, *Ayala v. Philadelphia Board of Public Education,* 453 Pa. 584 (1973) may also be found at 305 A.2d 877 (1973). When citing a court decision, one should cite both reporters; if only one citation is available, the regional reporter is considered as being the authoritative one. Federal court decisions are reported in the volumes of the National Reporter System according to the level of the federal court. Supreme Court decisions are reported in the United States Supreme Court Reporter (S. Ct.); [3] the decisions of the Courts of Appeal are reported in the Federal Reporter (F. or F.2d); and the decisions of the district courts are reported in the Federal Supplement (F.Supp.).

The National Reporter System also reports other kinds of decisions. The Federal Rules Decisions (F.R.D.) covers the opinions

---

3. Decisions of the Supreme Court of the United States are reported in two other places. The Court's official reports appear in United States Reports (U.S.). The third source is the United States Supreme Court Reports, Lawyer's Edition (L. Ed.). This last source includes parts of attorneys' briefs and numerous annotations not found in the other two sources.

of the federal district courts that are not designated for publication in the Federal Supplement. These kinds of decisions typically involve federal rules covering civil and criminal procedure. The National Reporter System also reports decisions of the Court of Claims (Ct. Cl.), and the Court of Customs and Patent Appeals (C.C.P.A.).

For ease in reporting, the system of volumes covering state court opinions is divided into nine regions. The following are the regions and the states they serve, the name of the set of volumes, the abbreviation for that set, and the states included in the region:

Atlantic (A. or A.2d) Connecticut, Delaware, Maine, Maryland, New Hampshire, New Jersey, Pennsylvania, and Vermont.

California (Cal. Rptr.) California.[4]

New York Supplement (N. Y. Supp.) New York.[5]

North Eastern (N.E. or N.E.2d) Illinois, Indiana, Massachusetts, New York, Ohio, and Rhode Island.

North Western (N.W. or N.W.2d) Iowa, Michigan, Minnesota, Nebraska, North Dakota, South Dakota, and Wisconsin.

Pacific (P. or P.2d) Alaska, Arizona, California, Colorado, Hawaii, Idaho, Kansas, Montana, Nevada, New Mexico, Oklahoma, Oregon, Utah, Washington, and Wyoming.

South Eastern (S.E. or S.E.2d) Georgia, North Carolina, South Carolina, Virginia, and West Virginia.

Southern (So. or So.2d) Alabama, Florida, Louisiana, and Mississippi.

South Western (S.W. or S.W.2d) Arkansas, Kentucky, Missouri, Tennessee, and Texas.

Preceding each court opinion is the syllabus of the decision. It also contains information helpful to the researcher. It gives the title of the decision (the parties to the case), the court deciding the case, the date the case was argued and decided, the date a rehearing was granted or denied, and a synopsis of the case. The synopsis contains the following information: the facts and

4. *The California Reporter,* begun in 1960, contains all decisions of the California Supreme Court and approved decisions of lower California appellate courts no longer published in the Pacific Reporter since 347 P.2d. *The California Reporter* duplicates the state reports beginning with 53 Cal. 2d and 177 Cal. App. 2d.

5. *The New York Supplement,* begun in 1888, contains all decisions of the state's highest court, the Court of Appeals, since 1847, and many lower court decisions.

summary of the decision, digest paragraphs (references to points of law that are keyed to the American Digest System by a key number), and a list of attorneys arguing the case. Headnotes (the digest paragraphs) are numbered consecutively to correspond to the subject matter in the text of the opinion.

The headnotes of the court opinion are broken down by sections, and each section is given a number: a key number. That number identifies the subject matter of the opinion around which the major point of law was resolved. The summaries should not be used in lieu of an actual reading of the court opinion which follows the headnotes.

§ 2.4. Shepard's Citations.

Shepard's Citations is a system that provides a history of a reported court decision and a treatment of that decision. In like manner, it provides a history of a statute and indicates court decisions having an effect on that statute. The value of *Shepard's* is that it gives up-to-date authority on both court decisions and statutes so that a researcher may rely on the applicable court holding.

Shepard's Citations has a number of units which cover legal reporting systems. Each of the states with a reporter in the National Reporter System has a unit, each of the regional reporters has a unit, and each of the three levels of federal courts has a unit. In essence, the units of *Shepard's* correspond to the units of the National Reporter System.

In addition to the history and treatment of a court decision, *Shepard's* is also useful for finding similar decisions to a case under consideration.

The process of checking the status of cases or statutes in the various reporters is known as "Shepardizing." References to *Shepard's* are to case citations in the various reporters in the National Reporter System. One secures the appropriate unit of *Shepard's* that corresponds to the page of the opinion in the reporter and turns to the page in *Shepard's* that treats the case. The following is a partial treatment of the case, *West Virginia*

State Board of Education v. Barnette, 319 U.S. 624, 63 S. Ct. 1178, 87 L. Ed. 1628 (1943):

-624-

(87LE1628)
(63SC1178)
(147ALR674)
s47FS251
319US^{2}588
320US^{2}708
j321US113
321US^{2}165
j321US^{2}174
321US^{5}665
322US^{2}86
323US^{2}527
323US^{2}545 [6]

With the aid of "Abbreviations — Analysis, Cases," at the front of the volume, one can then interpret the various entries. The following abbreviations are used in analysis:

HISTORY of CASE

a (affirmed)	Same case affirmed on appeal.
cc (connected case)	Different case from case cited but arising out of same subject matter or intimately connected therewith.
D (dismissed)	Appeal from same case dismissed.
m (modified)	Same case modified on appeal.
r (reversed)	Same case reversed on appeal.
s (same case)	Same case as case cited.
S (superseded)	Substitution for former opinion.

----

6. *Shepard's Citations.* Colorado Springs: Shepard's Citations, Inc. The example was taken from page 209 of the volume covering the above citation.

v (vacated)	Same case vacated.
US cert den	Certiorari denied by U. S. Supreme Court.
US cert dis	Certiorari dismissed by U. S. Supreme Court.
US reh den	Rehearing denied by U. S. Supreme Court.

TREATMENT of CASE

c (criticised)	Soundness of decision or reasoning in cited case criticised for reasons given.
d (distinguished)	Case at bar different either in law or fact from case cited for reasons given.
e (explained)	Statement of import of decision in cited case. Not merely a restatement of the facts.
f (followed)	Cited as controlling.
h (harmonized)	Apparent inconsistency explained and shown not to exist.
j (dissenting opinion)	Citation in dissenting opinion.
L (limited)	Refusal to extend decision of cited case beyond precise issues involved.
o (overruled)	Ruling in cited case expressly overruled.
p (paralleled)	Citing case substantially alike or on all fours with cited case in its law or facts.
q (questioned)	Soundness of decision or reasoning in cited case questioned.[7]

---

7. This example was taken from the explanatory material on the use of *Shepard's Citations.*

Through the above use of *Shepard's,* one can learn about the history of the case, including subsequent appeals and the disposition of those appeals. The treatment of a decision includes cases which have had some effect on it: whether followed, rejected, modified, expanded, or merely cited.

The treatment of statutes in *Shepard's* varies somewhat from the arrangement of court decisions. Constitutions are arranged by article and section, or amendment; legislative acts are arranged by date of enactment, chapter and section.

It may not be necessary to "Shepardize" each court decision in a lengthy research paper; however, one must not overlook the necessity of being certain that he is dealing with the most current applicable law.

§ 2.5. United States Law Week.

United States Law Week (U.S.L.W.) is a loose-leaf weekly publication that provides two main kinds of services. It supplies information about Congress and legislation in its General Law Section and about the United States Supreme Court in its Supreme Court Sections. Its value is in providing up-to-date information of the subjects it treats.

The General Law Section is a source for "slip laws" of Congress. It reproduces verbatim, in full, laws passed by Congress that are of general interest or importance. It has a section that contains short summaries and developments about recent legislation and court decisions. Finally, it contains quotations from very recent court decisions not yet reported elsewhere. The usefulness of this service is its being up-to-date in the selected areas it treats.

The second part, Supreme Court Sections, is divided further into two sections. One section covers the proceedings of the Court. It lists the cases filed with the Court, the cases docketed, a calendar of hearings scheduled, and a summary of the Court's orders. It frequently has supplementary articles on the work and decisions of the court.

The second section contains "slip" decisions of the Supreme Court. Since these decisions are mailed within a day of their being announced, subscribers such as libraries have access to the actual court decision within a week of its being handed down.

§ 2.6. Legal Encyclopedias.

Students of law may find two reference encyclopedias helpful in starting legal research. They are *Corpus Juris Secundum* (second body of law) (C.J.S., C.J.S.2d) and American Jurisprudence (Am. Jur., Am. Jur. 2d). These works are useful in that they provide an overview of a legal issue and support it with case citations.

The value of *Corpus Juris Secundum* is two-fold. It gives the researcher a notion of the state of law on a given issue and citations from which one can build a bibliography on that topic. The case citations are the specific cases from which the principles are derived.

Major content topics are arranged alphabetically in 101 volumes. An educator would refer to the major topic, "Schools and School Districts," which is covered in volumes 78 and 79. Under this topic there are 512 subtopics, each of which is discussed.

Below are listed several topics from the subtopic, "Pupils, and Conduct and Discipline of Schools."

      3. Control of Pupils and Discipline
          § 493. In general
             494. Rules and regulations
             495. —— Reasonableness and validity
             496. Outside school and school hours
             497. —— Homework
             498. —— Attendance at moving picture theaters and social parties
             499. —— Secret societies
             500. —— Athletic and sporting contests
             501. Violation of rules; offenses and punishment
             502. —— Corporal punishment
             503. —— Exclusion, expulsion, and suspension
             504. —— Readmission or reinstatement
             505. —— Actions for wrongful exclusion, expulsion, or suspension [8]

Each volume contains a word index for each major topic in it. In addition, a four-volume index accompanies the entire series. Cumulative annual pocket parts keep the citations up-to-date. It is necessary to refer to these annual supplements in order to collect

---

8. *Corpus Juris Secundum.* Brooklyn: The American Law Book Company. The example here was taken from Vol. 78, page 604.

the latest case citations that have accumulated since the original publication of the bound volume.

One may begin his research in *Corpus Juris Secundum* in one of two ways. He may go directly to the major topic, "Schools and School Districts," find the appropriate subtopic with the number to the left of it and, using the number, locate the topic in the text. A second way is by going to the index, finding the topic and subtopic there, and then proceeding to the topic in the text.

Within the text itself, the upper part of each page contains an analysis of the topic and relevant legal principles. The raised numbers in the text refer to footnotes at the bottom of the page. These footnotes come directly from the cases that support the principle of law. Since these principles are identified by the editors of *Corpus Juris Secundum* rather than by the courts, the researcher is advised to read the actual court opinion rather than rely exclusively on the comment in *Corpus Juris Secundum.*

Unlike *Corpus Juris Secundum,* its competitor, *American Jurisprudence,* is based upon selected rather than all court cases. It is a complete revision of its predecessor, *Ruling Case Law.* Its 82 volumes are organized similarly to *Corpus Juris Secundum.* It contains an index at the end of each volume with references to material in that volume. There is also a four-volume index to the entire set with cumulative pocket parts.

The topics in *American Jurisprudence* are arranged under the major heading of "Schools" in Volume 68. An example of the treatment of the subject of discipline follows.

F. DISCIPLINE AND PUNISHMENT

1. In General

§ 256. Generally; rights of parents and school
      authorities
§ 257. Punishable offenses
§ 258. Corporal punishment
§ 259. Detention after school hours

2. Suspension and Expulsion

§ 260. Generally
§ 261. Power of school authorities and
      directors

Because either of these two works is adequate for the educational researcher, it is not necessary to use both of them. One may, in fact, bypass them and begin research in the legal digests.

If one is researching a topic that involves only a state or local matter, he may prefer to rely on a state rather than a general encyclopedia. The *Pennsylvania Law Encyclopedia* is typical of a state encyclopedia. It has 45 volumes, three of which are a general index. Education topics are organized under "Schools," which is divided further into 177 subtopics. These subtopics are similar, but do not correspond exactly, to those listed under "Schools and School Districts" in the American Digest System.

§ 2.7. American Law Reports Annotated.

American Law Reports Annotated (A.L.R.(3d)) is a series of volumes that contains commentary on selected decisions and topics by legal authorities. The decisions and topics are selected for their general, broad interest. Topics of purely local or individual interest are not covered. Of the cases that are reviewed and analyzed, A.L.R. concentrates on topics in which there is difference of opinion. This source is useful in supplementing court decisions, for the subject matter is treated by authorities who present balanced arguments on a legal issue. An example of an entry from the index follows:

---

9. *American Jurisprudence* 2d. Rochester: The Lawyer's Co-Operative Publishing Company. This example was taken from Vol. 68, page 357.

RIGHT OF STUDENT TO HEARING ON CHARGES BEFORE
SUSPENSION OR EXPLUSION FROM EDUCATIONAL INSTITUTION.

§ 1. Introduction and scope, p. 904

Marriage or pregnancy of public school student as ground for expulsion or exclusion, or of restriction of activities. 11 ALR3d 996.

Validity of regulation by public school authorities as to clothes or personal appearance of pupils. 14 ALR3d 1201.

Participation of student in demonstration on or near campus as warranting expulsion or suspension from school or college. 32 ALR3d 864.

Liability of college or university to student enrolled in course of instruction terminated prior to completion. 51 ALR3d 1003.

Right to discipline pupil for conduct away from school grounds or not immediately connected with school activities. 53 ALR3d 1124.[10]

The indexes to A.L.R. are referred to as "Red Books." The entries are alphabetical, and the key lead word or subject identifies all references to an annotation on that subject. Topics in education are listed under "Schools."

A Supplement Service keeps the annotations current.

The following are features of the American Law Reports Annotated: 1. It contains a report of the entire court decision. 2. It gives the court opinion. 3. It gives a summary of the briefs of parties to the case. 4. It contains an annotation. The annotation supplements legal points covered in the opinion, treats lines of reasoning not covered by the courts, and identifies seemingly contrary decisions.

Approximately six volumes appear each year. Each digest covers its own arrangement of topics and subtopics. The annotations are not cumulative; that is, they do not repeat material covered in earlier volumes.

A.L.R.3d is the third of three companion sets of annotations of legal topics. The earliest one is A.L.R. which covers reports from 1919 — 1948. The second set, A.L.R.2d ran from 1948 — 1965. A.L.R.3d has been published since 1965.

---

10. *American Law Reports* 2d. Rochester: The Lawyer's Co-operative Publishing Company. This example was taken from the Later Case Service (covering Vols. 56-63 of ALR 3d), page 235.

§ 2.8. Legal Dictionaries.

As one engages in legal research, he realizes that words often have meanings other than when used in nonlegal circumstances. That is, law often has a vocabulary of its own. Not only should the researcher be aware of this, but he should also have access to and use terms as they are legally defined. There are a number of legal dictionaries that serve this purpose.

The most comprehensive of the legal dictionaries is *Words and Phrases.* It includes in its many volumes any word or phrase that has been defined in any case in American courts. Like the American Digest System, it covers reported cases from 1658 to the present.

Organizationally, definitions are arranged alphabetically. A word or phrase is defined by giving a digest paragraph followed by the citation to the case. The definition is in the court's own language except where it might be preferable to modify the language for ease in clarity and publishing.

Words and Phrases has a complete alphabetical index by subject headings. It contains numerous cross references and is kept up-to-date with annual cumulative pocket parts.

In addition to supplying definitions, *Words and Phrases* serves an additional function in legal research. One can locate pertinent cases through case citations to a definition. Seven paragraphs are devoted to the term, "expulsion." Paragraph three is listed below:

"Expulsion" means to eject, banish, or cut off from the privileges of an institution or society permanently. *John B. Stetson University v. Hunt,* 102 So. 637, 639, 88 Fla. 510.[11]

In addition to *Words and Phrases,* there are several excellent legal dictionaries in one or two volumes. These dictionaries are frequently revised and brought up-to-date since law constantly undergoes change. Among the standard dictionaries are *Ballentine, The Self-Pronouncing Law Dictionary; Black's Law Dictionary;* and *Bouvier's Law Dictionary and Concise Encyclopedia.*

Bouvier's first definition of "expulsion" is as follows:

EXPULSION (Lat. expellere, to drive out). The act of depriving a member of a body politic or corporate, or of

---

11. *Words and Phrases.* St. Paul: West Publishing Company. This example was taken from Vol. 15A, page 593.

a society, of his right of membership therein, by the vote of such body or society, for some violation of his duties as such, or for some offense which renders him unworthy of longer remaining a member of the same.[12]

In addition to the general legal dictionaries, there are also those for very specialized fields in law.

§ 2.9. Index to Legal Periodicals.

Many, if not most, law schools publish journals, typically referred to as law reviews. They contain leading articles on topical issues, notes and comments, case notes, and book reviews. The articles are typically scholarly, comprehensive treatments of current subjects. They are often written by a law professor, lawyer, judge, or a specialist on that subject. Somewhat like articles, the notes and comments are briefer and are often written by the abler law students in the host publishing school. Case notes involve treatment of a specific court decision, usually by a law student. Law books are reviewed in the book review section.

In order to identify periodical articles on legal subjects, one should refer to the *Index to Legal Periodicals,* the best known and most widely used source in its field. It corresponds to the *Reader's Guide to Periodical Literature* for those researching in education, and each of these publications has the same format. *Index to Legal Periodicals* contains a table of contents, an index, and a table of cases. It has references to legal journal articles plus a few other publications. It refers to printed material not only in the United States but also in Canada, England, Scotland, Ireland, Northern Ireland, Australia, and New Zealand.

The Index is published monthly except September. A permanent bound volume appears every three years. In between, there are periodically cumulative issues as well as an annual cumulative volume.

The Index consists of three parts. The first is a combined subject and author index. Subjects are arranged alphabetically and correspond similarly, but not exactly, to those used by the Key Number System. Thus, one may look under the author index if he knows the author's last name or under the appropriate subject

---

12. *Bouvier's Law Dictionary.* Kansas City: Vernon Law Book Company.

entry. The following are two entries from the September 1973 — August 1976 issue under "Schools and School Districts."

> Academic freedom in the public schools: the right to teach. NYU L Rev 48:1176-99 D '73
> Alternative schools for minority students: the constitution, the civil rights act and the Berkeley experiment. Calif L Rev 61:858-918 My '73 [13]

The second part is a table of cases. It lists court decisions for which there are case notes or case comments. It is organized on the plaintiff-defendant format.

The third part is a book review section. Books are listed under the last name of the author, followed by the title of the book and its publication date. Periodical citations of reviews then follow under each entry.

The use of the *Index to Legal Periodicals,* as well as the *Reader's Guide to Periodical Literature,* should give the researcher a comprehensive bibliography of journal articles on a given subject.

§ 2.10. Researching a Topic.

A major objective in undertaking a study of education law is to achieve an awareness of what law actually is. The methodology used in many education law classes is like that in most courses in a law school: the case study. It involves an analysis of many court decisions from which legal principles are derived. Study of case law is augmented with an analysis of statutory law — state and federal, where applicable.

Laws and court decisions are considered as being primary sources; these are the references that one should use initially. They may be supplemented later with secondary sources: annotations, legal encyclopedias, law reviews, educational articles, and books. Researchers who do not have access to a law library may have to undertake their study in secondary sources.

One begins his research by framing a problem as a legal issue. In framing the problem, one must necessarily define and possibly refine it to make it manageable. In the process of limiting the topic, one determines whether it has national or local import. If it has

---

13. *Index to Legal Periodicals.* New York: The H. W. Wilson Company. The examples were taken from the September 1973 to August 1976 volume, page 983.

national implications, the research must be extended beyond the laws and court decisions of a given state. An example of such a problem is the extent to which the First Amendment protects students in publishing a school-sponsored newspaper. If the problem is restricted to only one state, one then works with more limited resources. An example of a state or local topic is the maximum distance a student may be required to walk from his home to a school bus stop.

In treating an issue, one looks first to the statutes that may be controlling. In doing this, one also examines the federal and state constitutions to determine if either has any provisions on the topic. After collecting the appropriate statutes, one then builds a bibliography of court decisions. As noted in previous sections of this chapter, one may begin this search in several places.

Each court decision should be read and analyzed with care. A systematic approach will work to the researcher's advantage. One plan is to organize the study around four major areas: the facts, the question, the decision and rationale, and implications. Each is considered briefly below.

The facts. Who are the parties to the case? Who is suing whom? What factual situation occurred that precipitated a suit? What does the plaintiff base his case on — constitutional or statutory law, or something else? What is the defendant's response to the plaintiff's charge? What remedy is the plaintiff seeking?

The question. What is the court asked to decide? If one or more issues are involved, reduce the questions to their simplest form.

The decision and rationale. What is the court's actual decision? What are its reasons for deciding the way it did? Were there concurring and/or dissenting opinions? What was the reasoning of these judges?

Implications. Does the decision have local or general applicability? Is it consistent with previous rulings on the same subject? Does it set a precedent? What effect will it be likely to have on a school or school system?

After one has researched, analyzed, and begun to synthesize all relevant statutes and court decisions, he should examine secondary sources. Then, after synthesizing the primary and secondary sources, he should be able to state a definitive position on the given legal issue.

Since a court holding today may be overturned tomorrow, law is never static. Thus, law should be viewed as being controlling at a given point in time. It is consequently necessary for one to review constantly the state of law on an issue in order to be certain of being up-to-date.

PART II

LAW AND LOCAL BOARDS OF EDUCATION

Chapter 3

LOCAL SCHOOL DISTRICTS AND BOARDS OF EDUCATION

§ 3.0. Introduction.

According to a shibboleth, education is of national interest, a function of state government, and subject to local control. That statement is an over-simplification in that the three spheres of government are all very much involved in education and controls over it are found at all three levels. The truism exists, nonetheless, that much control of education still remains at the local level. The controlling body in the local school district is usually called a board of education, school committee, or board of trustees. Its primary function is the enactment of policy for the district.

The approximately 16,000 local school districts in this country are very diverse. They may be created out of counties, townships, municipalities, or by some other means. In size they vary from less than one hundred to thousands of square miles; in school population, from none (an inoperative district) to several hundred thousand pupils. Beyond what a state requires, programs may vary greatly among districts, for policies and regulations covering local matters depend on the will of the people and, specifically, on the decisions made by the board of education.

What these districts and school boards have in common under law is the focus of this Chapter. Since there is no national system of education, the powers and duties of these local school districts are determined, for the most part, by the laws of a given state. In that respect, one should not assume that the laws of one state apply to another. What is to be found in this Chapter are general principles illustrated with case law, that apply to the organization and governance of education at the local level.

§ 3.1. Status of Local School Districts.

It was indicated in Chapter One that, under our constitutional system, state governments were clothed with the legal responsibility for establishing and maintaining a system of public education. Thus, with two exceptions, a state has complete power with respect to determining the organization and control of local school systems. The two exceptions are conflicting constitutional provisions at the federal and state levels and conflicting legislative provisions at the federal level. It is fundamental that a constitutional provision is controlling over any other kind of law, and a federal statute is controlling over any constitutional provision or legislative law of a state.

Although the plenary power of states over education is considerable, state legislatures do not actually operate schools; rather, they provide for the operation of schools. The authority for this operation is delegated to a local governmental body. The name of the local body may vary from state to state and even within a state, but it takes the structure of a local school district. It is to this body that the state has given specified powers and duties in discharging a state function: education of young people. In delegating this responsibility, a state does not relinquish its control over education in general as well as over school districts in particular. This point was made by Edwards:

> Whatever agencies the legislature may select as the instruments for the execution of its educational policies, these agencies are completely subject to its control within constitutional limits. Since school districts are purely creatures of the state, they possess no inherent local rights — no rights at all in fact, except those with which they are endowed by the legislature. Their powers and the mode of exercise of these powers are defined by legislative act and may be added to, diminished, or destroyed as the legislature may determine.[1]

Since local school districts derive their power from the state, they have no inherent power of their own. Whatever powers they possess are those which the state has delegated to them. That delegated power may be enlarged, modified, or withdrawn if the state decides.

A local school district is both a political and a geographical entity. It is political in that it operates as an agency of the state, carries on a state function, has an organizational structure, and must rely on the will of the electorate it serves in order to achieve its purposes. It is geographical in that it has territorial boundaries which are, in fact, subdivisions of the state. The school boundaries are defined only for the purpose of establishing a school system, although they may or may not be coterminous with the political subdivision.

The relationship of the school district to the state is explained in another statement by Edwards:

> [T]he state may create new districts without regard to existing political boundaries or subdivisions, or it may use existing subdivisions, such as counties, townships, or cities. If a school district is carved out of the same geographical boundaries as a political subdivision, it should be recognized that the two perform different functions. The local political agency is created for the purpose of local self-government; the district is an instrument of state policy. It was not created to perform a local function.[2]

---

1. EDWARDS, THE COURTS AND THE PUBLIC SCHOOLS 84 (rev. ed. Chicago: University of Chicago Press, 1955).
2. *Id.* at 93.

The legislature is the source of control of education at the state level. As was stated previously, the legislature is limited, within the state, only by the constitution. In the exercise of its control, a state legislature can create, alter, consolidate, or abolish a school district. It can determine the taxing unit, impose special taxes, or order special elections — with or without the approval of the voters. It can determine the number of school board members, their terms of office, and the manner of their election. It can require that specified subjects be taught or not taught. In short, the state's power is nearly complete. The extent to which it exercises that power or delegates it to a local school district depends on a given state and more particularly on the will of the legislators. Thus, in some states there is a highly centralized system of education while in others, local school districts have considerable power.

§ 3.2. Powers of Local School Boards.

A local school board has no power of its own. The powers it does possess are those conferred upon it by the legislature. A school board cannot divest itself of any power or duty specifically authorized it. Conversely, it cannot grant itself any power which it otherwise does not possess. Where school board members derive any powers from the state's constitution, that power can be altered only by an amendment to the constitution. Similarly, where power is derived from the legislature, that power can be changed only by an act of the legislature.

Two recent cases serve as examples of a school board's abrogating its power. In one, a New Jersey board of education and the teachers' association entered into an agreement that delegated to an individual teacher or the teachers' association decisions about discussing controversies in the classroom. The court negated the agreement, for it noted that the legislature had mandated that the board was responsible for courses of study. This responsibility, the court held, could not be bargained away.[3] In the other case, an Iowa court held that a school board cannot delegate its rule-making power to a state high school athletic association.[4] An athlete had

---

3. Board of Educ. v. Rockaway Township Educ. Ass'n, 120 N.J. Super. 564, 295 A.2d 380 (1972).

4. Bunger v. Iowa High School Athletic Ass'n, 197 N.W.2d 555 (Iowa 1972).

been declared ineligible for competition under the association's rules because he had knowingly ridden in a car that contained alcholic beverages.

The laws that spell out the power and authority of school boards are often stated in general terms, for it would be impossible to foresee all the possible acts in which boards may engage. Even if they could be foreseen, it would be impractical to list all of them.

a. *Expressly Granted and Implied Powers.* In discharging its duties, a local school board can exercise those powers only expressly granted it, those powers implied from the ones expressly granted, and those necessary for accomplishing the purposes for which the board was created. Courts do not normally question the action of a school board in exercising its expressly granted powers, unless there is an abuse of it, for they are rather clearly spelled out by the legislature. School boards are more often challenged in the exercise of implied powers, for it is easier to allege that a board exceeded its power where it was not specifically stated that the board possessed it.

An expressly granted power is one that is stated in legislative acts. Examples of such powers include levying taxes, establishing an extracurricular activity program, and bargaining with a teachers' association. An implied power is one not spelled out in legislative acts, but considered necessary for a board to assume in order to perform duties legally imposed on it. The employment of an architect may be an implied power; building a school building may be an expressly granted power. Hiring a teacher is an expressly granted power; using funds in recruiting teachers may be an implied power.

Confusion sometimes exists as to whether or not a power is expressly granted or is implied. For example, the authority to "make all necessary and reasonable provisions for the best interests of the school system" provides for considerable interpretation of the exercise of that power. Generally, such a provision would not clothe the board with unlimited power, for where a board is given a large grant of power, the exercise of it is determined, not in light of the large grant but in specifically enumerated grants of power.

School boards may exercise their grants of power only as a corporate body. That is, school board action is legal only when the board members act in concert, as a unit, in a meeting. As individuals, its members possess no power. When a board is not in session, its members possess no authority; their legal status within the district is like that of any other citizen. An order or pronouncement by an individual board member is without legality.

If school boards go beyond their duly constituted authority, they act *ultra vires,* that is, beyond the scope of law. Their action is viewed as being that of individuals and not legal, hence it is not binding on the board. If challenged successfully, board action may be merely nullified, or board members may be sued as individuals. Courts have traditionally given board members benefit of the doubt where their actions actually exceeded their authority, unless there was a clear indication that their behavior was motivated by malice, greed, personal benefit, attempt to injure, or clear disregard of the law.

b. *Discretionary and Ministerial Acts.* Like power, actions by local boards of education may be classified into two categories. They consist of discretionary or ministerial acts.

A discretionary act is one which requires judgment of the board. Such action involves debate and discussion, and it is expected that a board deliberate fully before agreeing on an issue. Most of the board's actions fall within this category. Discretionary action cannot be delegated to a committee of the board, to subordinate educators, or to other agencies. Discretionary action includes such matters as selecting a school site, employing professional personnel, approving courses of study, and authorizing expenditures of funds. A school board may call on other people for assistance in considering discretionary matters, but the action involving approval or disapproval of such matters must be its own.

Courts are reluctant to interfere with school boards in the exercise of discretionary action. When it is recognized that a school board has such authority, the exercise of it in the normal course of events will not be challenged unless, of course, there is evidence of its abuse.

A ministerial act is one which does not involve judgment of the board. It is considered as being routine or mechanical. A board can delegate this action to another person. For example, the employment of professional personnel requires action by a full board — a discretionary action; the actual execution of the contract is mechanical — a ministerial act which may be exercised by the board chairman, for instance. Preparation of a budget may be a ministerial act, but board approval of it is discretionary.

Recent court cases of the mid-1970's involving discretionary and ministerial actions have focused, for the most part, on personnel matters. The issues have often centered on procedural rather than substantive issues. Two cases are included here as examples. A California court held, in 1973, that the revocation of a teacher's license was a ministerial act; moreover, it was a duty in this instance. The teacher had earlier been convicted of a sex crime; the contract had been revoked by the state board of education. The court held that the state board had acted properly in maintaining the integrity of the schools.[5]

In a case decided the following year, the question involved the procedure used in dismissing a teacher. Here, the court ruled against the school board, for it had failed to give reasons and provide procedural due process for the employee. The court ruled that, by failing to supply both reasons and procedural due process, the board had failed in a ministerial act that could lead to members' liability.[6]

§ 3.3. Meetings of School Boards.

In order for any action by a school board to be considered as being legal, it must transpire in an official board meeting. The meeting itself must conform to law. Where there are statutory provisions that require specifically that certain conditions exist at a meeting, those provisions must be met. Although laws of the fifty states vary, some general statements may be made concerning the legality of school board meetings. One would need to examine the statutes of his given state to ascertain if they apply here.

a. *Notice of Regular Meetings.* It is a fundamental principle that every board member shall be entitled to notice of meetings. That serves to alert the member that a meeting will transpire as well as to allow him opportunity to prepare for it. Courts have held that notice is for the benefit of board members rather than the public, and unless a statute authorizes it, the public is not entitled to

---

5. Purifoy v. State Bd. of Educ., 30 Cal. App. 3d 187, 106 Cal. Rptr. 201 (1973).
6. Van Buskirk v. Bleiler, 77 Misc. 2d 272, 354 N.Y.S.2d 93 (1974).

notice. Some states require that public notice shall be given of meetings, as, for example, in a local newspaper.

If the meeting is a regularly scheduled one and the board, in its rules of organization, has established a fixed date, time, and place for all its meetings, further notice is not necessary. If there is any deviation from the standard schedule, notice is required for that meeting.

The meeting may be held anywhere within the school district, unless statutes authorize otherwise. Unless statutes specifically provide for it, a meeting cannot be held outside the district.

b. *Notice of Special Meetings.* In addition to its regular meetings, boards of education often have special meetings. They, too, must conform to law. A special meeting requires special notice in that it has been called for a special purpose. Generally, notice must include date, time, place, and the business to be transacted. Any business transacted other than what was stated in the notice would not be considered as being legal.

Some states specify the number of days' notice that a board member must have prior to a special meeting. Where statutes are silent on this question, courts have ruled that a reasonable period of time is all that is required. That time may be variable in consideration of a number of factors such as ease in communicating with the members and the amount and complexity of items for consideration.

The notice may be written or otherwise, depending on the statutes. In the absence of a law, written notice is not required.

There are three exceptions to the notice requirement for special board meetings. If all board members are together and agree to act, notice would not be necessary in that it had already been served. However, if one board member objects, the board could not act under such terms of notice. Similarly, after a meeting has begun, a board member could not object and have his action sustained.

The second exception is when it would be physically impossible for a board member to attend. For example, if one were hospitalized with a serious illness or on an African safari, rendering it impossible to attend, in either case, on one or two days' notice, a special meeting would not otherwise be invalidated.

A third exception is when there is an emergency. Where an

attempt to get board members together would exacerbate the problem, the action of one or two board members, on behalf of the entire board, would be upheld. This kind of action constitutes an exception also to the requirement that the board act as a whole or a corporate body. Such action is rarely exercised.

c. *Closed Meetings.* Many states have statutes which require that all school board meetings be open, that is, that the public be allowed to attend. The thinking is that a school board is a public body which transacts public business; consequently this business should be conducted openly rather than secretly. This holds true for most, but not all, school board action.

Some deliberations by a school board do not lend themselves to open meetings, therefore, closed meetings may be allowed, unless they are forbidden by law. Statutes typically specify what kinds of business can be transacted in a closed meeting. For instance, it would be unwise for a school board to decide publicly that it had four school sites under consideration, for it could lead to land speculation, forcing up prices, and political pressure on board members to select a given site. This point was made by an Illinois court on a challenge to a school board that had met secretly in deciding to purchase land. In ruling that the meeting was legal, the court stated:

> To hold otherwise would either greatly handicap the ability of school boards to deal for real estate or would drive the boards to informal get-togethers instead of regular meetings. Public knowledge of board intentions and actions resulting from compulsory public deliberative sessions when considering the purchase of real estate would destroy any advantage to be gained from negotiation and would work a severe detriment upon the board and the public they represent.[7]

Similarly, some personnel transactions are better handled in a closed session. A morals charge against a teacher, without merit, could well damage that individual's reputation beyond repair. It would be better to have the hearing privately.

The North Carolina legislature in 1971 provided for closed

---

7. Collinsville Community Unit School Dist. No. 10 v. White, 5 Ill. App. 3d 500, 283 N.E.2d 718 (1972).

sessions of boards of education or its committees for the following matters:

1. Acquisition of property
2. Negotiations with employee groups
3. Conferences with legal counsel and other deliberations concerning prosecution, defense, settlement, or litigation of any judicial action in which the school board is a party or directly affected
4. Any matter constituting a privileged communication
5. Student discipline cases
6. Strategy for handling an existing or imminent riot or public disorder
7. Appointment, discipline, or dismissal of personnel.[8]

d. *Executive Sessions.* Unlike a closed meeting, an executive session is a conference by the board in private. It is held for the purpose of discussion only and not for formal action. The general rule is that matters considered in an executive session must be formally ratified in an open meeting. Even if a board agrees on a matter in an executive session, the matter must still be acted upon in an open meeting. The degree of action taken in an executive session may be subject to challenge. In a North Dakota school district, a school board met in an executive session, in violation of the state's "sunshine law" and voted not to renew a teacher's contract. At a subsequent open meeting, the board affirmed, without discussion, its earlier action. The court held that the dismissal was void in that it was the product of an earlier illegal meeting.[9]

In an executive session, another school board voted not to renew a teacher's contract. The board did not officially act, however, on the matter at the open meeting, and it sent a letter of dismissal to the teacher. Later, the board ratified its action, but the court held that the board had acted improperly.[10]

In a North Carolina case, a school board, in a work session,

---

8. N.C. GEN. STAT. § 318.1-318.7 (1971).
9. Peters v. Bowman Public School Dist. No. 1, 231 N.W.2d 817 (N.D. 1975).
10. Kerns v. School Dist. No. 6, 515 P.2d 121 (Col. 1973).

selected an agent to pick a school site. The board was challenged for holding an illegal meeting, but the court held that the briefing session was legal, for the board had formally ratified its action at an open meeting.[11]

A question of a school board's legality in purchasing land was considered in the previous subsection. The court held that the state's public meeting law contained an exception for considering the acquisition and sale of land:

> All official meetings at which any legal action is taken by the governing bodies of . . . school districts . . . shall be public meetings except . . . meetings where the acquisition or sale of property is being considered, provided that no other portion of such meetings shall be closed to the public.[12]

In what seems to be a consensus of what courts have held concerning holding closed sessions, a Louisiana court ruled that a school board may hold informal sessions without notice to the public for the purpose of exchanging ideas rather than making binding commitments requiring board action.[13]

e. *Rules of Procedure.* Where states require that specific rules of procedure be followed in conducting school board business, these rules must be followed. Although many states prescribe some operating rules, they are not often all-inclusive. As a result, local school boards are free to supplement with their own rules. The general rule of law is that, in the absence of controlling statutes and rules, strict adherence to technical rules of procedure is not required. The reason for this is that it is not so important to have a board comprised of strict parliamentarians or to be the best possible adherent to Robert's Rules of Order, but rather to have an orderly system for the transaction of business. Thus, a board has considerable autonomy in determining the extent to which it wishes to be formal or informal, rigid or flexible.

It should be made clear, however, that when a board adopts its own rules of procedure, they are as binding as statutes. Failure to follow them can, if challenged, nullify board action. This was

---

11. Eggiman v. Wake County Bd. of Educ., 22 N.C. App. 459, 206 S.E.2d 754 (1974).

12. Collinsville, *supra*, note 7.

13. Reeves v. Orleans Parish School Bd., 281 So. 2d 710 (La. 1973).

made clear in an Ohio case.[14] A school board had approved a rule providing that school bus drivers involved in five accidents causing police investigation would be dismissed. A driver, after little sleep the previous night, was involved in an accident. Although there were no injuries, the board dismissed him. The court held for the driver, citing the board regulation. The judges observed that it might be the better part of wisdom if the driver were relieved of his responsibilities, but to do so would be a violation of established procedure.

In a teacher dismissal case, a state statute regarding board procedure was cited as controlling the issue.[15] At the meeting in which a teacher was dismissed, a roll call vote was not held, and members' votes were not recorded, both violations of state law. The statute provided:

> . . . any vote or action thereon (employment, hiring, etc. of any public employee) must be taken in public meeting with the vote of each member (of the school board) publicly cast and recorded.
> Any other action taken in violation of the above provisions shall be invalid.[16]

The court held that the board's failure to record the votes as prescribed was more than harmless error; it constituted invalid action.

In a New Hampshire case, the court upheld school board action where parliamentary procedure was not followed.[17] The court pointed out that no statutes were violated. A board meeting was invalidated in a Missouri school district where two members got together and decided to have a meeting without notifying a third member. They called for a special election which, the court held, was invalidated.[18]

In the final case in this subsection, a board was called to task for violation of a technical matter on the general procedures it had

---

14. State *ex rel.* Edmundson v. Board of Educ., 2 Ohio Misc. 137, 201 N.E.2d 729 (1964).

15. Oldham v. Drummond Bd. of Educ., 542 P.2d 1309 (Okla. 1975).

16. OKLA. STAT. tit. 25, § 201 (1972).

17. Lamb v. Danville School Bd., 102 N.H. 569, 162 A.2d 614 (1960).

18. Stewart v. Consolidated School Dist., 281 S.W.2d 511 (Mo. 1955).

approved.[19] Louisiana statutes give a school board the right to adopt its own rules of order, and the board adopted Robert's Rules of Order. They were violated in a meeting involving the election of a superintendent. At one board meeting, fourteen of fifteen members were present, and Broussard was elected by a 7-6 vote, with apparently one abstention. The board chairman ruled that Broussard was not elected in that he needed eight votes, or a majority of the total board. At a later meeting in which all fifteen members were present, Broussard was removed by an 8-7 vote and a replacement was elected.

The court held that Roberts' Rules of Order provide that, normally, when a quorum is present, a majority vote is usually sufficient to carry any motion. According to Roberts', a quorum is a majority of the members, and a quorum was present at the first meeting when Broussard was elected by a 7-6 vote. The vote to remove him was invalid since he could be removed only for cause.

In order for a board meeting to be legal, a quorum must be present. State statutes generally specify what constitutes a quorum; it is usually a simple majority. Where a quorum does not exist, a board cannot act, otherwise its actions would be deemed as being that of individuals rather than of a board. Where vacancies exist on a board, that does not reduce the number needed for a quorum.

f. *Voting.* Rules governing voting in school board meetings are included in statutes or rules of procedure. These rules often prescribe the method for voting as well as the number of votes required to approve an action.

Individual roll call votes may or may not be required in all kinds of voting. When they are required, they should identify the name of each board member and how he voted on the specific question. Where roll call votes are not required, the number of affirmative and negative votes cast is sufficient.

When a quorum is present, a majority vote is usually sufficient except for special, designated situations, such as the dismissal of professional personnel, in which case a larger number than a simple majority is usually required. Many people feel that when a school board decides a matter unanimously, the better it is for

---

19. State *ex rel.* Broussard v. Gauthe, 262 La. App. 105, 265 So. 2d 828 (1972).

the district. It may be sound thinking in terms of politics or psychology, but it is not a legal consideration.

A board member attending a meeting has a duty to vote; failure to do so is an abrogation of his responsibility. There are some cases on record of a member in attendance not voting on an issue. According to prevailing law, his vote is viewed as acceding to the decision of the majority. An example of this situation occurred in a case over fifty years ago.[20] Of a seven-member board, three voted in favor of a contract, two opposed it, and two did not vote. The court held that the motion carried by a vote of five to two.

In a more recent case from Missouri, a three-member board was considering an annexation issue. One voted for it, one against it, and one refused to vote. The court held that the issue was approved. It observed:

> There were two of the three members of the School Board present and by their presence constituted a quorum for the transaction of business and it became and was the duty of each member to vote for or against any proposition which was presented to them. Mr. Eveland voted in favor of submitting the question of annexation and Mr. Williams did not vote. . . . It was his duty to vote for or against the question submitted. . . . When a member of a school board sits silently by when given an opportunity to vote, he is regarded as acquiescing in, rather than opposing, the measure, and is regarded in law as voting with the majority.[21]

Bolmeier notes one exception to the general rule of one acquiescing with the majority when he fails to vote and that exception is "when a statute *requires* the affirmative vote of all members present." [22]

School board members cannot delay their voting by leaving the room while remaining in the vicinity. Various courts have held that, technically, those members are still viewed as being in attendance.

g. *Minutes.* Evidence of what a school board has decided is revealed through the records the board has kept. The minutes provide legal evidence of the matters that were transacted. Not

---

20. Collins v. Janey, 147 Tenn. 477, 249 S.W. 801 (1923).

21. Mullins v. Eveland, 234 S.W.2d 639 (Mo. 1950).

22. E. C. BOLMEIER, THE SCHOOL IN THE LEGAL STRUCTURE 167 (2d ed. Cincinnati: W. H. Anderson Company, 1973).

only do the minutes supply evidence but, if necessary, they also reveal the intent of the board.

Board members cannot, as individuals, speak for the board itself. It is only through the minutes that a board actually speaks. The minutes serve several purposes: to reveal what a board has done, to provide guidance for the present board, to serve as a resource for future boards, and to serve as a record for citizen or public inquiry. In short, minutes indicate what a board actually did and how it acted.

Most school boards keep rather sophisticated forms of minutes. While desirable, it is not legally required. So long as they reflect what a board of education actually did, minutes need not be formal or technical. The major objective is accuracy and clarity. A full statement on what should be included in minutes is given by Brown:

> Generally, business to be covered in minutes should include names of all those present, including those who come late, with arrival noted, actions upon all communications to the board, reports of all standing and special committees and action taken thereon, business manager's report, including therein a financial statement of the general account, building fund, sinking fund, monthly vouchers, bids, purchases, the superintendent's report, including therein personnel changes, those employees hired and discharged or retiring, curriculum changes or suggestions, changes in policy to be discussed, future meeting sites and dates.
> When policy is to be changed, minutes should include a copy of the old and new policy, complete salary schedules when adopted, names of all visitors giving presentations, and recording of board action of all resolutions, including recording by name the number of ayes and nays.[23]

A school board can amend or correct its minutes. Although it does not have to take place at the next meeting, it should be done within a reasonable period of time. The amending or correcting cannot be done to satisfy the whims of a member or even the entire board; rather, the content must reflect actual board action. Minutes cannot be altered after a meeting on the basis of information by

---

23. Brown, "Records of School Board Meetings," Ch. 2 in LEGAL PROBLEMS OF SCHOOL BOARDS, (Arthur A. Rezny ed., Cincinnati: W. H. Anderson Company, 1966).

or political pressure from citizens unless the change reflects actual board decisions.

School board minutes become official when formally approved by the board. Courts have held that the notes of minutes do not constitute board minutes. States vary with respect to requirements for the actual execution of the minutes. In some states all board members must sign them; in others, the signature of the president and the secretary is sufficient. After formal approval and the required signatures, minutes are then considered as being public documents and may be inspected by interested persons.

§ 3.4. Office-Holding of Board Members.

a. *Selection of Board Members.* There is no uniformity among the states with respect to requirements for becoming a local school board member. Even within some states, requirements vary.

The number of board members varies from three to over twenty. The modal number is usually from five to nine. The larger the total school district population, the greater the tendency to have large school boards, thus large city school systems tend to have large school boards.

Board members are selected in a variety of ways. Over four-fifths of the local school board members in this country are elected, most often in a nonpartisan election. In some states, however, board members run in a partisan election. Where board members are appointed, it is by a variety of ways: by local judges, grand jury, city council, mayor, governor, or by the legislature.

Qualifications for office are minimal. Among the requirements are citizenship, a minumum age, and residency within the district. Other more general requirements might state that a candidate be of good character and have an interest in education.

Most board members serve without pay. Traditionally, they have been viewed as rendering a public or civic service, and a salary would be inimical to that thinking. Although they receive no salary, some board members have received modest expense allowances. More recently, however, some larger affluent school districts have begun to pay board members a salary of several thousand dollars a year.

Terms of office vary among, and sometimes within, states. A

typical term is from two to six years with members serving overlapping terms. The member with the most seniority does not automatically accede to the presidency or chairmanship of the board.

b. *Restrictions on Office Holding.* When one becomes a school board member, he may have to forego some opportunities that he might otherwise be entitled to. He may, for example, be restricted in the employment of his relatives; he may be ineligible for another office; and he may not do business with the school district. Each of these three restrictions will be examined briefly.

1. EMPLOYMENT OF RELATIVES. Common sense dictates that a school board member should not employ his relatives in a school district that he serves. To do otherwise would be to create a conflict of interest or the possibility of a conflict of interest. Statutes often specify the classes of relatives ineligible for employment, or in more lenient states, statutes may specify that so long as the related board member disqualifies himself from voting on the employment of his relative, the individual may, on getting a favorable vote, be employed.

In a 1977 decision from West Virginia, a court held that a superintendent was not disqualified from holding office simply because he and a board member were married to sisters.[24]

A 1976 case concerned a New York law that forbade more than one member of a family from serving on the same board of education. A wife sought a seat on the Albany school board; her husband was already a member. The court held that the law was sound in that it provided for a broader representation of the school community and it allowed individual members to debate issues with their fellow board members objectively and independent of intimate relationships.[25]

2. DUAL OFFICE HOLDING. Most states have provisions in their constitutions or statutes that forbid the holding of two offices simultaneously. Since board members are viewed as being officers, they are thus ineligible to hold a second office which would be in conflict with the first one. Incompatibility exists when a superordinate-subordinate relationship exists or when the offices

---

24. State *ex rel.* Anderson v. Bd. Educ., 233 S.E.2d 703 (W. Va. 1977).
25. Rosenstock v. Scaringe, 387 N.Y.S.2d 716 (N.Y.A.D. 1976).

are in different branches of government. For example, one could not be a board member as well as a local judge who would rule on school controversies; one could not be a board member and a member of city council which appoints board members and acts on the school's budget.

It has often been held that when one holding a public office accepts another one incompatible with the first one, he automatically resigns the first office. The general principle was modified, however, by a New Jersey court in 1971.[26] The mayor appointed a teacher to fill a vacancy on the school board. The appointment was challenged, and the defendant argued that his acceptance of the board position vacated his teacher's position. The court responded that "Here, defendant teacher was bound by his teaching contract for the school term and was not legally free to abandon one public job for another."

In Pennsylvania the question of the legality of a supervisor's being a member of a school board was litigated.[27] The supervisor was employed by an intermediate school district (a conglomerate of a number of local school districts) and served as a board member for one of the constituent districts. The court held that the two positions were not incompatible in that an intermediate school district is not a school district. The law prohibited only the executive director and the assistant executive director from serving on the intermediate board.

Teachers are considered as being employees, not officers. Even so, they are ineligible to serve as a board member in the district in which they work. They may be eligible, however, to serve as a board member in the district in which they reside but do not work.

In Illinois, in 1977, a court held that a generally-worded statute did not forbid wives of board members from being employed as teachers in that district.[28] Although it appeared that the issue was moot, the court elected to rule on the matter because of the public interest in it. It relied on a provision of the state's Corrupt Practices Act that provides:

No person holding any office, either by election or

---

26. Visotcky v. City Council, 113 N.J. Super. 263, 273 A.2d 597 (1971).

27. Commonwealth *ex rel.* Waychoff v. Tekavec, 456 Pa. 521, 319 A.2d 1 (1974).

28. Hollister v. North, 50 Ill. App. 3d 56, 365 N.E.2d 258 (1977).

appointment under the laws or constitution of this state, may be in any manner interested, either directly or indirectly, in his own name or in the name of any other person, association, trust or corporation, in any contract or the performance of any work in the making or letting of which such officer may be called upon to act or vote.[29]

The court also relied on a statute that provided that a married woman has the right to contract as if she were single and a right to her earnings as her own separate property.

3. CONFLICT OF INTEREST. Another fundamental principle of law is that a school board member cannot have an interest in a contract with an agency he administers. Were he to do so, he would tend to profit from the association. For example, a school board member who was also an insurance broker, wrote a contract for the school district with his firm. His action was inconsistent with the statutes which forbade any school board member from having an interest in any contract made by the board. The court held that the member's action constituted a basis for removal from office.[30]

In another case, a conflict of interest was found to exist in Kentucky when two school board members were declared ineligible for continuing in office.[31] One had sold $55.06 of supplies to the home economics department; the other had continued briefly after his election to supply transportation to the school system. Both were in violation of the statute that provided that no person shall be eligible for office as a school board member, who at the time of election, was involved in the sale of any property, supplies, or services for which school funds were spent.

c. *Disqualification for Office.* When a school board member has been appointed for an indefinite or non-fixed term, he may be removed arbitrarily without cause and without notice. Incident to the power of appointment is the power of removal. Where a school board member has been elected to serve for a fixed term of office, he cannot be removed prior to the expiration of that term except for cause. Cause may involve a number of reasons: malfeasance, misconduct, inefficiency, incapacity, neglect of duty, absence from meetings, illegal expenditures, or financial interest in contracts.

---

29. ILL. REV. STAT. ch. 102, § 104 (1973).
30. People v. Becker, 112 Cal. App. 2d 324, 246 P.2d 103 (1952).
31. Commonwealth *ex rel.* Matthews v. Coatney, 396 S.W.2d 72 (Ky. 1965).

In the case of appointed school board members, the removal may be by the appointive body, or it may be by another agency designated by the statutes. Another method of removal is by a recall election in which a stated number or percentage of the electors petition for a special election to determine if the member may continue in office.

For the removal of an elected board member, notice and hearing are typically required. Generally, a formalized court procedure is not held, and one is not entitled to a jury trial.

Chapter Four
TORT LIABILITY

§ 4.0. Introduction.

A tort is a civil wrong, other than a breach of contract, for which a court will provide a remedy in the form of damages. The wrong grows out of harm to an individual by the unreasonable conduct of others. The remedy is premised on the notion that one should be allowed to recover something, usually money, from the one who harmed him.

At all levels, school personnel are faced with the potentiality of accidents. The educational environment cannot be made accident-proof, for despite the best efforts of all concerned, accidents do occur. An injured party may or may not be able to recover in damages for his injury; this depends on a number of factors. This chapter will treat those factors and others, including the elements of due care, the nature of immunity of various categories of school personnel, and the current status of tort law in the educational sector.

§ 4.1. Intentional Interference.

Torts involve two major categories: intentional interference and negligence. The former grows out of one person invading the rights of another, at which point he commits an intentional tort. Assault and battery fall into this category. Assault is an overt attempt to injure another person physically. Although it does not involve actual physical contact, an individual's behavior or demeanor is such as to put another in a state of peril or to threaten him. Shaking a fist menacingly may constitute assault. Battery involves actual physical contact with another. It is often used in conjunction with and may be the end product of assault.

a. *Assault and Battery.* There have been relatively few assault and battery cases in education, presumably because administrators and teachers have been given considerable discretion in the discipline of school children. Occasionally, however, a parent may sue in the belief that a teacher or principal used extreme methods in controlling student behavior. In a 1974 case from Illinois, a parent sued the school district, charging teachers and school officials with intentionally abusing, attacking, and intimidating her children. She maintained that the child's nervous system and learning abilities had been damaged. The court dismissed the suit. It held that a teacher has the right in Illinois to inflict reasonable corporal punishment as well as to chastise a student verbally. It also held that a teacher cannot be sued for liability unless there is proof of malice.[1]

In a 1973 case it was held that a teacher did not commit assault and battery on a student while restraining him in class. The student had spoken defiantly, used vulgar language, and refused to leave the classroom when ordered. The teacher then moved toward the student to evict him at which point the student threatened the teacher. The teacher immobilized the student's arms and led him toward the door at which point the student extricated himself, swung, and broke a window. His arm was cut. The court ruled that

---

1. Gordon v. Oak Park School Dist. No. 97, 320 N.E.2d 389 (Ill. App. 1974).

the teacher had used reasonable force and no assault and battery attached.[2]

b. *Defamation.* Another category of intentional interference is defamation. Defamation includes two categories: slander and libel. Slander is a spoken word which defames or injures a person's reputation. For one to be successful in a slander suit, a malicious intent to injure must be proven. Libel involves an injury to a person through the medium of printed material.

Like assault and battery, slander and libel suits occur infrequently in education. An example of a libel suit was decided by the California courts in 1975. Parents wrote a letter to their principal, charging that one of the teachers "displayed an utter lack of judgment or respect, had been rude, vindictive and unjust, misused her authority, and had given failing grades to students she did not like." [3] The letter expressed the hope that the teacher would correct her personality defects.

The teacher countered the charges by alleging that the statements were designed to harass her. She then sued the parents for libel.

Both the trial and appellate courts held that the teacher had failed to state a cause of action for libel. Both courts recognized that the parents had used normal channels to communicate their concerns. Further, the communications were held to be privileged, that is, protected in that they had been made through official channels to responsible parties. The court recognized that a teacher may expect to receive unfavorable criticism:

> One of the crosses a public school teacher must bear is intemperate complaint addressed to school administrators by overly-solicitous parents concerned about the teacher's conduct in the classroom. Since the law compels parents to send their children to school, appropriate channels for the airing of supposed grievances against the operation of the school system must remain open.[4]

---

2. Simms v. School Dist. No. 1, 508 P.2d 236 (Ore. App. 1973).
3. Martin v. Kearney, 124 Cal. Rptr. 281, 283 (Cal. App. 1975).
4. *Id.* at 283.

§ 4.2. Negligence.

a. *Criteria of Negligence.* The second major category of torts is negligence, a subject with which this chapter is primarily concerned. Negligence involves conduct by one person that falls below an established or acceptable standard which results in an injury to another person. The standard is a variable one, that is, negligence under one situation may not be under another circumstance. Courts must decide such cases on the basis of the factual situation against a general set of criteria. These criteria typically include four questions: (1) Within the given situation, did one owe a standard of care, a duty, to another? That is, was the individual expected to supervise, maintain a safe environment, or give proper instruction? (2) Did one fail to exercise that standard of care or duty? That is, was the individual derelict in supervising, maintaining a safe environment, or in giving instructions? (3) Was there an accident in which a person was injured? Did one actually suffer some kind of loss or injury? (4) Was the failure to exercise due care the proximate (direct) cause of the injury? The cause of the injury must first be established, then it must be shown that there was some connection between it and one's failure to exercise due care.

b. *Defenses Against Negligence.* One should not assume that, whenever there is an injury, another person is always to blame. Many accidents occur and many tort suits are filed, without the injured party recovering anything. The burden is usually upon the plaintiff (the one bringing the suit) to prove that the defendant was negligent, that is, that he actually was directly responsible for the accident. His negligence could take several forms. It could involve misfeasance — performing an act wrongfully, malfeasance — performing an unlawful act, or nonfeasance — failing to perform a required act.

Several defenses apply in tort actions. Any one, if established, will absolve the defendant of liability. Some districts may, for example, claim immunity from suit on the basis of the state legislature not allowing its agents to be sued. Individual school personnel have no such defense, for through the years they have been subject to tort suits for their negligence. The extent of school district immunity will be explored later in this Chapter.

A second defense is contributory negligence. Under this defense, if it is shown that the injured individual directly and fully contributed to his injury, no one else is to blame. An example is a 1974 case in New York in which a secondary school student, against the instructions of his physical education teacher, participated in gymnastic activities without proper equipment. The appellate court held that the student had contributed directly to his injury.[5]

Closely allied to contributory negligence is a third defense, comparative negligence. Under this defense both a plaintiff and a defendant are jointly held responsible for the accident. The court settlement will properly adjust any damages to the degree of negligent responsibility of either party. This is illustrated in a 1967 case in which a defendant was held for one-half the costs, the principal for one-fourth, and the board of education for one-fourth. The defendant was responsible in that he had injured another pupil at the school's pickup site before school; the other two parties were responsible for failure to supervise and for seeing that there was supervision.[6]

The fourth defense is assumption of risk. An individual understands, appreciates, and agrees that, in undertaking an activity, he subjects himself to a possible injury, for one cannot guarantee the safety of another. This applies particularly in activities that are considered as being potentially dangerous. For example, when an athlete tries out for the football team, he risks an injury. In any activity one assumes "normal" risks, but not those risks growing out of the negligence of another.

§ 4.3. School District Immunity.

For many years school districts were held not liable for negligence suits. This action was premised on the notion that a school district is an agency of the state, and, like the state, it is not liable in its corporate capacity unless the legislature has specifically ruled otherwise. Further, it was viewed that a school district's funds are trust funds — earmarked for educational purposes and not for payment for damages.

---

5. Passafora v. Board of Educ., 353 N.Y.S.2d 178 (App. Div. 1974).
6. Titus v. Lindberg, 228 A.2d 65 (N.J. 1967).

a. *Historical Precedents.* The precedent for the long-established principle of tort immunity of school districts goes back almost 200 years to a decision of an English court, *Russell v. Men of Devon.*[7] The factual situation involved a wagon broken down as a result of a bridge being out of repair. The wagon owner sued the men of the county, for they were responsible for maintaining the roads. In affixing no negligence, the court held that neither law nor reason supported the action. If a suit were allowed, it would likely lead to many such suits which would mean that all inhabitants of the county would have to pay. It also held that the legislature, not the courts, should be the source for allowing such suits. It concluded by stating that it was better for an individual to sustain an injury than the public an inconvenience.

The *Russell* decision was accepted as precedent in this country. The first real test of its application came in 1812, and it involved a similar situation to the one in *Russell.* The Massachusetts court held that public or quasi-public corporations are not liable for negligence.[8] Thus, the precedent for the immunity of school districts in this country was established and remained in effect until 1959. That year, in a case in Illinois, a state court held that a school district was liable for damages to a student injured in a school bus accident.[9] The bus had left the road, hit a culvert, exploded, and burned. The student suffered severe and permanent burns for which he sought compensation of $56,000. In its precedent-making decision, the court reasoned that liability should naturally follow negligence. The notion that "The king can do no wrong" was held to be outmoded. Further, education was viewed as being a big business, for school districts have large budgets with which to conduct their affairs.

The *Molitor v. Kaneland* decision started a movement in other states to abrogate the immunity doctrine. Several approaches have been followed since 1959. One has been for the legislature to abrogate the immunity doctrine; another has been for the courts to abrogate it. In some states it has been adhered to, modified, or operates on an insurance-waiver theory. Although the number

---

7. Russell v. Men of Devon, 100 Eng. Rep. 359, 2 T. R. 667 (1788).
8. Mower v. Leicester, 9 Mass. 237 (1812).
9. Molitor v. Kaneland, 163 N.E.2d 89 (Ill. 1959).

changes, to date, approximately half the states now allow school districts to be sued.

b. *Governmental and Proprietary Functions.* One reason why courts have been reluctant to tamper with school district immunity has been because of their recognition that schools perform a governmental function. As such, they are instrumentalities of the state and, thus, act as the state itself. Some courts have distinguished, however, between what a district is required to do and what it elects to do. They have held the former to be governmental and the latter proprietary. One court characterized a proprietary function as follows: the school is not required to perform it, it can be carried out by a commercial agency, and it is used to raise money.[10] Consequently, some, but not all, courts have held school districts to a higher standard of care in performing a proprietary as opposed to a governmental function. Other courts have held that any such distinction is an artificial rather than a real difference.

§ 4.4. School Board Immunity.

Through the years courts have made a distinction between the immunity of school boards as corporate entities and school board members as individuals. When board members act within the scope of their legislatively prescribed or implied authority, they are acting as a corporate body. So long as they act honestly and in good faith, within their prescribed authority, they will not be held liable for an injury growing out of an error of judgment. That is, they cannot be sued for conscientious mistakes or errors in judgment. Courts have reasoned that to rule otherwise would be to deprive a community of potentially valuable civic leadership.

§ 4.5. School Board Member Immunity.

a. *In General.* In contrast to the corporate action of a board of education, board members have been successfully sued as individuals. It is only when the members of a board of education exceed their authority that they may be liable — as individuals, not as a corporate body. In order to hold a member liable, it must be shown that he was motivated by malice, corrupt motive, or attempt

---

10. Morris v. School Dist., 144 A.2d 737 (Pa. 1958).

to injure. Otherwise, board members have considerable discretion, make many decisions involving judgment, and are not subject to suit.

b. *Liability Under the Civil Rights Act.* The above standard was the general holding of courts for many decades. However, in the mid-1960's an old law was rediscovered which changed the status of the immunity of individual school board members. That law is the Civil Rights Act of 1871. Section 1983 of that act provides as follows:

> Every person who, under color of any statute, ordinance, regulation, custom or usage of any State or Territory, subjects or causes to be subjected any citizen of the United States or other person within the jurisdiction thereof to the deprivation of any rights, privileges or immunities secured by the Constitution and laws shall be liable to the party injured in an action at law, suit in equity or other proper proceeding for redress.[11]

The above act provides that, in education, school board members and school administrators who deprive employees of their constitutional rights may be personally liable. An injured person may sue simply to have the wrong corrected (a suit in equity) or he may sue for monetary damages. Federal district courts have original jurisdiction in such cases.

1. SUITS BY TEACHERS. A variety of court actions have been brought by teachers under this act. They include an illegal dismissal of a black teacher who was a civil rights advocate,[12] and an illegal dismissal of a teacher who refused to shave a beard grown over winter vacation.[13] A federal court in Georgia ruled that a school board was liable for refusing to employ a teacher solely on the ground that she lived in a commune.[14] In contrast to the above cases in which teachers successfully defended their First Amendment rights, a teacher in Massachusetts was held not to have that Amendment's protection. He had carried and fondled a mannequin in public and was dismissed for that reason. The court held that freedom of speech and expression did not extend to him

---

11. 42 U.S.C. § 1983 (1871).
12. Johnson v. Branch, 364 F.2d 177 (4th Cir. 1966).
13. Lucia v. Duggan, 303 F. Supp. 112 (D. Mass. 1969).
14. Doherty v. Wilson, 356 F. Supp. 35 (M. D. Ga. 1973).

in such circumstances.[15] A teacher was not upheld for exercising freedom of speech in distributing literature that contained deliberate, misleading statements tending to antagonize the school board and administration.[16] Other cases have been litigated, for the most part based on denial of rights under the First and Fourteenth Amendments.

2. SUITS BY STUDENTS. The liability of school board members was extended under Section 1983 to students by a 1975 decision of the Supreme Court of the United States.[17] In its narrow holding, the Court ruled that school board members may be sued by students who are denied constitutional rights. This case involved a denial of due process in a suspension hearing for mixing an alcoholic drink with fruit punch at a school function. The girls admitted having done it, and a suspension hearing was held before the school board. Neither the girls nor their parents were asked to attend. A second hearing was held two weeks later, at which time the board announced the conclusions which had been reached during the previous meeting. This meeting was attended by the girls, their parents, and counsel. The school board did not alter its punishment — expulsion for the remainder of the school term which amounted to three months.

In its reasoning, supporting the board, the Court recognized that school board

> action taken in the good-faith fulfillment of their responsibilities and within the bounds of reason under all the circumstances will not be punished and that they need not exercise their discretion with undue timidity.[18]

The Court recognized that school officials have some degree of immunity for their acts. They may make a mistake and not be held liable for it. So long as they act sincerely and with a belief that they are doing right, they will be protected by qualified good-faith immunity under Section .1983. The criterion that the Court expressed in determining if liability applies is as follows:

> [A] school board member is not immune from liability for damages under § 1983 if he knew or reasonably should

---

15. Wishart v. McDonald, 367 F. Supp. 336 (D. Mass. 1973).
16. Vanderzanden v. Lowell School Dist. No. 71, 369 F. Supp. 67 (D. Ore. 1973).
17. Wood v. Strickland, 420 U.S. 308, 95 S. Ct. 992, 43 L. Ed. 2d 214 (1975).
18. *Id.* at 321.

have known that the action he took within his sphere of official responsibility would violate the constitutional rights of the student affected, or if he took the action with the malicious intention to cause a deprivation of constitutional rights or other injury to the student.[19]

With respect to awarding damages, the Court held it would be appropriate only "if the school board member has acted with such an impermissible motivation or with such disregard of the student's clearly established constitutional rights that his action cannot reasonably be characterized as being in good faith." [20]

§ 4.6. School Employee Immunity.

The immunity traditionally enjoyed by school boards has never been extended to school employees. Superintendents, principals, and teachers have always been subject to tort suits for their own negligence. When one's actions fall below a standard of care expected of the average person, resulting in an injury, negligence is established. The behavior expected of school personnel is that which is measured against what a reasonably prudent person, one of ordinary intelligence and prudence, would do, or should have done, in the same or similar circumstances. Against that standard, a court will then determine whether liability may be imposed.

A key element in the determination of negligence is the matter of forseeability. An administrator or a teacher is expected to "Take reasonable care to avoid acts or omissions he can reasonably forsee would be likely to injure." [21] An educator is expected to forsee the possible consequences of an action or a condition and then take measures, where necessary, to remedy them. For example, in the ordinary course of a work day, it may involve removing shattered glass in a corridor, warning students to keep away from workers pruning a large tree, adding supervisors to a bus loading area where fights have recently occurred, or giving special instructions prior to undertaking an experiment in chemistry.

a. *Supervision.* Both administrators and teachers are expected

---

19. *Id.* at 322.

20. *Id.* at 322.

21. Seitz, *Tort Liability of Teachers and Administators for Negligent Conduct Toward Pupils,* 20 CLEV. STATE L. REV. 556 (1971).

to supervise students. A general charge in a tort suit is that an educator failed to supervise or failed to supervise properly.

Although no one standard of what constitutes adequate supervision exists, some generally accepted principles do prevail. For an administrator, adequate supervision involves the assignment of a qualified teacher to the activity he is directing. It includes making known to the teacher a set of general expectations. It means making periodic visits or inspections to ascertain if the teacher is meeting those conditions set for him. It also involves periodic inspection of the building, grounds, and facilities to determine that no apparent hazards exist or to see that maintenance corrects inadequacies.

For a teacher, adequate supervision involves due care commensurate with the circumstances. Older students need less direction than younger ones; mature students need less direction than less responsible ones. Low risk activities require less supervision than potentially dangerous ones. Van Der Smissen has pointed out that a teacher must "be alert to conditions which may be dangerous to participants, such as rowdyism, defective premises, lack of use of protective devices or safety equipment, and the age-skill experience of the participants in relation to the assumption of risks." [22]

Courts recognize that students cannot be held to the same degree of care as adults, consequently less is expected of them; more is demanded of teachers who supervise them. In spite of this notion, a teacher cannot possibly supervise all students constantly at all times of the day and in all places at school. Continuous supervision is not necessarily required, but that does not imply that a teacher should not be vigilant. An Indiana court absolved a teacher of liability who was out of the room when a student was injured.

> [W]hat constitutes due care and adequate supervision depends largely upon the circumstances surrounding the incident such as the number and age of the students left in the classroom, the activity in which they were engaged, the duration of the period in which they were left without supervision, the ease of providing some alternative means of supervision and the extent to which

---

22. VAN DER SMISSEN, LEGAL LIABILITY OF CITIES AND SCHOOLS FOR INJURIES IN RECREATION AND PARKS 115 (1975 Supp., Cincinnati: W. H. Anderson Co., 1975).

> the school board has provided and implemented guidelines and resources to insure adequate supervision.[23]

In the above case, the elementary school teacher demonstrated to the satisfaction of the court that she had properly prepared the class for independent activity, that the students were responsible, there was no evidence of previous misconduct, and the students were not engaged in any hazardous activity. She could not have predicted that a student would bring a dangerous substance to school and that it would explode.

Courts remain in disagreement over a teacher's liability while not in the classroom. Some recognize that a teacher's mere presence is enough to discourage student misconduct while other courts recognize that a teacher's presence is no guarantee against spontaneous misbehavior.

Supervision also involves the corollary of instruction. Together, they constitute the basis for many tort suits involving teachers and administrators. Moreover, a school district may be held liable for lack of supervision of its personnel. Several court decisions, treated briefly, relate to the nature of both supervision and instruction.

Liability was established in a 1975 case in Louisiana, and the injured student was awarded damages of over $100,000.[24] He was seriously injured when his science project, a simulated volcano, exploded. The project was constructed of molded clay and mud around a glass bottle into which a metal can containing powder from a firecracker had been inserted.

While the student was waiting for the school bus, the volcano erupted and caused the boy to lose three fingers. Negligence was established in the following manner: 1. Neither the teacher nor the administration had imposed any regulations regarding the project. 2. No one had assumed any overall supervision for the display. 3. The principal had not required any reports or set any guidelines for Display Day. 4. The teacher had not determined what substances were to be used and what ones were dangerous.

A second case, decided also in 1975, established the negligence

---

23. Miller v. Griesel, 308 N.E.2d 701, 707 (Ind. 1974).
24. Simmons v. Beauregard Parish School Bd., 315 So. 2d 883 (La. App. 1975).

of a school district and the non-negligence of a teacher.[25] It illustrates arguments propounded by the plaintiff in establishing, and the defendant in refuting, a case of negligence. It involved a student injured in a high risk activity, a physical education class. While performing on a trampoline, she suffered severe injuries. The activity was required of all freshmen and, although the student was apprehensive about doing a "front drop", her teacher encouraged her to do so. Only one teacher supervised the 20-25 students performing on three or four trampolines; however, each trampoline was surrounded by spotters while the teacher alternated among each group. At the time of the accident the teacher was ten feet away watching another student.

The teacher was charged with negligence for failing to supervise closely and for forcing a reluctant student to engage in the stunt.

The school district was charged with negligence for failing to provide proper supervision for beginning students, to increase supervision as injuries increased, to require the use of a safety harness, to provide more teachers and student leaders per class, to separate beginners from experienced performers, and to test beginners on the trampoline.

In defense, the school district cited the following safety precautions: It had certified instructors present at all times. Student spotters were to be stationed around each trampoline in use. Before any student undertook an exercise, safety principles were to be taught and demonstrated. Finally, students were not to be forced to do any stunt.

The court ruled that, under the school code, the plaintiff was not bound to a standard of proof of wilful and wanton misconduct in the supervision of students in school activities before any liability can be imposed on the defendant. Using a lesser standard of care, the court took note of a number of injuries in the classes and imposed negligence on the district.

School personnel were held not to be negligent as a result of a student drowning.[26] The youth, aged eleven, was enrolled in a school-sponsored summer program. The class of seventeen was

---

25. Chilton v. Cook County School Dist. No. 207, Maine Township, 26 Ill. App. 3d 459, 325 N.E.2d 666 (1975).

26. Wong v. Waterloo Community School Dist., 232 N.W.2d 865 (Iowa 1975).

supervised by one teacher plus six helpers, some of whom could not swim. The entire class was in the swimming pool at the time of the drowning. The deceased was last seen at the shallow end of the pool; his body was found at the deep end.

The court rejected all claims by the plaintiff and held that the evidence did not support negligence on the part of school personnel. Other facts to consider were the inherent dangers of swimming, a possibility of bodily malfunction, and an individual's own negligence.

In an accident in an unsupervised area of the school grounds, a Hawaiian court held that the absence of supervisory personnel was not the proximate cause of a student's injury.[27] "The duty to supervise does not require that every portion of the buildings be supervised. If certain areas are known to be dangerous, or should have been known to be dangerous, that requires supervision. There was no evidence that this area was dangerous." [28] The accident occurred when a student was hit in the eye as she was leaving school.

There was reasonable supervision, the court held, in that three adults supervised the bus loading area, one adult supervised the cross-walk at the street in front of the school, the vice-principal generally toured the campus, the principal stationed himself on an elevated walkway where he could see much of the campus, and teachers supervised hallways as the students left the building. These kinds of supervision were sufficient to relieve the district of any liability. The court recognized that if certain areas are known to be dangerous, they require supervision. Since there was no evidence that the area of the injury was dangerous, school officials had no duty to supervise there.

Litigation has also involved supervision before and after school as well as during the lunch hour. A school is responsible for students on their way to and from school as well as while they are at school. This does not mean, however, that school personnel must supervise children several blocks away from school nor that they can insure a safe environment away from school.[29] It does mean that authorities may set down reasonable rules and regula-

27. Miller v. Yoshimoto, 536 P.2d 1195 (Hawaii 1975).
28. *Id.* at 1200.
29. Oglesby v. Seminole County Bd. of Pub. Instr., 328 So. 2d 515 (Fla. 1976).

tions to which students are expected to conform. (See, for example, *Titus v. Lindberg*, § **4.2.a.**) Therefore, students may be held accountable to school authorities for misconduct occurring while on their way to and from school. A New Jersey court ruled that a principal was responsible, in part, beyond the school property itself, for providing a safe place for students in a heavily used area adjacent to school property.[30] The area was well known and often used as a short-cut for students during the noon hour and after school. Although a hazard existed, school authorities had taken no measures to have it corrected.

Reasonable supervision is necessary also during the noon hour. However, extraordinary supervision is not required. Thus, on a cold snowy day, a teacher was not expected to remain outside the building during the noon hour in supervising students returning from lunch.[31]

In one of the largest tort settlements in history, a case in California recognized the negligence of several people, resulting in permanent disability to the injured student, and a multi-million dollar settlement.[32] The charge was failure to supervise and to diagnose and provide proper treatment for an injury.

The accident occurred on a school playground in a summer program sponsored jointly by the school district and the city. While the program supervisor was inside a building, two boys became involved in a fight. One boy hit another on the head with a softball bat. When he learned of the fight, the supervisor separated the two boys. The injured one mounted his bicycle and rode home. His skull was fractured, an artery was torn, and a blood clot had formed, bringing pressure on the brain.

The boy's father took him to the hospital where various personnel acted negligently. His admission was delayed because of incorrect information given an intern. The people initially examining him had not determined correctly the severity of the injury; the suggestion was made that he should be admitted for observation. The boy exhibited the following behavior: drop of

---

30. Caltavuturo v. City of Passaic, 307 A.2d 114 (N.J. 1973).
31. Lawes v. Board of Educ., 266 N.Y.S.2d 364 (N.Y. 1965).
32. Niles v. City of San Rafael, 116 Cal. Rptr. 733 (Cal. App. 1974).

pulse, headache, swollen tissues, grogginess, sleepiness, irritability, perspiring, loss of color, and vomiting.

A staff member suggested that the father take his son home and observe him there. The father was not given any guidelines for determining change in behavior. He did, however, take the boy home but returned within three hours. The diagnosis this time was intracranial bleeding. The child remained in a coma for forty-six days. He became permanently disabled. The brain damage was irreparable, although his mental capacities were otherwise unaffected. Physically, he has only slight movements of the right hand and foot, is mute but can communicate by eye movements.

The jury awarded the boy $25,000 from the city and the school district and $4,000,000 from the hospital and the director of the outpatient clinic. The former had failed to provide proper supervision on the playground; the latter had failed to attend the plaintiff and treat him properly. That failure had aggravated the injury. Testimony revealed that, had the child been treated properly, he would have had an excellent chance of recovery.

b. *Instruction.* As mentioned in the previous section, instruction is often a part of supervision. According to Root, evidence of reasonable instruction includes:

> explaining and demonstrating how equipment operates, how materials should be used, and the proper performance of procedures or exercises; explaining the inherent dangers of equipment, materials, and procedures; instructing on methods of avoiding danger; requiring students to use protective devices; checking that equipment and materials are being used properly; checking that students are proceeding properly; and enforcing all safety rules.[33]

The previous section on supervision pointed out that school districts, administrators, and teachers may be liable for lack of supervision. In contrast, in the area of instruction, responsibility lies more specifically with a teacher. Courts look to the sufficiency of instruction in terms of the circumstances of a case. They determine if, in view of a given learning activity or experience,

---

33. Suzanne Root, Administrators' and Teachers' Perceptions of the Duty of Due Care in Preventing Student Injury. (unpublished doctoral dissertation, Temple University, 1977), at 70.

there was reasonable instruction. Since this is often difficult to determine, courts often rely on the testimony of experts. These experts may be called on to testify if a given activity has educational value, was appropriate for the specific group of students in question, and if the instructions were sufficient and appropriate. Judgments are often made about the appropriateness of an activity in terms of a child's size, age, and skill.

Instructional care can also mean other things. It may include posting, demonstrating, and distributing safety regulations, reviewing and reinforcing safety measures, warning students of potential dangers, screening students before they undertake an activity, and testing students to ascertain their mastery of safety information and procedures.

The following case illustrates the liability of a teacher for failure to warn a student of a potential danger.[34] The student had constructed a cannon in a machine shop, taken it home and later loaded it, causing it to fire. The explosion blew off two fingers and part of a palm and wrist. Even though the accident did not occur at school, the teacher was negligent in not giving proper instructions to the pupil.

In another case, a teacher was charged with negligence for failing to enforce rules and regulations and for not supervising.[35] A non-class member was repairing his auto with an acetylene torch when a spark ignited the gas tank. The tank exploded, killing one student and seriously injuring another.

c. *Facilities.* Another responsibility of school authorities is to provide buildings, equipment, and grounds that are safe for students. While one cannot assure that a school environment will be accident-free, he must be prudent in lessening the possibility of an accident. Although educators have no control over building and safety codes, they are responsible for inspecting the place for defects, reporting hazardous conditions, and taking temporary measures, if necessary, in protecting people against possible harm until the hazard is removed. If considerable time elapses before a problem can be corrected, one may, for example, warn people to

---

34. Calandri v. Ione Unified School Dist., 33 Cal. Rptr. 333 (1963).
35. Dutcher v. City of Santa Rosa High School Dist., 290 P.2d 316 (Cal. 1957).

stay clear of an area, post signs about the hazard, close off the area completely, or station supervisors there.

Time is a key element in determining if liability exists for unsafe conditions. Courts ask how long a problem existed, how long authorities had knowledge of it, and if there has been sufficient time to correct it.

Major responsibility for providing a safe environment rests with a school board. It is responsible for landscaping grounds, constructing buildings, and providing equipment. Defects in those areas lie not so much with teachers and administrators as with a board. A teacher's responsibility is in the careful use of such facilities. When conditions are determined to be unsafe, a teacher should present evidence, with documentation, to the principal who, in turn, would request that the matter be corrected. Both teacher and principal should retain a copy of the report. In the meantime, one should use good judgment in determining whether to avoid an area or discontinue using a facility or equipment considered in need of correction.

Several cases follow, which illustrate problems concerning safe facilities that arise at school and their disposition by courts. In Kentucky, a suit was brought against a board of education for allegedly permitting an excavation to remain unfilled. On the morning after a child had attended a ball game at school, his body was found at the bottom of that pit. The court ruled that governmental immunity in that state prevented any recovery.[36]

A different ruling was handed down in Pennsylvania in a case in which the immunity doctrine was abrogated.[37] The plaintiffs brought suit against the School District of Philadelphia for an injury to a student, aged fifteen, whose arm was caught in a shredding machine in an upholstery class. They alleged successfully that the district had failed to have a proper safety device for the machine, maintained defective machinery, and failed to warn children of the defective machinery. The state's Supreme Court agreed.

A New York court ruled, over three decades earlier than the Pennsylvania court, that, for failure to provide a protective apron

36. Smiley v. Hart City Bd. of Educ., 518 S.W.2d 785 (Ky. 1975).
37. Ayala v. Philadelphia Bd. of Educ., 305 A.2d 877 (Pa. 1973).

for a student operating a lathe, the school district was negligent.[38] The court referred to the state statute requiring that the board of education furnish equipment necessary for the efficient management of educational activities.

A wet gymnasium floor, on which a basketball player slipped and injured his back, was held not to be dangerous.[39] Hence, the boy could not recover. The boy's coach had not questioned the condition of the floor; the opposing coaches and the referees did not think the matter serious enough to cancel the interscholastic game.

There was no requirement that a school district supervise a Saturday morning baseball game on the premises of an elementary school.[40] A child, injured by a bicycle, could not collect damages.

In another case, an injured child collected $50,000 in damages from a city and the local school board.[41] She was brain-injured when, on a swing set, a steel support pole dislodged and struck her on the head.

The school board had purchased used equipment on property owned by the city. The area was unsupervised. It was held that the city had a duty to exercise reasonable care in erecting and maintaining the park. It did not have to have notice of a defective condition to render it liable, for here it had actually created the hazard.

Responsibility for safe facilities includes not only grounds and classrooms, but corridors as well.[42] A loose rail on a stairway separated from the wall, causing a child to fall five or six steps on a marble stairway. The fact that the railing had been loose for several months established a *prima facie* case of negligence.

d. *Field Trips.* The same principles of tort law apply on field trips as they do at school. Responsibility may be shared, however, by non-school personnel who may also be involved in the activity, for example, the group's host and the transportation carrier may be subject to liability. It is also possible that an injured student may have been negligent.

---

38. Edkins v. Board of Educ., 41 N.E.2d 75 (N.Y. 1942).

39. Nunez v. Isidore Newman High School, 306 So. 2d 457 (La. App. 1975).

40. Orsini v. Guilderland Central School Dist., 46 A.D.2d 700, 360 N.Y.S.2d 288 (1974).

41. Watts v. Town of Homer, 301 So. 2d 729 (La. App. 1974).

42. Wiener v. Board of Educ., 48 A.D.2d 877, 369 N.Y.S.2d 207 (1975).

Liability waivers, or release forms, are often used by school authorities prior to students undertaking a field trip. Since a district or its employees cannot actually waive away their responsibilities, liability waiver forms may diminish the possibility of a suit, otherwise their essential purposes are in informing parents and securing permission for the trip.[43]

Persons on field trips are considered as being either licensees or invitees. Although courts are not in full agreement, a student on a field trip is generally considered as being a licensee. A licensee is one who is on the premises of another by permission rather than by invitation. Since a visitor is there at the convenience of the host, the host owes his guest no more than a duty to abstain from actually harming him. In contrast, an invitee is one who is on the premises of another by invitation of an owner. An owner has a greater care of duty in protecting the visitor from injury. Not only must the premises be safe, but the owner also has a duty to warn a visitor of possible dangers. This principle was stated in *Nunez:*

> An owner or occupier of lands or buildings must take reasonable and ordinary care to protect invitees from any dangerous conditions on the premises. He must also warn them of any latent dangerous defects in the premises and inspect the premises for any possible dangerous conditions of which he does not know.[44]

In a case involving a drowning on a class outing, it was held that a high school principal had given adequate instructions concerning the activity.[45] In another case, action was brought against a museum, a school district, and two teachers for injuries sustained by a boy, aged twelve, who was assaulted while on tour of a museum. The court dismissed the suit, for it was the intervention of a third party, the assaulter, who actually brought on the injury.[46]

---

43. The only known exception to this holding is by an appellate court in Georgia which disallowed a claim by an individual who had signed a liability waiver prior to being injured in test-driving a motorcycle. Cash v. Street and Trail, Inc., 136 Ga. App. 463 (1975).

44. Nunez, *supra* at 458.

45. Cox v. Barnes, 469 S.W.2d 61 (1971).

46. Mancha v. Field Museum of Natural History, 5 Ill. App. 3d 699, 283 N.E.2d 899 (1972).

e. *Medical Treatment.* To a limited extent, an educator stands in place of a parent (*in loco parentis*). One such occasion is during an emergency. Even here, however, that responsibility is limited. An administrator or teacher is not expected to, nor should he, treat a sick pupil; that is a function of one trained in medicine. An educator's responsibility is limited only to administering first aid after having determined that one needs attention. Even here, Kigin cautions:

> Whether or not to administer treatment subsequent to the injury of a pupil constitutes a risk that must be taken with the hope that the court or jury would hold the defendant blameless for what he does or does not do. This is based on prudence. By reason of the relationship of the teacher to the pupil (*in loco parentis*) the teacher is obligated to do the best he can for the pupil in the event of an injury. It is to the teacher's distinct advantage to be trained in at least the rudiments of first aid.[47]

Like Kigin, Appenzeller cautions that teachers are expected to administer life-saving first aid when needed, but they are not expected to go beyond that. First aid is limited to giving temporary care until one can secure the services of a physician.[48]

An educator can be charged with excessive treatment of a student. A coach acted negligently in allowing an injured pupil to be taken off a football field without a stretcher. The movement of the player aggravated the injury.[49]

An educator can also be charged with doing too little. During football practice a boy became ill from exhaustion and began vomiting. Twenty minutes later the bus took him and his teammates to the school. The boy was placed on the floor of the cafeteria and later taken to the shower room where he was placed on a blanket. One of the coaches placed an ammonia capsule by the boy's nose. The coaches then reviewed the first aid manual but refused to call a doctor. It was a parent who noted that the boy needed professional attention immediately. The child's mother was

---

47. DENIS J. KIGIN, TEACHER LIABILITY IN SCHOOL-SHOP ACCIDENTS 97 (Ann Arbor: Prakken Publications, Inc., 1973).

48. H. APPENZELLER, ATHLETICS AND THE LAW 208 (Charlottesville: The Michie Company, 1975).

49. Welch v. Dumsmuir Joint Union High School Dist., 326 P.2d 663 (Cal. 1958).

called, she called a doctor, and he sent the boy to a hospital. He suffered heat exhaustion and irreversible shock and died the next day. The court drew two conclusions: that the delay in getting medical attention caused his death and that the coaches had attempted to administer first aid in a negligent manner.[50]

A 1942 case has long been cited over the matter of untrained people attempting to give medical treatment.[51] A boy, aged ten, had an infected finger although it did not prevent his playing ball. Two teachers decided to treat the infection. They kept the boy after school and immersed his hand for approximately ten minutes in a pan of boiling water. The hand was permanently disfigured. Since no emergency existed and neither teacher had medical training, the situation did not justify the teachers' action.

§ 4.7. Accountability.

Traditionally, courts have been reluctant to second-guess school authorities and their evaluation of a teacher's competence. More often than not, judges first confine their review to procedural matters by insuring that all channels were properly followed. Then, they ascertain if the board's action was supported by sufficient evidence and whether the members' action was arbitrary or capricious.

That traditional stance of courts concerning review of school performance is now in a transitional period in the second half of the 1970's. A number of factors are responsible for this change. Many states have instituted competency-based programs which spell out instructional objectives and attempt to measure what is learned. Parents, in revolting against tax increases for education, have demanded more of schools in general and greater achievement of their children. Students have begun to sue school districts for failure to learn or achieve, and administrators are subject to increased controls in supervising teachers and in evaluating their performance.

As of mid-1978 it is unclear as to what legal trends will develop on the matter of teacher accountability. So far, there have been very few court decisions which provide guidance. In a 1974

---

50. Mogabgab v. Orleans Parish School Bd., 239 So. 2d 456 (La. App. 1970).
51. Guerrieri v. Tyson, 24 A.2d 468 (Pa. 1942).

decision, a teacher's dismissal was upheld for her students having scored low on standardized achievement tests. The improvement of test scores was a primary objective of the school system, and she had failed to produce the results expected of her.[52]

In a more celebrated case in California, a high school graduate sued his school district for what he deemed to be an inadequate education.[53] He filed his suit for damages on two basic tort theories: negligence and false representation. He claimed the district was negligent in teaching, promoting, and graduating him. He claimed the district falsely represented to his mother that he was performing at or near grade level in basic skills.

Under California law, an employer is not liable for the conduct of its employee unless it is first established that the employee would be personally liable for his conduct on some acceptable theory of liability. Further, before damages can be awarded, four conditions must exist: 1. The plaintiff must show a legal cause of action. 2. The cause must be stated in the complaint alleging facts showing a care of duty to the plaintiff. 3. The complaint must show negligence constituting a breach of duty. 4. There must be an injury to the plaintiff as a result of the breach of duty. The court concluded that it was not certain that the plaintiff had suffered injury within the meaning of the law of negligence.

In treating the complexity of the problem, the appellate court revealed the difficulty of clearly establishing negligence for a student's not learning:

> On occasions when the Supreme Court has opened or sanctioned new areas of tort liability, it has noted that the wrongs and injuries involved were both comprehensible and assessible within the existing judicial framework.... This is simply not true of wrongful conduct and injuries allegedly involved in educational malfeasance. Unlike the activity of the highway or the marketplace, classroom methodology affords no readily acceptable standards of care, or cause, or injury. The science of pedagogy itself is fraught with different and conflicting theories of how or what a child

---

52. Scheelhaase v. Woodbury Community Central School Dist., 488 F.2d 237 (8th Cir. 1973), *cert. denied,* 417 U.S. 969 (1974).

53. Peter W. v. San Francisco Unified School Dist., 131 Cal. Rptr. 854 (Cal. App. 1976).

should be taught and any layman might—and commonly does—have his own emphatic views on the subject. The "injury" claimed here is the plaintiff's inability to read and write. Substantial professional authority attests that the achievement of literacy in the schools, or its failure, are influenced by a host of factors which affect the pupil subjectively, from outside the formal teaching process, and beyond the control of its ministers.[54]

In a New York case on the same subject, the judge dismissed the suit.[55] Although the judge felt the matter should be reviewed by a higher court because of the issue involved, he ruled that there was no precedent in the state for attaching liability to a school district for failing to educate a student. The student, aged eighteen, and an unemployed carpenter, alleged that he could not read menus, had to take his driver test orally, and had to rely on his mother for filling out a job application. His parents claimed that teachers promoted him and although he received some special help in the lower grades, it was not until his senior year that he received special tutoring. His reading improved from second to third grade level. The parents charged the administration for failure to provide facilities and personnel, to advise them of the child's difficulty, and to take proper precautions for his condition.

In a number of other states, similar cases have been filed charging negligence for a student's not learning, but to date, rulings have not been issued. The limited case law thus makes the legal status of accountability uncertain.

§ 4.8. Preventing Injuries.

Approximately 50 to 60 tort suits in education are decided each year by courts of record in this country. That number does not reflect the many legal actions settled before they actually reach court nor the many more accidents in which there was no suit. The real objective in being knowledgeable about tort law, however, is not so much in winning a court case but in preventing injury. An educator should seek to provide a healthy and safe environment that lessens the likelihood of accidents.

---

54. *Id.* at 860-61.

55. Donohue v. Copiague Union Free School Dist., No. 77-1122 (Supreme Court, Suffolk County, New York, August 31, 1977).

The cases that have been treated in this chapter are very few in comparison to the thousands that courts have decided through the years. They should alert the reader to the fact that courts are not always in agreement in determining negligence. Where questions of fact are in dispute, a jury trial is held; where questions of law are involved, a judge resolves them.

How can injuries be prevented? There is no guaranteed system for doing so, but precautions can be taken. The following precautions are aimed for school board members, administrators, and teachers:

1. Employ responsible people. These people, at all levels, should be mature and safety conscious.

2. Know the extent of one's authority. Failing to act or overacting can constitute a tort.

3. Be familiar with the rights of one's subordinates. Today, denying a subordinate the exercise of his constitutionally protected rights can be the basis of a tort suit.

4. Award contracts to competent firms in doing business with the school. Responsible people should be engaged in work for the school, whether it be routine maintenance or large-scale construction.

5. Be sensitive to potential problems. One should not overlook a small problem, for it could mushroom into a very serious one.

6. Gear work to the students. A teacher should consider a student's age, maturity, and ability in making assignments.

7. Teach attitudes and responsibilities. Teaching students to be careful and to respect dangers inherent in some learning experiences may be as important as the mastery of subject matter. In like manner, an administrator should instruct teachers about their attitudes and care in helping provide a safe learning environment.

8. Make periodic inspections. The administrator should routinely inspect the entire facility; a teacher should routinely inspect his classroom.

9. Report problems promptly. First, report to the proper authorities that a condition needs correcting, then do what is wise in preventing an injury until the problem is in fact corrected.

10. Avoid overcrowding. Accidents are less likely to occur where people move freely in noncongested areas.

11. Get rid of junk. Waste materials tend to clog a facility, create sanitary and fire hazards, and invite accidents.

12. Exercise reasonable supervision. Extraordinary care is not required; the care of a reasonably prudent person is the standard.

In addition to the safety guidelines listed above, an educator is advised to be covered by liability insurance. Practices vary with respect to its availability, but it is often available to members of a union or professional association. Like administrators and teachers, school board members should also be covered. Law tends to be more exact with respect to an individual member's being covered as distinguished from a school board. There are no problems in a board's purchasing liability insurance, but some states do not state clearly that public tax funds may be used in covering individual board members.

A few states have "save-harmless" statutes. These provide that, in the event of a tort suit, a defendant's legal fees and damage claims will be paid for him.

Many tort suits that reach the courts are decided in favor of an educator, but there are enough decisions otherwise to warrant one to exercise the care of a reasonably prudent person.

Chapter Five

COLLECTIVE NEGOTIATIONS

§ 5.0. Introduction.

Collective bargaining in public education is a phenomenon of the 1960's and 1970's. Although organized labor grew rapidly in this country within the last century, its power as a body had less recognizable influence on the schools. Moreover, courts were reluctant to give unions more power, and they often ruled against strikes and picketing. However, once bargaining began in education, it grew rapidly until today, more than half the states have some kind of legislation which, in varying degree, mandates or permits some kind of bargaining between teachers and school boards.

Three acts by Congress have had considerable impact on organized labor in the private sector. The passage of the Wagner Act (National Labor Relations Act or NLRB) of 1935 is viewed as being a milestone in the development of organized labor. The act, designed to limit the power of management, protects the right of employees to organize and bargain. It also grants to employees the right to strike and picket. Its constitutionality was tested and upheld in 1937.[1]

Twelve years after the passage of the NLRB, Congress attempted to reverse some of the power assumed by unions with the enactment of the Taft-Hartley Act. Another landmark statute was the 1959 Landrum-Griffin Act, designed to regulate the internal affairs of unions.

When public employees began to organize much later than private employees, they followed the pattern set by private business. Legislation authorizing bargaining in public education was first enacted by the General Assembly of Wisconsin in 1959. Other States then began to follow the Wisconsin lead.

The growth of organized labor in public education has not been universally received with approval. Some people view education as being too vital a public function to have it subjected to work stoppages or other kinds of interruptions. Other people have reasoned that a school board cannot delegate authority vested in it by the legislature to another body for decision-making.

A school board may bargain because the legislature authorizes it or because it agrees to. A Louisiana court held, in 1974, that, in the absence of specific legislation, the school board had the authority to negotiate with teachers if it were determined that the process would more effectively and efficiently accomplish its objectives and purposes.[2] An Iowa court tempered the above holding when it ruled that it would be an improper delegation of authority for a school board to enter into a collective bargaining agreement within the industrial context. It held that it would be acceptable to enter into an agreement based on meet-and-confer procedures since that action had no binding effect on the board. It ruled further that all decisions regarding wages, working conditions, and grievances resided with the board.[3]

---

1. National Labor Relations Bd. v. Jones and Laughlin Steel Corp., 301 U.S. 1, 57 S. Ct. 615, 81 L. Ed. 893 (1937).

2. Louisiana Teachers Ass'n v. Orleans Parish School Bd., 303 So. 2d 564 (La. App. 1974).

3. Service Employees Int'l v. Cedar Rapids Community School Dist., 222 N.W.2d 403 (Iowa 1975).

three designated days not originally listed. The court observed, moreover, that the school board had initially contracted the right to fix the number of teaching days.[42]

A California court held in 1977 that paying school teachers for a holiday before Easter was valid and any effect of that action on religious institutions was indirect and incidental.[43]

Courts have tended to rule that the length of a school day is a term and condition of employment. A New York court held that, in the absence of a statutory prohibition or countervailing public ~licy, a school board is free to negotiate on this subject.[44] ailarly, a New Jersey court had held three years earlier that the tension of a school day is a subject of negotiation in that it relates rectly to financial and personal considerations.[45]

5. ACADEMIC FREEDOM. In labor disputes in education, the subject of academic freedom has had limited litigation. Because academic freedom is so closely allied with one's constitutional rights under the First Amendment, it is not usually surrendered to a union agreement. Further, when disputes on this issue do occur, they are not usually subject to arbitration. That point was made clear in a New Jersey court decision in 1972.[46] Under the union agreement, there was a provision that a subject was deemed proper for teaching if it was appropriate for the maturation level of students. When a seventh grade teacher attempted to teach about abortion and the superintendent attempted to stop it, the court held that courses offered and subjects taught could not be a condition of employment.

Under different conditions but still involving the issue of speech, a California court held that a school board could restrict a teacher's freedom of speech.[47] The teachers' association had sought to

---

42. Adamich v. Ferguson-Florissant School Dist., 483 S.W.2d 629 (Mo. App. 1972).

43. California School Empl. Ass'n v. Sequoia Union H. S. Dist., 136 Cal. Rptr. 594 (Cal. App. 1977).

44. New York City School Bds. Ass'n v. Board of Educ., 383 N.Y.S.2d 208 (App. Div. 1976).

45. Board of Educ. v. Englewood Teachers Ass'n, 311 A.2d 729 (N.J. 1973).

46. Board of Educ. v. Rockaway Twp. Educ. Ass'n, 120 N.J. Super. 564, 295 A.2d 380 (1972).

47. Los Angeles Teachers' Union v. Los Angeles City Bd. of Educ., 74 Cal. Rptr. 461 (Cal. 1969).

circulate in the schools a petition on school finance which would be forwarded to the Governor, State Superintendent of Public Instruction, and the City Board of Education. The court ruled that such action amounted to political activity and consequently had no place within the school itself.

Academic freedom was one of the issues in a Supreme Court decision in 1976.[48] The Court held that a teacher has a right speak out at a meeting of the board of education on a subcurrently under negotiations. Such statements do not connegotiations, the Court ruled, for the teachers had not a to bargain, nor were they authorized to do so. The Court the teachers were exercising the First Amendment right protected them in speaking out on public issues.

The litigation arose when two teachers violated a state law permitted only union representatives to speak out on matter negotiation. The teachers had mailed a letter to union members the subject of fair share, and they later circulated a petition calli for a one-year delay in implementing that provision until it could be studied more fully. The results of the questionnaire were presented to the board of education. The union then filed an unfair labor practice complaint for allowing the teachers to make the presentation.

The Supreme Court saw that the board meeting was public and to deny the teachers the right to speak would be, in effect, to inhibit all such speech since any aspect of public school operations is a potential subject of bargaining.

6. PROFESSIONAL GROWTH. Negotiations over activities involving professional growth have included a number and variety of issues, but one theme tends to run through all the litigation. It involves being rewarded for enhancing one's position through various kinds of professional activities or being penalized for a lack of professional growth.

In a Wisconsin case, teachers objected to loss of salary for the time they missed to attend a convention. Their petition was not upheld, for they were representing a minority union association and the school board had not agreed to pay them. Further, state law

---

48. City of Madison Joint Dist. No. 8 v. Wisconsin Empl. Rel. Comm'n, 429 U.S. 167, 97 S. Ct. 421, 50 L. Ed. 2d 376 (1976).

did not specifically provide for days off for teachers of a minority union to attend a convention.[49]

A Massachusetts court ruled that it was proper for an arbitrator to determine a salary position for a teacher. The teacher had added a vocational-education certificate to his regular academic certificate but was not given a salary increase. The Court ruled that such action amounted to paying the teacher as little as possible and was not within the purview of educational policy.[50] The arbitrator had properly ruled that the teacher was entitled to the same salary as a new teacher with dual certification.

A New Jersey court ruled that a sabbatical leave is a term and condition of employment. As such, it was legitimate for teachers to enter into binding arbitration on such a subject.[51]

When a teacher did not enter into any professional growth activities, a school board attempted to fire her. The court held that her contract could not be terminated for that reason, although her salary could be frozen.[52]

7. NONRENEWAL OF TEACHERS' CONTRACTS. One of the current crucial issues in personnel administration is the suspension of teachers for lack of pupil enrollment. A number of school systems have already experienced the trauma of having to reduce the teaching force, an action that will likely continue for another decade. This issue along with teacher dismissal is treated in another Chapter in this book. However, it will be dealt with briefly here insofar as it touches on negotiations. Several cases will serve as examples of subjects of bargaining on termination of teachers.

Unquestionably, the authority to employ and dismiss teachers resides with the board of education, and the board cannot bargain away this right. It can, however, share this responsibility with a teachers' union in defining terms and in determining procedures that relate to employment. In doing this, the board still retains the authority to employ and dismiss.

A New York statute governed the abolition of teaching positions, but that did not prohibit the teachers' association from bargaining

---

49. Board of Educ. v. Wisconsin Empl. Rel. Comm'n, 191 N.W.2d 242 (Wis. 1971).

50. School Comm. v. Gallagher, 344 N.E.2d 203 (Mass. App. 1976).

51. South Orange-Maplewood Educ. Ass'n v. Board of Educ., 370 A.2d 47 (N.J. 1977).

52. Hefner v. Board of Educ., Grundy County, 335 N.E.2d 600 (Ill. App. 1975).

on a definition of seniority to include past non-consecutive service when layoffs were contemplated.[53]

A school board cannot give up its authority to abolish teaching positions to a collective bargaining agreement. This was the essence of a 1975 decision. No charges were brought against the teachers nor had they been disciplined in any way; their release was simply a result of the abolition of positions.[54] A Washington court also held that a school district is not obligated to negotiate the nonrenewal of teachers' contracts. In this situation, the contracts of two hundred teachers were not renewed, and the teachers unsuccessfully sought relief from the courts.[55]

A New York court held that a contract provision that purported to give teachers absolute job security except in cases of unsatisfactory performance is a permissive subject of bargaining.[56]

A union agreement can provide for five additional days of notification prior to the termination of teachers, over and above what is required by a statute, if the school board agrees to it.[57] It can also contain provisions for notice and termination. In so holding, the court overruled an arbitrator who had concluded that a teacher's service had been improperly terminated and that she should be reappointed and paid for lost salary.[58]

Another general subject of reduction-in-force relates to termination for other than lack of enrollment. For the most part, nontenured teachers have limited rights with respect to dismissal proceedings. The contract of a nontenured teacher could be terminated for absences beyond a specified three-month period of temporary incapacity. The board was also within its power in adopting a regulation defining temporary incapacity.[59]

---

53. Board of Educ. v. Lakeland Fed'n of Teachers, 381 N.Y.S.2d 515 (N.Y. 1976).

54. Schwab v. Bowen, 363 N.Y.S.2d 434 (N.Y. 1975). *See also* Carmel School District v. Carmel Teachers Ass'n, 348 N.Y.S.2d 665 (N.Y. 1973).

55. Spokane Educ. Ass'n v. Barnes, 517 P.2d 1362 (Wash. 1974).

56. Board of Educ. v. Yonkers Fed'n of Teachers, 386 N.Y.S.2d 657 (App. Div. 1976).

57. Associated Teachers of Huntington v. Board of Educ., 64 Misc.2d 443, 303 N.Y.2d 469 (1969).

58. Board of Educ., Central School Dist. v. Harrison, 46 A.D.2d 674, 360 N.Y.S.2d 49 (1974).

59. Elder v. Board of Educ., 208 N.E.2d 423 (Ill. App. 1965).

Two nontenured teachers alleged that an agreement gave them many rights enjoyed by tenured teachers. They had been dismissed for reasons stated in the school code. The court ruled that the school board could not enter into an agreement that was in conflict with the school code.[60]

A Pennsylvania court ruled that the propriety of a teacher's dismissal was subject to arbitration on the basis that the issue dealt with wages, hours, and conditions of employment. The school board had objected to arbitration on the ground that it was an unlawful delegation of power.[61]

§ 5.2. Required Union Membership.

Public education has not accepted a union shop which requires that employees join the bargaining unit that represents them. It has subscribed to an agency shop which requires a non-union member to pay a fee to cover his share of the costs of the services he receives. However, in 1974, a Pennsylvania court held that agency shop agreements are illegal under the state's Public Employee Relations Act since that statute provides only for a maintenance-of-membership provision.[62] This provision means that at the time an agreement is negotiated, the members of the bargaining unit must agree to remain a member of the union for the duration of the contract.

The Supreme Court of the United States ruled in 1977 that a teachers' union could require non-union members to pay a service charge to cover the expenses of activities related to bargaining, but it could not require them to pay for support of political and ideological activities. This, the Court held, would be in violation of the teachers' First Amendment rights.[63]

A Pennsylvania court held, in 1976, that a school board could not terminate a teacher's contract for refusing to pay membership dues. That reason was not one of the enumerated causes for termination as specified in the codes.[64]

---

60. Wesclin Educ. Ass'n v. Board of Educ., 331 N.E.2d 335 (Ill. App. 1975).

61. Board of Educ. v. Philadelphia Fed'n of Teachers, 346 A.2d 35 (Pa. 1975).

62. Pennsylvania Labor Rel. Bd. v. Zelum, 329 A.2d 477 (Pa. 1974).

63. Abood v. Detroit Bd. of Educ., 429 U.S. 209, 97 S. Ct. 1782, 52 L. Ed. 2d 261 (1977).

64. Dauphin County Technical School Educ. Ass'n v. Dauphin County Area Vocational-Technical School Bd., 357 A.2d 721 (Pa. Cmwlth. 1976).

A New York court upheld a dues check-off system for teachers. This was in spite of an attempt by the state's Public Employment Relations Board to punish the union by revoking dues check-off privileges.[65] This system provides for the employer to withhold dues from one's paycheck and forward them to the union.

§ 5.3. Impasse.

When the negotiating parties fail to come to an agreement, impasse results. When that situation occurs, several avenues are possible. One is the use of mediation. This involves a third party, a disinterested person, working with one or both sides in order to have someone modify a position in order to come to an agreement. A mediator cannot in and of himself impose a solution.

A second avenue is the use of a fact-finder. This person conducts hearings and amasses evidence from both parties; he may collect data from others as well. At the conclusion of the hearing, the fact-finder will file a report, with recommendations. Unlike a mediator, who tends to work discreetly, a fact-finder helps to marshal public opinion in effecting an agreement.

a. *Strikes.* Failure to reach an agreement through the parties to a contract, or by the intervention of a third party, can result in a strike. Although teachers' strikes are illegal in most states, a few states do allow them. In the first court opinion on this issue, the Supreme Court of Errors of Connecticut held that strikes were illegal, although it was legal for teachers to organize and bargain collectively over salaries and working conditions.[66] In some states where strikes are illegal, teachers have nonetheless struck.

In holding that a strike against government is illegal, the Supreme Court of Florida rejected the teachers' contention that their status constituted involuntary servitude.[67] Courts have also upheld the constitutionality of laws that specifically forbid strikes.[68]

---

65. Buffalo Teachers' Fed'n v. Helsby, 435 F. Supp. 1098 (S.D.N.Y. 1977).

66. Norwalk Teachers' Ass'n v. Board of Educ., 138 Conn. 269, 83 A.2d 482 (1951).

67. Pinellas County Classroom Teachers' Ass'n. v. Board of Pub. Instr., 214 So. 2d 34 (Fla. 1968).

68. City of New York v. DeLury, 23 N.Y.2d 175, 295 N.Y.S.2d 901, 243 N.E.2d 128 (1968).

The Supreme Court of the United States upheld the dismissal of teachers who engaged in an illegal strike.[69] Wisconsin law forbade teachers' strikes but that did not deter teachers, who struck in 1974, after negotiations had failed. After they had been reminded twice that their strike was illegal and had been invited to return to work but did not, the school board then voted to dismiss eighty-six teachers. The Court also dealt with other issues to be treated later in this Chapter.

A New York court ruled that refusing to attend a back-to-school night constitutes a strike.[70] The teachers pointed out that this activity was not covered in the contract, but the court relied on the past practice of teachers having attended these meetings, with two exceptions, for the previous seventeen years. Similarly, a New Jersey court ruled that teachers' resigning from sponsorship of extracurricular activities constituted an illegal strike.[71] The activities were not a part of the contract and teachers refused to direct them. The court ruled that the school board could assign these activities without any extra compensation.

b. *Injunctions.* One tactic that a school board uses against a strike is an injunction. It is a court order that forbids an action, in this instance, a strike. It will be issued only after a school board has made a proper showing that the strike would result in grievous damage to the public. The Supreme Court of Michigan required, as a proper showing, evidence of "violence, irreparable injury, or breach of the peace." [72] The New Hampshire Supreme Court ruled that an injunction would not automatically be issued, even though it was contrary to state law for public employees to strike.[73]

In a Rhode Island case, the school district demonstrated irreparable harm to the school calendar by a strike. More specifically, it pointed out interference with student learning,

---

69. Hortonville Joint School Dist. No. 1 v. Hortonville Educ. Ass'n, 426 U.S. 482, 96 S. Ct. 2308, 49 L. Ed. 2d 1 (1976).

70. Bellmore-Merrick H. S. Dist. v. Bellmore-Merrick United Secondary Teachers, Inc., 378 N.Y.S.2d 881 (N.Y. 1975).

71. Board of Educ. v. Asbury Park Educ. Ass'n, 368 A.2d 396 (N.J. Super. 1976).

72. School Dist. for City of Holland v. Holland Educ. Ass'n, 380 Mich. 314, 157 N.W.2d 206 (1968).

73. Timberlane Regional School Dist. v. Timberlane Regional Educ. Ass'n, 114 N.H. 245, 317 A.2d 555 (1974).

inability to serve lunches to needy children, and a disadvantage to seniors entering the labor market at a very late date.[74]

c. *Sanctions.* A sanction is a device to punish, in some way, a party to a contract for having taken a position or engaged in some action which offended a second party. The sanction may be directed against a group or an individual. The intended effect is to get one's demands met or to punish one for what he did. This device was approved by the National Education Association in 1962. Its legality is not fully clear.

When a board of education attempted to dismiss a teacher solely for having engaged in union activity, the court held that this cannot be done.[75] Similarly, a teacher cannot be dismissed solely for being critical of the administration's posture in negotiating sessions.[76]

A New Jersey court ruled against teachers on a different matter. When a board of education decided not to rehire three nontenured teachers, one of them being the president of the local teachers' association, thirty-one of forty-seven teachers decided to resign, effective two weeks before the end of the school year. In supporting the teachers, the local and state associations imposed sanctions by sending notices to state members and to preparatory institutions within the state and in neighboring states. The state's supreme court held that the intended purpose of the resignations was to support the refusal of others to work. This action was as illegal as a strike.[77]

d. *Picketing.* In Chapter 8 *infra,* it may be seen that, outside the classroom, teachers have very broad rights of free speech under the First Amendment. Picketing is one form of speech, but it is not protected under the First Amendment as a form of pure speech. While a teacher has a right to express himself or take a position on an issue, that right is not without limits. The exercise of that right becomes more critical when it is attached to a work stoppage.

Teachers were restrained from picketing which was designed solely to induce a breach of contract.[78] The Supreme Court of

74. Menard v. Woonsocket Teachers' Guild, 363 A.2d 1349 (R.I. 1976).

75. McLaughlin v. Tilendis, 398 F.2d 287 (7th Cir. 1968); Muskego-Norway Consolidated Schools Joint Dist. No. 9 v. Wisconsin Empl. Rel. Bd., 35 Wis. 2d 540, 151 N.W.2d 617 (1967).

76. Roberts v. Lake Central School Corp., 317 F. Supp. 63 (N.D. Ind. 1970).

77. Board of Educ. v. New Jersey Educ. Ass'n, 53 N.J. 29, 247 A.2d 867 (1968).

Illinois held that a court could issue a temporary injunction without notice and hearing when teachers were picketing and striking.[79]

e. *Penalties.* In spite of laws forbidding strikes, teachers have engaged in them in order to have their demands met. When a strike is settled and an agreement ratified, the parties often agree not to penalize the striking teachers. This action is viewed as a major move in "closing ranks" and proceeding with business. However, some school districts have sought and been successful in punishing teachers for striking. The punishment may take the form of dismissal, fines, or low ratings.

A Kansas court upheld the right of the school district to dismiss striking teachers.[80] However, the leading case on this subject is *Hortonville District v. Hortonville Education Association,* decided by the Supreme Court of the United States in 1976.[81] The facts were previously stated in § **5.3.a.** After the teachers' contracts had been terminated, three basic issues were before the High Court: bias of the school board as a hearing body, property and liberty interests of teachers, and due process in hearings. The Court held that the school board was not biased in serving as a hearing tribunal in conducting termination hearings. Although it was acknowledged that the board was familiar with the case, that fact was insufficient to disqualify it, for there had been no evidence that the board was incapable of judging the issue fairly. There had also been no evidence that the board had a personal or financial interest in the matter so as to create a conflict of interest nor was there evidence of personal animosity.

On the issue of property or liberty interests, the Court noted that the teachers had expected their jobs would remain open, and this constituted a property right.

On the third issue, due process, the Court used a balance test: the interest of the teachers in continued employment versus the interest of the school board in governmental and policy decisions.

---

78. Board of Educ. v. Ohio Educ. Ass'n., 13 Ohio Misc. 308, 235 N.E.2d 538 (1967).

79. Board of Educ. v. Kankakee Fed'n of Teachers, 46 Ill. 2d 439, 264 N.E.2d 18 (1970), *cert. denied* 403 U.S. 904 (1971).

80. Seamen Dist. Teachers Ass'n v. Board of Educ., 217 Kan. 233, 535 P.2d 889 (1975).

81. *Supra,* note 69.

It held that the board's interest in considering alternative responses to the strike in serving the cause of education outweighed the teachers' interest in continued employment.

Some courts have upheld fines of teachers for striking. A New Jersey court held that fines as well as imprisonment were appropriate penalties for being in contempt of an anti-strike statute.[82] In 1977, a New York court upheld the imposition of fines on a teachers' union and its leaders who had defied a back-to-work order during a strike.[83] A California court held that a school district can sue for monetary damages as a result of an illegal strike.[84]

The Pennsylvania Supreme Court held that formal letters of reprimand and unsatisfactory ratings for a semester constituted discipline within the meaning of the negotiated contract.[85]

§ 5.4. Arbitration.

Arbitration is a means of enforcing a contract when one grieves an action. It is a substitute for filing a court suit and is viewed as being quicker and less expensive than a law suit. It involves a third party conducting a hearing, gathering evidence, and issuing a ruling. The parties may voluntarily agree to accept the decision of the arbitrator as in advisory arbitration or agree, in advance, to accept the decision of the arbitrator as in compulsory arbitration.

Differences often exist over whether a grievance is arbitrable. The outcome often hinges on the language of the contract, and the presumption is usually in favor of a broad interpretation over the arbitrability of a dispute. Disputes over the arbitrability of grievances hinge mainly on teacher personnel problems: assignment, dismissal, and nonrenewal.

Courts are not in full agreement as to the scope of an arbitrator's authority in ruling on cases of teacher dismissal and whether an arbitrator can order reinstatement. A Maine court held that the state statutes forbade grievance arbitration on teacher dismissal

---

82. *In re* Block, 50 N.J. 494, 236 A.2d 589 (1967).

83. Board of Educ. v. Lakeland Fed'n of Teachers, 399 N.Y.S.2d 61 (App. Div. 1977).

84. Pasadena Unified School Dist. v. Pasadena Fed'n of Teachers, 140 Cal. Rptr. 41 (Cal. App. 1977).

85. Lewisburg Area Educ. Ass'n v. Board of School Dist., 376 A.2d 933 (Pa. 1977).

and nonrenewal.[86] This ruling preceded action by the legislature which provided that just cause for permanent teachers could be negotiated by school boards.

Teachers in Newark, New Jersey, made a better case for arbitration when they alleged that their nonreemployment did not comply with procedural rights guaranteed under the contract. The court agreed and held that this matter was mandatorily arbitrable.[87] A Pennsylvania court held that a teacher could not be discharged for nonpayment of union dues, but that the dispute was a proper subject for an arbitration hearing.[88] A Vermont court held that an arbitrator exceeded his authority in ordering the reappointment of a teacher. The school board had not participated in the arbitration, and it was not bound to do so.[89]

A New Jersey court held that the statutory power to reduce personnel resides with a board of education, not an arbitrator. A nontenured teacher has no right to employment, and the decision not to renew is a discretionary one for the board. Thus, that issue is not subject to arbitration.[90]

For failure to appoint a local candidate as a principal despite a clause in the contract which favored local candidates if their qualifications were equal to non-local candidates, a school board did not have to submit its decision to arbitration.[91] Another court reversed an arbitrator's decision that had reassigned a teacher on the basis of degree requirements. The court held that, under the contract, it was intended that a master's equivalency be the same as a master's degree.[92]

Courts have also been asked to review decisions of arbitrators with respect to sabbatical leaves. The Connecticut Supreme Court upheld an arbitrator who supported a guidance counselor's claim

---

86. Superintending School Comm. v. Winslow Educ. Ass'n, 363 A.2d 229 (Me. 1976).

87. Newark Teachers v. Board of Educ., 373 A.2d 1020 (N.J. Super. 1977).

88. Appeal of Jones, 375 A.2d 1341 (Pa. Cmwlth. 1977).

89. Fairchild v. West Rutland School Dist., 376 A.2d 28 (Vt. 1977).

90. Board of Educ. v. Englewood Teachers Ass'n, 375 A.2d 669 (N.J. App. Div. 1977).

91. Berkshire Hills Regional School Dist. v. Gray, 369 N.E.2d 736 (Mass. App. 1977).

92. Matter of Lewisburg Area Educ. Ass'n, 371 A.2d 568 (Pa. Cmwlth. 1977).

to a sabbatical leave.[93] In contrast, a Pennsylvania court overturned an arbitrator's decision that had granted a teacher full salary for a half year's sabbatical leave.[94] Where a school district had agreed to a broad binding arbitration provision in a negotiated contract, it could not set aside an arbitrator's ruling on a sabbatical leave, in charging that he had exceeded his powers.[95]

A Massachusetts court held that an arbitrator can fashion remedies regarding tenure but he cannot grant it. The authority for granting tenure belongs exclusively to the school board.[96]

§ 5.5. Summary.

Collective negotiations in public education are very new. As a result, there are not enough court decisions on specific issues to arrive, justifiably, at global conclusions. Furthermore, judges have handed down what seem to be conflicting opinions involving the same or similar questions. However, their holdings have been based on an interpretation of law as it applies to a local school district contract or existing state statutes. Thus, these decisions have often been resolutions of very specific and narrowly-defined issues.

The degree to which states and local school districts engage in bargaining varies greatly, ranging from no bargaining in some states to highly sophisticated unionization in others. Where bargaining is allowed, the issues subject to the negotiations process range from mandatory to permissive or prohibitive bargaining.

The Supreme Court of the United States has issued three specific rulings on negotiations in public education. It has protected teachers in exercising freedom of speech at a school board meeting; upheld the right of school boards to dismiss teachers who engage in an illegal strike; ruled that a school board can serve as an impartial tribunal in dismissing striking teachers; and held that

---

93. Board of Educ. v. Bridgeport Educ. Ass'n, 377 A.2d 323 (Conn. 1977).

94. Allegheny Valley School Dist. v. Allegheny Valley Educ. Ass'n, 360 A.2d 762 (Pa. Cmwlth. 1976).

95. Rochester City School Dist. v. Rochester Teachers' Ass'n, 394 N.Y.S.2d 179 (App. Div. 1977).

96. School Comm. of Danvers v. Tyman, 360 N.E.2d 877 (Mass. 1977).

non-union members can be required to pay dues to cover union expenses so long as they are not routed for political purposes.

Courts have iterated that school boards retain their authority when engaged in the bargaining process. However, decisions have made it clear that this authority is now shared with unions. Although a board has the responsibility for making policy, it must consult with a union on a variety of matters until, in effect, the teachers' union does help to shape educational policy.

Chapter Six

FINANCE

§ 6.0. Introduction.

As creatures of state and local government, public schools are almost completely funded by tax dollars. Despite the fact that federal and state tax revenues form a financial support base for public education, the lion's share of all money utilized to establish and maintain public schools generally comes from localities. Throughout the history of public education in this nation, the local property tax has served as the major producer of public school funding.

Suffice it to say, reliance on local property tax revenues is not without problems. This "property tax dependence," has caused a certain unevenness of development throughout state educational systems; not only visible when comparing one state to another, but, even more so, when comparing one public school system to another within the same state. As the results of the National Education Finance Project (NEFP) revealed, "The fundamental result of heavy reliance on property taxes to support public schools is that the quality of a child's education is largely determined by the wealth of the school district in which he lives." [1]

To understand the problems of contemporary public school finance, one must first examine some fundamentals of school district fiscal management. A discussion of the legal prerogatives

---

1. K.F. Jordan and K. Alexander, eds., FUTURES IN SCHOOL FINANCE (Bloomington, Indiana: Phi Delta Kappa, 1975).

and restraints placed upon local school officials for the fiscal affairs of their local school districts (or divisions) is of paramount importance.

§ 6.1. Local Boards and the Power to Tax.

As stated in other sections of this book, local boards of education possess no inherent authority. They only possess authority and powers either expressly or impliedly granted by statute. The power to tax for school purposes is no exception to the rule.

According to *American Jurisprudence,* ". . . school districts have no inherent power of taxation, and may exercise such power only under a valid delegation by the legislature." [2] Only a state legislature can "make a school district a taxing [entity] and delegate to the board of that district power to levy and collect a tax the object of which is the raising of a fund for school purposes." [3]

The statutes of each state are different regarding the power of local school boards to raise and collect taxes for schools. Thus, in some states local school boards are "fiscally independent," while in other states they are "fiscally dependent." Independent school districts outnumber dependent ones.

a. *Fiscally Independent School Boards.* Fiscally independent school boards are granted legal authority by the state legislature to set the *ad valorem* tax rate on real property (not personal and intangible property), and to collect taxes for support and maintenance of the local schools. In the State of Florida, for example, local school authorities levy and collect taxes for school purposes. Local school boards need not depend on the local county or city governments for their source of local school tax revenues. [4] Likewise, in Georgia and Missouri, state law grants local public school boards authority to tax property for the support and maintenance of schools. [5]

2. 68 *American Jurisprudence* 2d 428 (Rochester: The Lawyer's Co-Operative Publishing Co. 1973).

3. *Id.* at 429.

4. *See,* for example, Gulesian v. Dade County School Bd., 281 So. 2d 325 (Fla. 1973). It should be pointed out, however, that Florida State law sets a legal limit on the tax rates that can be set by local school boards.

5. *See,* for example, Board of Comm'rs of Newton County v. Alligood, 214 S.E.2d 522 (Ga. 1975), and Enright v. Kansas City, 536 S.W.2d 17 (Mo. 1976).

b. *Fiscally Dependent School Boards. Corpus Juris Secundum* tells us that state statutes in some jurisdictions provide "for the apportionment of school taxes to different political subdivisions possessing territory in the school district." [6] The governing board of that political subdivision, and not the local school board, (*e.g.*, city council or county supervisors), "has the duty to apportion school taxes as may be designated by the statute." [7]

In the Commonwealth of Virginia, local school boards, by law, cannot levy or collect taxes for school purposes. The local municipal governmental agency is the tax levying authority. Local school boards also must go to their local governmental body for appropriations and budget approval.[8]

Another example of fiscal dependence can be found in a 1973 Pennsylvania court decision. According to the Pennsylvania Commonwealth Court, in that state, the power to assess or reduce assessment on property within a school district belongs to the city tax assessor and not to the local school board.[9]

Generally, state statutes require that increases in tax levies by political subdivisions be submitted to popular referendum. And, that taxes for school purposes shall not be raised without first receiving approval by popular vote of the community.[10] However, there have been exceptions to this procedure. For example, the New Jersey Commissioner of Education recently certified a local school board's raising of additional school funds by taxation, when the local board found it necessary to do so because of voter reluctance to approve funds for necessary school expenditures.[11]

§ 6.2. Indebtedness and Expenditure of Funds.

Generally, state legislatures, within constitutional limitations,

---

6. 79 *Corpus Juris Secundum* 183 (Brooklyn: The American Lawbook Co., 1952).

7. *Id.*

8. VA. CODE, § 22-126.1, *et seq.* (1975). *See also,* Bradley v. School Bd., 462 F.2d 1058 (4th Cir. 1972), *motion denied,* 409 U.S. 910, 93 S. Ct. 239, 35 L. Ed. 255 (1972).

9. Leopard Indus., Inc. v. Toanone, 310 A.2d 440 (Pa. 1973).

10. Recent voter resistance to increases in property taxes (for school purposes) has been experienced in the States of California and Minnesota. *See also,* Street v. Maries City School Dist., 511 S.W.2d 814 (Mo. 1974), and State *ex rel.* Daoust v. Smith, 371 N.E.2d 536 (Ohio 1977).

11. *In re* Upper Freehold Regional Bd. of Educ., Dec. of N.J. Comm. of Educ. (1978).

delegate legal authority to local school boards to incur indebtedness and to expend funds solely for the conduct and maintenance of the public schools.[12] All indebtedness and expenditures of local school boards, to be judged proper, must be made in accordance with state constitutional and statutory mandates,[13] and must be a part of an approved budget. "After the budget has once been approved by the designated reviewing body the board of education is free to transfer amounts from one item to the other as they see fit, providing the total amount approved is not exceeded." [14]

The administration of a school district's approved annual budget and the day-to-day fiscal management of school district matters are legal duties of local school boards. What is more, it is the legal prerogative of a local school board to exercise a degree of discretion it deems necessary in the performance of these duties.[15]

Local school boards are legally accountable for all debts incurred, and for all funds expended during the duration of an approved budget. In 1977, for example, a California appellate court held that, by state statute, taxpayers have standing to sue local school districts for "waste" of funds.[16]

§ 6.3. School Property.

Generally, tax dollars pay for school property. School sites are acquired, school buildings are erected, and school supplies and equipment are purchased with funds raised through taxation. And, even though some federal funding and state funding are made available for such matters, most of these tax dollars are raised locally.

---

12. 79 C.J.S. 7 (1952). *See,* for example, Buse v. Smith, 247 N.W.2d 141 (Wis. 1976).

13. Northampton Area Bd. of Educ. v. Zehner, 360 A.2d 793 (Pa. 1976).

14. BOLMEIER, SCHOOL IN THE LEGAL STRUCTURE, 185 (2d ed. Cincinnati, Ohio: The W.H. Anderson Co., 1973). *See,* for example, De Nunzio v. Board of Educ., 396 N.Y.S.2d 236 (N.Y. 1977), wherein parents challenged budgetary cuts in educational services for handicapped children.

15. Weary v. Board of Educ., 360 N.E.2d 1112 (Ill. 1977).

16. Los Altos Property Owners Ass'n v. Hutcheon, 137 Cal. Rptr. 775 (Cal. 1977). *See also,* Bethlehem Steel Corp. v. Board of Educ., 397 N.Y.S.2d 882 (N.Y. 1977), wherein taxpayers challenged a school board's adopted budget as exceeding the board's authority.

Some experts in school law adhere to the notion that all public school property is state property, no matter what is the source of its funding. Since public education is legally a state function, they argue, school property is state property, to do with as the state sees fit. Others argue, however, that local school districts usually depend on local tax sources for support of new property. Therefore, school property is local property. Whether one attitude is more accurate than the other can only be determined by a careful examination of the school code of each state.

Typically, determining whether or not new school buildings are needed; whether or not existing school buildings are to be renovated, closed, or demolished; where new school buildings are to be located; and matters of supply and equipment are all granted by state statute to local school boards. State law and budgetary constraints will determine the funding and the financial methods and procedures that must be adhered to by the local boards.

According to Hazard, "Funds for capital expenditures for major school plant improvement and new construction generally come from the sale of bonds." [17] And, he states, authority for a local board of education to sell bonds is not implied. It must be granted by state law, and it usually requires approval by popular vote of school district residents.[18]

§ 6.4. Uses of School Buildings and Grounds.

Absent state law to the contrary, decisions on matters of use of school buildings and grounds are usually the local school board's to make.

In Virginia, for example, a local school board, or the division superintendent where board policy permits, must approve the use of school buildings and grounds. And, it is the legal prerogative of the local board, or its agent, to adopt all reasonable rules and regulations necessary to protect school property when in use.[19]

---

17. HAZARD, EDUCATION AND THE LAW, 485 (2d ed. New York, N.Y.: The Free Press, 1978).

18. *Id.* at 485-6. *See,* for example, Butsche v. Coon Rapids Community School Dist., 255 N.W.2d 337 (Iowa 1977), Nance v. Williams, 564 S.W.2d 212 (Ark. 1978), and Cuka v. School Bd., 264 N.W.2d 924 (S. Dak. 1978).

19. VA. CODE, § 22-147, *et seq.* (1975).

According to Virginia law, local school boards may permit use of school property under their control "as will not impair the efficiency of the schools." [20] Further, local boards may impose specific conditions for said usage.[21] This includes use of property during school hours, after school hours, on weekends, and during official school vacation periods.

§ 6.5. Challenges to State Finance Schemes.

In the late 1960's, litigation began to appear attacking state public school financing systems.[22] The school finance cases came from the courts in two distinct waves. One wave has been referred to as *McInnis*-type cases (largely unsuccessful), while wave two became known as the *Serrano*-type cases (largely successful).[23] Petitioners in these actions presented similar claims saying that state educational finance schemes, based upon property-tax revenues, discriminated unfairly between classes of children, conditioning their free access to equal educational opportunity by "accident of their birth."

a. *McInnis-Type Cases.* In 1968, a class action suit was brought on behalf of parents and public elementary and secondary school students in four school districts located in Cook County, Illinois. Plaintiffs in the case, *McInnis v. Shapiro*,[24] claimed that the Illinois system of public school finance violated their equal protection guarantees under the Fourteenth Amendment. Additionally, they claimed that state statutes permitted a wide variation of expenditures per student among Illinois public school divisions. A permanent injunction was sought forbidding further distribution of tax funds in reliance on state statutes.

---

20. *Id.* at 127.

21. *Id.* at 128. *See also*, the discussion of "Uses of School Property" by Piele and Forsberg in THE YEARBOOK OF SCHOOL LAW, 1975, 77-8 (Topeka, Kansas: NOLPE 1975).

22. Portions of this section of the chapter are taken directly from R.S. Vacca, *The Courts and School Finance: A Reexamination,* in FUTURES IN SCHOOL FINANCE: WORKING TOWARD A COMMON GOAL 119-34 (K.F. Jordan and K. Alexander eds. Bloomington, Indiana: Phi Delta Kappan, 1975).

23. J.D. Lucas, *Serrano and Rodriguez — An Overextension of Equal Protection,* 2 NOLPE SCHOOL LAW JOURNAL 18-20 (1972).

24. 293 F. Supp. 327 (N.D. Ill. 1968), *aff'd mem. sub nom.,* McInnis v. Ogilvie, 394 U.S. 322 (1969).

A three-judge, United States District Court, upon hearing plaintiffs' allegations, ruled against them. The district court reached its conclusion based upon three points. First, in their opinion, the Fourteenth Amendment did not require that public school expenditures be made solely on the basis of "educational need." Second, "educational expenses" were not the "exclusive yardstick" for measuring the quality of a child's educational opportunity. Finally, the *McInnis* court added a further dimension to its opinion; namely, that there were no "judicially manageable standards" by which a federal court could determine if and when the Equal Protection Clause is satisfied or violated.

Since the Illinois finance scheme was found to show an absence of any form of invidious discrimination, the suit was dismissed for no cause of action. In the district court's opinion, ". . . the General Assembly's delegation of authority of school districts appears designed to allow individual localities to determine their own tax burden according to the importance which they place upon public schools." The inequity of funds between school districts, said the court, is "an inevitable consequence of decentralization." [25]

That same year, a similar action was heard by a three-judge United States District Court in Virginia. *Burruss v. Wilkerson* involved a challenge brought by parents in Bath County, Virginia, who claimed that because of the Virginia system of public school finance, their children were being denied educational opportunities equal to those enjoyed by children attending public schools in other districts of the state.

The district court dismissed the plaintiffs' action, convinced that the deficiencies and disparities existing between public school districts in Virginia were not the results of purposeful discrimination by the State. The blame, said the court, "is ascribable solely to the absence of taxable values sufficient to produce required moneys." [26]

In both *McInnis* and *Burruss,* the courts were willing to leave it to the respective state legislatures to remedy the existing inequities. Thus, as the nation entered the decade of the 1970's,

---

25. *Id.*

26. 301 F. Supp. 1237 (W.D. Va. 1968), 310 F. Supp. 572 (W.D. Va. 1969), *aff'd mem.,* 397 U.S. 44 (1970).

state educational finance systems remained intact as subsequent courts consistently adhered to the *McInnis* precedent.[27]

b. *Serrano-Type Cases.* A new judicial attitude toward problems of school finance had its roots in a matter heard on appeal by the Supreme Court of California. In *Serrano v. Priest,* plaintiff parents and their children sought to enjoin the State of California and Los Angeles County school officials from carrying out and implementing what plaintiffs claimed was an unconstitutional school finance system.[28] The California school finance scheme, they argued, because it relied heavily on local property taxes, caused substantial disparities in per pupil revenues available to individual school districts. Such a system was not fiscally neutral because it discriminated against poor school districts, and, ultimately, the children enrolled in those districts.[29]

In remanding the case back for trial, the California Supreme Court opined that the California finance scheme made "the quality of a child's education a function of the wealth of his parents and neighbors." [30] Additionally, the high court found that even state grants to local school districts actually helped to widen the financial gap between poor and affluent school districts.[31]

Six weeks after *Serrano,* a United States District Court in Minnesota held, in *Van Dusartz v. Hatfield,* that the Minnesota system of public school finance (which made spending per pupil a function of school district wealth) violated the equal protection guarantee of the Fourteenth Amendment.[32] In reaching its decision, the district court held, as would subsequent courts in other states, that students in public elementary and secondary schools enjoy a right to have the level of spending for their education unaffected by variations in the taxable wealth of their school district or their parents.[33]

The *Van Dusartz* court did not require absolute uniformity of

---

27. *See,* for example, Hargrave v. Kirk, 313 F. Supp. 944 (M.D. Fla. 1970), *judgment vacated, sub nom.,* Askew v. Hargrave, 401 U.S. 476 (1971).
28. 96 Cal. Rptr. 601, 487 P.2d 1241 (1971), 135 Cal. Rptr. 345 (1977).
29. *Id.*
30. *Id.* at 1244.
31. *Id.* at 1248.
32. 334 F. Supp. 870 (D. Minn. 1971).
33. *Id.* at 872.

school expenditures. Rather, the court looked to the state legislature to remedy the situation. It encouraged the state "to adopt one of many optional financing schemes which do not violate the equal protection clause." [34]

c. *San Antonio v. Rodriguez.* The two-year period between 1971 and 1973 saw major changes take place in several states as legislatures and state boards worked to revise their public school finance schemes. In 1973, the United States Supreme Court, by a vote of 5-4, brought an end to the *Serrano*-type attitude that depicted public education as a fundamental interest protected by the United States Constitution. *San Antonio Independent School District v. Rodriguez* [35] marked a return to a judicial attitude that saw public education as basically a responsibility of states and not directly a federal matter.

Rodriguez was originally decided by a three-judge United States district court in Texas. The district court held for the plaintiffs, finding the State of Texas public school finance scheme (which relied heavily on the local property tax) unconstitutional. The district court did not require that Texas spend equal amounts of money on every child. What the court did advocate, however, was that Texas establish an educational finance structure built upon "fiscal neutrality," and not a structure where access to educational opportunity was conditioned by local wealth.[36]

The State of Texas appealed the decision to the United States Supreme Court where the district court was reversed. Mr. Justice Powell voiced the majority opinion for the High Court, which rejected appellees' rationale on two vital points.

First, since appellees were unable to specifically describe the class of "poor" who were being discriminated against, it must be concluded "that the Texas system does not operate to the secular advantage of any suspect class." [37] Justice Powell then pointed out that the Supreme Court has never held that "wealth discrimination

---

34. *Id.* at 877.

35. 411 U.S. 1, 93 S. Ct. 1278, 36 L. Ed. 2d 16 (1973), *rev'g,* 337 F. Supp. 280 (W.D. Tex. 1973).

36. 337 F. Supp. 280 (W.D. Tex. 1973), *rev'd,* 411 U.S. 1, 93 S. Ct. 1278, 36 L. Ed. 2d 16 (1973).

37. *Rodriguez, supra,* 411 U.S. 1.

alone provides an adequate basis for invoking strict scrutiny...." [38]

Second, the importance of public education (a service provided by the state) does not in and of itself "determine whether it must be regarded as fundamental for purposes of examination under the Equal Protection Clause." [39] Further, stated Justice Powell, education "... is not among the rights afforded explicit protection under our Federal Constitution. Nor do we find any basis for saying it is implicitly so protected." [40]

Mr. Justice Powell concluded the majority opinion by making specific reference to the financial disparities existing among various Texas public school districts. The solution to such problems, however, "... must come from the lawmakers and from the democratic pressures of those who elect them." [41]

d. *Post-Rodriguez and the Future of School Finance.* In the months following *Rodriguez,* cases were decided by state appellate courts revealing a judicial trend of future litigation concerning public school finance. One such decision was handed down by the Supreme Court of New Jersey.

In *Robinson v. Cahill,* [42] the Supreme Court of New Jersey upheld a superior court ruling that New Jersey's system of financing its public elementary and secondary schools (at that time) was unconstitutional. In rendering its decision, the superior court said that the State's finance system discriminated against pupils in districts with low real property wealth, and it discriminated against taxpayers by imposing unequal burdens for a common state purpose. [43]

The New Jersey Supreme Court, Chief Judge Weintraub, for a unanimous court, agreed with the lower court's final determination. New Jersey's educational finance system, said the high court, which relied heavily on local taxation and which led to great disparities in dollar input per pupil, had no relation to that state's own constitutional mandate to furnish "a thorough and

---

38. *Id.*
39. *Id.* at 1295.
40. *Id.* at 1297.
41. *Id.* at 1348.
42. 119 N.J. Super. 40, 303 A.2d 273 (N.J. 1973).
43. 289 A.2d 569 (N.J. 1973).

efficient system of public schools." [44] The New Jersey Supreme Court ordered that the state legislature immediately devise a new financial scheme for public education in that state.

Milliken, et al. v. Green, et al. is a similar case, from the Michigan Supreme Court. In *Milliken,* the court held that that state's system of school finance (consisting of local, general, and *ad valorem* property taxes and school aid appropriations), relied on the wealth of local school districts. That reliance resulted in substantial inequality of maintenance and support of public elementary and secondary schools, denying equal protection of the laws as guaranteed by the Michigan Constitution.[45] Said the court, there is "... an inherent inequality in the school district property tax bases which creates unequal support for the education of Michigan children." [46]

The Michigan Supreme Court did not require absolute equality in the distribution of state educational resources to each child in public school. No court has yet demanded that.

In December, 1977, the Court of Common Pleas of Hamilton County, Ohio, found that state's system of school finance in violation of the Ohio Constitution. To that court, among other things, the statutory system which the legislature established for the financing of public elementary and secondary schools establishes invidious classifications among school children in violation of the equal protection clause of the Ohio Constitution.[47]

Horton v. Meskill is a 1977 decision. Decided by the supreme court of Connecticut, *Horton* involved an appeal of a superior court judgment declaring the Connecticut system of financing public elementary and secondary schools (in effect in 1974), violative of the state constitution, but not the federal constitution.[48]

The Supreme Court of Connecticut relied heavily upon *Rodriguez* and *Robinson* and held, among other things, that in Connecticut the right to education is so basic and fundamental that any infringement of that right must be "strictly scrutinized."

---

44. 303 A.2d *supra,* at 273.

45. 389 Mich. 1, 203 N.W.2d 457 (Mich. 1972), amended Michigan Supreme Court No. 53809 (Dec. 14, 1973).

46. *Id.,* at 462-63.

47. Brinkman v. Gilligan, No. C-3-75-304 (S.D. Ohio 1977).

48. 172 Conn. 615, 376 A.2d 359 (Conn. 1977).

Further, stated the court, public school students in that State are entitled to equal enjoyment of the right to elementary and secondary education, and any system of financing that education which depends "primarily on a local property tax base without regard to the disparity in the financial ability . . . to finance an educational program and with no significant equalizing state support," cannot pass "strict judicial scrutiny." The state legislature, said the high court, is the proper body to fashion a constitutional system of educational finance.[49]

The phrase "public education is a fundamental entitlement of all children of school age" must not be interpreted generally. Thus courts will not automatically utilize the "strict scrutiny test." *Hernandez v. Houston Independent School District* [50] offers an example of a recent case wherein the interpretation of this phrase is crucial.

Appellants in *Hernandez* were several children who lived within the Houston Independent School District who, admittedly, were citizens of Mexico and who lacked any proof to support the legality of their presence in the United States. As the basis of their suit they argued that the school system's enforcement of Section 21.031 of the Texas Education Code (1975), which provided for a tuition-free public education for children who are either citizens of the United States or "legally admitted aliens," constituted a violation of the due process clause and equal protection clause of the United States Constitution and the Constitution of the State of Texas.[51] As their relief appellants sought and were denied at trial, among other things, an order requiring the school district to admit *all* children between the ages of 5 and 18 (who resided with a parent or guardian within the school district) and to provide them with a tuition-free education.

In affirming the lower court's decision, the Court of Civil Appeals of Texas relied on *Rodriguez* and said that a "tuition-free education is not a 'fundamental right' guaranteed by the Constitution of the United States." [52] Therefore, Section 21.031 of

---

49. *Id.* at 374-376.
50. 558 S.W.2d 121 (Tex. 1977).
51. *Id.* at 122-123.
52. *Id.* at 124.

the Texas Education Code was not to be subjected to "strict judicial scrutiny." The statute in question, said the court, does bear a rational relationship to a legitimate state purpose. Moreover, a "child should have no greater rights to a free education, due to his unlawful presence, than those rights he would have had if he had not come to this country." [53]

Finally, the Texas court declared that the legislature, not the judiciary, was the proper body to fashion the system of public school finance and management. And, within the limits of reason, the legislature's efforts to solve the complexity of problems should be respected.[54]

§ 6.6. Summary.

As this nation's public school systems entered the 1970's, they faced growing financial crises. Across this country, school systems found themselves in serious financial trouble as bond issues and other tax referenda met defeat at the hands of voters. In some states the situation became so critical that whole school systems had to close early because budgets were spent.[55]

Suffice it to say, the American way of educational finance, built upon a local property tax base, had to experience change if public schools were to remain in existence. Beginning in the 1971-72 school year, through such cases as *Serrano, Robinson,* and *Milliken,* needed reform was started.

According to Callahan and Wilken (National Conference of State Legislators), following *Serrano* (in 1971) more than twenty states made fundamental changes in their funding policies. Increased state funding commitments, say these experts, instead of increased local dependence, became the major thrust in finance-reform states.[56]

Apparent in the post-*Rodriguez* era (since 1973) is a move among the various states to make statutory and policy changes aimed at

---

53. *Id.*

54. *Id.* at 124.

55. See S. Landsman, *"Can Localities Lock the Doors and Throw Away the Keys?"* 7 J. OF LAW AND EDUC. 431-47 (July, 1978).

56. J.J. Callahan and W.H. Wilken, "School Finance Reforms: Do they Remain Equitable?" (Unpublished Paper, San Antonio, Texas: American Education Finance Association Conference, 1977), at 1, 3.

carrying out state constitutional mandates regarding educational opportunity for all children. Clearly, the legal responsibility for ensuring financial access to a quality education for each child fell directly upon state legislatures and state boards of education.

As this nation moves into the 1980's, parents and other concerned citizens will insist that the quality of a child's education not be measured only by dollar input. Public school systems will be required to show that children have progressed and are "better" for what schools have done to, with, and for them.

In their insistence on fiscally neutral systems of school finance, courts of law have never demanded that equal dollars must be spent on every child. Future courts will maintain this attitude and will insist that states provide differing resources to meet differing student needs. The responsibility will be on each state to see to it that this goal is reached. Thus, throughout the states, changes in tax policies, taxing structures, and school system organization and administration are inevitable as public education moves into the next decade.

PART III

LAW AND PROFESSIONAL STAFF

Chapter Seven

EMPLOYMENT AND JOB SECURITY

§ 7.0. Types of School District Employees.

Basically, there are two types of categories of employees working within public school systems. One category includes individuals who provide support services for the system (*e.g.,* maintenance and custodial care of buildings and grounds, maintenance and operation of buses and other vehicles, operation of the cafeterias, provision of clerical and secretarial services), and is generally referred to as the nonprofessional, classified, or noncertificated staff.

The second category of school system employees contains the professional or instructional staff members. Superintendents of schools, building principals, curriculum supervisors, guidance counselors, school psychologists, school social workers, and classroom teachers belong to this group. Typically, to be eligible for employment (full-time or part-time), in one of the aforementioned positions, an individual must initially possess a valid *certificate* issued by the state. In some state statutes, however, local school boards may employ individuals not holding full-force certificates in one of the above professional capacities on a temporary, substitute, or emerging basis, or through issuance of a provisional or special certificate (*e.g.*, vocational-technical teachers).

Generally, local school boards cannot legally pay professional staff members who do not hold bona fide certificates, or who do not meet some special exception allowed by law. A recent Wisconsin case demonstrates that a school board can terminate a teacher who is not certified to teach a particular subject, even though that teacher taught that same subject for eight years prior to termination. The board's reason for termination was that she, the teacher, was uncertified for her job.[1]

§ 7.1. Certification.

As used in school law, the term *certification* is synonymous with the term *license*. That is to say, the state, by issuing a certificate to an individual is giving its formal permission to that person to practice his or her profession (teaching, administration, psychology, etc.) in the public schools of that state. Thus, a certificate legally grants entrance to practice, but does not ensure that the individual holding the certificate will gain employment.

---

1. Grams v. Melrose-Midora Joint School Dist. No. 1, 245 N.W.2d 730 (Wis. 1977). For another case involving the termination of a teacher who, for several years of teaching, lacked proper certification, *see* Chapman v. Board of Educ., 394 N.Y.S. 2d (App. Div. 1977). See also, Chambers v. Board of Educ., 397 N.Y.S. 2d 436 (App. Div. 1977).

Certificates are not employment contracts. As Bolmeier has commented regarding teacher certification:

> The teacher's certificate is, in essence, a document indicating that the holder has met legal qualifications required by a particular state to follow the teaching profession in that state. It does not, by itself, give the holder the right to demand a teaching position.[2]

Colleges of education do not grant certificates. Local school boards do not issue certificates. Generally, state law (the legislature) delegates the legal authority to grant and issue certificates of professional practice in the public schools to the state board of education (in some states, called boards of regents).[3] Although the state board maintains legal authority for the issuance of certificates, it often delegates the administrative tasks of processing applications for certificates, evaluating transcripts, and other such matters to the state department of education (sometimes called the state department of public instruction). Thus, persons usually apply to the state department of education (or state department of public instruction), but are formally granted the certificate by the state board of education itself.

In some states, agencies other than the state board of education may be involved in the certification process. For example, school psychologists might be certificated through a state board of psychological examiners, while school nurses might receive their licensure through a state board of nursing or state board of health.

The certificate itself usually grants licensure for a specific professional position (*e.g.*, as a "teacher" in the public schools of a state). Specific *endorsements* are placed on the certificate and may be added to the certificate, as demonstrated by the person's

---

2. E.C. BOLMEIER, SCHOOL IN THE LEGAL STRUCTURE 189, (2d ed. Cincinnati, Ohio: The W.H. Anderson Co., 1973). According to *American Jurisprudence*, "...teachers' licenses or certificates, like other licenses, possess none of the elements of a contract protected by the due process clause of the Fourteenth Amendment...." 68 AM. JUR. 2d, 462 (1973). *See also,* Wardwell v. Board of Educ., 529 F.2d 625 (6th Cir. 1976).

3. As the Supreme Court of Alabama said in a recent decision, "The individual boards of education in Alabama have nothing whatever to do with certification of teachers. That is done by the State Board of Education." Bramlett v. Alabama State Tenure Comm'n, 341 So.2d 727 (Ala. 1977).

professional training (*e.g.*, social studies, English, and reading, grades 1-12). Generally, local school boards are encouraged not to assign professional personnel to positions for which they are neither certified nor endorsed. If such an assignment is made, the board should, within reason, see to it that the professional immediately pursue additional training for the new job. Local boards of education may prescribe additional requirements for personnel over and above state requirements.

Generally, state statutes require that professional certificates be renewed after a given period of time — frequently every five or six years. During that period, professionals often return to the university to pursue the additional courses necessary to renew their certificate.[4]

Revocation of certification is different from removal or dismissal from employment. While a local school board can legally remove or dismiss a superintendent, principal, supervisor, counselor, teacher, or other professional employee, state commissioners and state boards are generally the only ones legally able to revoke a certificate. Additionally, state statutes usually specify grounds and procedures for certification revocation,[5] and these statutory mandates must be adhered to. Generally, courts of law will not intervene in a certificate revocation matter unless an individual has lost his certificate on grounds not specified in statute, or if mandatory procedures were not followed.[6] What is more, courts will also insist that plaintiffs exhaust administrative remedies available before taking their complaint into court.

§ 7.2. Legal Status of Professional Employees in Schools.

All professionals in public school systems are employees of their local school board. And, since local school boards are *quasi-municipal* corporations legally constituted to carry out a state

---

4. Pointek v. Elk Lake School Dist., 360 A.2d 804 (Pa. 1976).

5. Moral unfitness, sexual misconduct, lack of requisite qualifications, willful neglect of duties, use or sale of illegal drugs, and involvement in criminal activity offer examples of grounds cited for revocation of teaching certificates by state boards.

6. 68 Am. Jur. 463 (1973). For a recent case involving the revocation of a teacher's certificate *see:* Shore v. Board of Examiners of New York City, 392 N.Y.S.2d 328 (N.Y. 1977).

governmental function (providing public education), professionals in local school systems are, legally, public employees.

An examination of the professional hierarchy within public school systems, however, reveals the existence of differences in legal status among professional employees. The major difference concerns those professional employees who hold legal status as school *officials* or *officers,* and those who occupy legal status solely as *employees.*

According to *Black's Law Dictionary,* an officer

> . . . is one who is invested with some portion of the functions of the government to be exercised for the public benefit. . . . An officer is distinguished from an employee in the greater importance, dignity, and independence of his position, in requirement of oath, bond, more enduring tenure, and fact of duties being prescribed by law.[7]

Individuals who occupy status as school officials or officers are entrusted with *authority* to do what is necessary for the well-being of the schools and to exercise independent discretion in the administration of school board policy. Decision-making authority and the possession of legal prerogatives to control the behavior of employees within the school system organization are major characteristics of school officialdom.

Most professionals in public school systems occupy legal status solely as *employees* of the school board and not as officers or officials. How is the term employee legally defined and how does it differ from that of officer, previously defined? As one source states,

> The status of "employee" arises where one is engaged by another person to perform work or services as directed and controlled by the other person's promise to pay wages, salary, or compensation for such services, and where there is a contract between employer and employee. . . .[8]

---

7. BLACK'S LAW DICTIONARY, (4th ed. St. Paul, Minn: West Publishing Co., 1951), at 1235.

8. *Words and Phrases,* (permanent ed. St. Paul, Minn: West Publishing Co., 1952), at 531.

The absence of any reference to employee decision-making authority, coupled with the notion of performance of work as directed and controlled by the employer, and the presence of a contractual agreement (including compensation for services rendered) are significant elements in understanding the differences existing between the status of an official and that of an employee.

a. *The Legal Status of Superintendents.* Legally, local superintendents of schools are both employees of the school board and administrative officers of the local school division (district). Superintendents are contracted by the school board (usually for a term fixed by state law), to serve as the board's chief administrator and educational advisor. As employees of the school board, superintendents are contracted by and work directly for the school board; and, they are accountable to the board for the performance of their professional tasks. Like any other board employee, they are subject to dismissal from employment.

As officers of the school system, however, superintendents are generally granted independent discretion by the board to make decisions (undergirded by board policy), on the many administrative problems that might occur in the daily operation of the school system. And so long as the superintendent does not violate state law, state board regulations, or local board policy, a school board generally will not interfere with the superintendent's decisions.

In some states, statutory provisions have been interpreted to specifically grant "officer" status to local superintendents of schools. Ohio offers an example of one such State. According to *Ohio Jurisprudence,*

> Under earlier statutes, the superintendent of schools was regarded merely as the agent or employee of the board of education. . . . But inasmuch as the statute now provides that a superintendent of schools is the executive "officer" for the board of education of the school district, and speaks of a vacancy in the "office" of superintendent, it would seem that the General Assembly had definitely characterized a superintendent of schools as a public officer, as distinguished from a public employee. . . .[9]

---

9. 48 *Ohio Jurisprudence* (2d) 810 (1966).

State statutes usually specify legal duties of local superintendents of schools,[10] with the proviso that boards of education have the prerogative to assign all other duties that they, the board, deem necessary for the overall operation of the school system.

Thus, the legal status of the local school superintendent can be determined only by examination of pertinent state law. Whether or not a superintendent of schools gains tenure in that capacity is another matter that must be studied on a state-to-state basis (statutes and court decisions).[11]

b. *The Legal Status of Principals.* Despite the fact that building principals are granted considerable discretion by local school boards and superintendents to conduct the day-to-day business of their individual schools, courts have consistently held that principals are not public officers. School principals are *employees* of the school board, appointed and assigned by that board to carry out administrative duties within a given school building.

Generally, the legal status of principals is determined by interpretation of state statute. In some states (*e.g.*, the Commonwealth of Virginia), continuing contract status (tenure), as a principal is specifically enumerated in statute, and is achieved after serving three probationary years in that position.[12] On the other hand, however, in states like Ohio, Tennessee, Illinois, and California, courts have interpreted state law to say that all administrative and supervisory personnel achieve tenure as teachers and not as administrators or supervisors.[13]

---

10. In New York State, for example, the several powers of local superintendents of schools are specifically enumerated by statute. 52 *N.Y. Jurisprudence* 85 (1967).

11. Recently, the Supreme Court of California ruled that *California Education Code* only provides tenure as a *classroom teacher* and not as an administrator or supervisor. Therefore, an associate superintendent of schools for business in the Jefferson Elementary School District (with eight years of service in that position), did not have a property interest in his administrative position. *Barthuli v. Board of Trustees,* 139 Cal. Rptr. 627 (1977). *See also,* Seyfang v. Board of Trustees, 563 P.2d 1376 (Wyo. 1977).

12. VA. CODE, § 22-217.9.

13. For recent cases on point *see* Coe v. Bogart, 519 F.2d 10 (6th Cir. 1975), Danno v. Peterson, 421 F. Supp. 950 (N.D. Ill. 1976), Barthuli v. Board of Trustees, 139 Cal. Rptr. 627, 566 P.2d 261 (1977), and Lane v. Board of Educ., 348 N.E.2d 470 (Ill. 1976).

School boards possess the legal prerogative granted by state statute to reassign principals to any principalship or supervisory position within the school system for which they are qualified. Also, boards can reassign principals to classroom teaching positions provided the board acts in good faith and state tenure statutes are not violated. In *Lane v. Board of Education,* a principal of five years challenged his board's decision to reassign his teaching duties, claiming that he had a property interest in his principal's position. In holding for the board, the appellate court interpreted the Illinois code and ruled that the plaintiff's property right was in his position as a certified employee and not in his administrative position. Thus, the school board could transfer him to any job for which he was qualified and adjust his salary accordingly.[14] The sections below discuss the legal aspects of assignment, reassignment, transfer, and demotion of administrators.

c. *The Legal Status of Supervisors.* Unlike the individual working in business and industry who holds the title "supervisor" and exercises certain *line* (command) responsibilities, the supervisor in a public school system is generally classified (legally) as acting in a staff position possessing no administrative responsibilities. Supervisors in educational settings are usually hired to help in curriculum development and to assist teachers and administrators to improve instruction.

Legally, supervisors are generally certified by the state to practice their specialty, but they do not acquire tenure in their supervisor's position. Some states (*e.g.*, Virginia), do allow for continuing contract status as a supervisor (after serving three years of probation in that capacity), while in other states (*e.g.*, California), an individual acquires tenure only as a classroom teacher.

The legal status of supervisors in public school systems is that of an *employee* of the school board. Supervisors are not *officers* of the school system.

d. *The Legal Status of Counselors.* Generally, state education codes require that all individuals serving as guidance counselors

---

14. 348 N.E.2d 470 (Ill. 1976). *See also,* Conte v. School Committee of Methuen, 356 N.E.2d 261 (Mass. 1976).

in public school systems be certified for that position by the state. Certificates for counselors may be issued by state boards of education or, as has happened recently in some states, by boards of professional licensure (such boards also license psychologists and others who work as professional counselors).

Counselors in schools usually acquire tenure as classroom teachers and not as counselors. Such a determination is made under the control of appropriate state law and, in some situations, pertinent state court opinions.

In 1977, the Supreme Court of California heard the appeal of a public school attendance counselor who, after serving two years in that position, was reassigned by his board to classroom teaching duties and was reduced in salary. The counselor held both a classroom teacher's certificate and that of a counselor in the State of California. The Supreme Court of California affirmed the decision of the lower court which was adverse to appellant's claim.[15] The California Education Code, stated the court, "provides in effect that employees holding both teaching and counseling certificates shall acquire permanent status only as a classroom teacher, and not as counselors."[16] Thus, the court continued, "We hold that an employee with both teaching and counseling certificates acquires permanent status as a classroom teacher regardless of the position held by that employee at the completion of the probationary period."[17]

Counselors in public school systems are professional employees of the system. Legally, they in no way hold official (officer), status in school systems.

§ 7.3. Selection and Assignment of Employees.

State law provides that local school boards possess legal authority to contract and to be contracted with. Thus, all employees enter into employment contracts with local boards of education and not with administrators. It follows, therefore, that boards of education also possess legal authority to nonrenew contracts with employees and to dismiss employees under contract when cause

---

15. Thompson v. Modesto City High School Dist., 139 Cal. Rptr. 603 (1977).
16. *Id.* at 607.
17. *Id. See also,* Capella v. Board of Educ., 367 A.2d 244 (N.J. 1976).

exists to take such action (state statutes usually specify cause for dismissal).

a. *Selection of Employees.* The administrative tasks associated with recruitment and selection of personnel are usually delegated by school boards to school system personnel offices, generally under the supervision of an assistant superintendent of schools, or a director of personnel. Legally, however, the ultimate selection authority of all personnel employed in public schools (certificated and noncertificated), resides with the board of education of the particular school system. To put it another way, courts have held consistently that only local boards of education (not superintendents or principals), possess legal authority (specified in state law), to contract with (hire) personnel employed by their school system.[18]

In addition to compliance with state law and their own policies, school boards must likewise comply with federal law and policy regarding recruitment, selection, and hiring of employees. Recent examples of federal laws (intended to remove any forms of discrimination), having direct impact on board employment prerogatives are Title VII of the Civil Rights Act of 1964, Title IX of the Education Amendments of 1972, and Section 504 of the Rehabilitation Act of 1973. Additionally, policies and guidelines from such federal agencies as the Office of Economic Opportunity (OEO), the Department of Health, Education and Welfare (HEW), and the decrees of federal courts (especially recent cases wherein 42 U.S.C., Section 1983 has been applied to claims of employment discrimination), have also changed and reshaped the employment practices of local school boards.

b. *Recommendation.* Where state statutes specify that teachers and other personnel be employed by local boards of education, upon recommendation of the superintendent of schools, courts of law have held that contracts are not binding absent said recommendation.[19] A statutory procedure requiring a recommendation of employees by the superintendent has been held not to constitute an illegal delegation of board authority.[20]

---

18. Marsh v. Birmingham Board of Educ., 349 So. 2d 34 (Ala. 1977). *See also,* School Board v. Goodson, 355 So. 2d 308 (Fla. 1976).

19. *See,* for example, Bonar v. City of Boston, 341 N.E.2d 684 (Mass. 1976).

20. Hembree v. Jefferson City Bd. of Educ., 337 So. 2d 9 (Ala. 1976).

An example of a state statute requiring the recommendation of the superintendent is found in the CODE OF VIRGINIA. According to Section 22-217.9, of the Code,

> The school board of any division upon recommendation of the division superintendent may employ an administrator or administrators called principals and assistant principals. [21]

School boards are not required to accept the personnel recommendations of superintendents or building principals. Moreover, personnel recommendations of superintendents and principals are not legally binding in and of themselves. As a Florida appellate court held (interpreting the School Code of Florida), in *School Board of Leon County v. Goodson:* [22]

> The School Board is to have exclusive authority to form contracts with the instructional personnel of the school system. The Board may accept or reject the recommendations of the superintendent who, in turn, may accept or reject the recommendations of the school principals. Neither a superintendent nor a principal, acting individually or collectively, may enter into a contractual agreement with a teacher without express approval of the School Board.[23]

Thus, it can be said that local school boards retain ultimate legal authority to contract with (hire), professional personnel even though authority to initially *recommend* personnel may be placed by statute within the purview of school administration.

c. *Assignment.* Courts of law have consistently held that local school boards must have enough latitude to effectively administer the operation of public school systems.[24] Assignment and reassignment of professional personnel to positions and to schools within systems are areas of school district operation wherein courts have, over the years, firmly established school board discretionary prerogatives. Absent any statutory or contractual provisions to the contrary, local boards of education are generally free to assign all personnel to any one position or combination of

---

21. VA. CODE, § 22-217.9.
22. 335 So. 2d 308 (Fla. 1976).
23. *Id.* at 310.
24. Hudson v. Independent School Dist. No. 77, 258 N.W.2d 594 (Minn. 1977).

positions for which they are qualified. Said assignments must be reasonable and must be made on nondiscriminatory bases.

The power of local school boards to reassign and transfer professional personnel does not end when personnel tenure is achieved. According to *American Jurisprudence:*

> The right to continued employment in a position of the same rank or grade as that to which a teacher has been "elected" under a tenure law has been recognized, although within reasonable limits a school board has power to change the assignment of a permanent teacher so long as the work assigned is of a rank and grade equivalent to that by which the permanent status was acquired and the assignment is one for which the teacher is qualified.[25]

Additionally, suggests *American Jurisprudence,*

> "tenure statutes do not guarantee to a teacher the right to continue in a particular school. . . . Employment under a continuing service contract does not prevent a board of education from transferring a teacher from one school to another or from one class of teaching position to another, unless the contract specifies the school or class of position. . . ."[26]

§ 7.4. Board Authority and Teacher Personnel.

Local boards of education possess considerable legal authority in dealing with professional personnel. It has been held that local boards possess the legal prerogatives for making all personnel decisions necessary for the "best interests of the school system."[27] What is more, as the United States Supreme Court held in *Adler v. Board of Education,* " . . . school authorities have the right and duty to screen the officials, teachers, and employees as to their fitness to maintain the schools as a part of ordered society. . . ."[28]

The legal authority to employ, assign, transfer, suspend, nonrenew, and dismiss teacher personnel belongs to the local

---

25. 68 AM. JUR. 157 (1973).

26. *Id.* 157-58.

27. Morelli v. Board of Educ., 42 Ill. App.3d 722, 358 N.E.2d 1364 (Ill. 1976).

28. 342 U.S. 485, 72 S. Ct. 380 (1952), at 385. *See also,* Singston v. King, 340 F. Supp. 314 (W.D. Va. 1972).

school board. Teachers in public school systems contract with the school board and not with superintendents or building principals.[29]

School board decisions in personnel matters will not be interfered with by courts of law unless it is proved that the board acted arbitrarily, capriciously, or beyond the scope of its duly constituted authority.[30] Moreover, the legal presumption is that boards of education act in *good faith* when making personnel decisions. Thus, according to Levin:

> ... Unless the school board has dismissed, transferred, demoted, or disciplined its employees for constitutionally impermissible reasons or has failed to provide the requisite procedural safeguards, it has proved difficult for employees to successfully challenge such actions.[31]

Over the years, however, school board authority and control over teachers have received much attention as increasing numbers of complaints reached courts of law. Cases have been taken to the courts challenging almost every aspect of board regulation and censure of teacher behavior. As Hamilton observed more than two decades ago,

> The list of rules and regulations affecting teachers which have been challenged is a very long one. They vary from rules concerning tenure, salary, duties, leaves of absence, and other such important matters, to the length of the teacher's skirt or where or how she will spend her time outside of school hours.[32]

Local school boards continue to reassign, reprimand, discipline, and discharge teachers for a variety of reasons. Some reasons cited in recent litigation are: admitted homosexual activity,[33] insubordination,[34] excessive and improper use of corporal punishment,[35] wearing a beard in violation of school board

---

29. Hart v. School Bd., 340 So. 2d 121 (Fla. 1976).

30. *Morelli, supra,* at 1369.

31. B. Levin, *"Employees."* In P.K. Piele (Editor-in-Chief), THE YEARBOOK OF SCHOOL LAW 1976 (Topeka, Kan.: NOLPE, 1977), at 129.

32. 13 BI WEEKLY SCH. LAW LET. (October 15, 1953), at 66.

33. Burton v. Cascade School Dist., 512 F.2d 850 (9th Cir. 1975).

34. Thompson v. Wake County Bd. of Educ., 230 S.E.2d 164 (N.C. 1976).

35. Board of Educ. v. Shank, 542 S.W.2d 779 (Mo. 1976).

regulations,[36] cruelty to students,[37] persistent neglect of professional duties,[38] distributing ACLU materials and participating in ACLU activities,[39] out-of-wedlock pregnancy,[40] incompetency,[41] lack of classroom discipline,[42] below-average grades and test scores attained by students,[43] lack of tact in handling professional matters,[44] incapacity for teaching because of a sex-change operation,[45] and a variety of other causes too numerous to list.

The above causes are made complex in that most are not included in or defined by state statute or school board policy; and, "may not occur at all during the teacher's classroom work performance. They can occur on the job before school, after school, on the playground, in the halls, in the cafeteria, and during preparation periods."[46]

When evaluating teachers' fitness, school boards are not restricted in considering teachers' in-school and in-class behavior only. As a New Jersey superior court held, local school boards have the duty of determining the general issue of "teacher fitness."[47] Regarding the actual scope of a teacher's fitness (per se), the court said:

> A teacher's fitness may not be measured "solely by his or her ability to perform the teaching function and ignore the fact that the teacher's presence in the classroom might, nevertheless, pose a danger of harm to the

---

36. Morrison v. Hamilton County School Bd., 494 S.W.2d 770 (Tenn., 1973), *cert. denied,* at 414 U.S. 1044.

37. Rolando v. School Directors, 358 N.E.2d 945 (Ill. 1976).

38. diLeo v. Greenfield, 541 F.2d 949 (2nd Cir. 1976).

39. Woqdward v. Hereford, 421 F.Supp. 93 (N.D. Tex., 1976).

40. Brown v. Bathke, 416 F.Supp. 1194 (D. Neb. 1976).

41. Filliard v. Board of Educ., 343 N.E.2d 704 (Ill. 1976).

42. Hagerstrom v. Clay City, 343 N.E.2d 249 (Ill. 1976).

43. Klein v. Boehmer, CV75-L-70 (D. Neb. 1976).

44. Mt. Healthy City School Dist. v. Doyle, 429 U.S. 274, 97 S. Ct. 56, 50 L. Ed. 2d 471 (1977).

45. *In re* Tenure Hearing of Grossman, 321 A.2d 253 (1974), *cert. denied,* 429 U.S. 897 (1976).

46. 1 COLLECT. BARG. QUART. (1976), at 1.

47. Gish v. Board of Educ., 145 N.J. Super. 96, 366 A.2d 1337 (1976).

students for a reason not related to academic proficiency." [48]

§ 7.5. Teachers' Tenure as Job Security.

To protect themselves from possible excessive exercises of school board authority and to establish job security, teachers have, over the years, relied on the existence of tenure statutes. Tenure (or continuing contract as it is called in some states), is conferred by state law and can be changed or repealed by legislative enactment only. Thus, to discover how tenure status and its specific guarantees are attained, one must examine the specific statutes of a given state.

Tenure in public education systems is not a guarantee of permanent employment. Tenure laws were meant in their inception and are meant now "to give job security to certified employees who meet the necessary qualifications and who satisfactorily have served the probationary period...."[49] Once attained, therefore, tenure exists to protect competent teachers from unlawful, arbitrary, and capricious board actions and to provide orderly procedures (enumerated in state statutes) to be followed if and when cause for a teacher's dismissal is established.

Recent court decisions have placed the meaning of teachers' tenure under a federal constitutional overlay of *substantive* and *procedural due process,* as guaranteed by the Fourteenth Amendment. Between 1972 and 1976, courts, (federal and state), consistently applied the United States Supreme Court's holdings in *Board of Regents v. Roth,*[50] and *Perry v. Sindermann*[51] to matters of teacher personnel. *Roth, Sindermann,* and their progeny added a second dimension to teachers' job security. In addition to boards and administrators providing state tenure guarantees to those who qualify for them, so too were personnel decisions to be free from any constitutional violations. Thus, taken together, these two cases balanced school board personnel prerogatives with teachers' constitutional rights.

---

48. *Id.* 1342.
49. Thompson v. Modesto City H. S., 134 Cal. Rptr. 496 (1977).
50. 408 U.S. 564, 92 S. Ct. 2701, 33 L. Ed. 2d 548 (1972).
51. 408 U.S. 593, 92 S. Ct. 2694, 33 L. Ed. 2d 570 (1972).

a. *The Probationary Teacher.* As previously discussed, state legislatures create tenure, and tenure guarantees and protections accrue to professional employees who qualify for them. Typically, a probationary period must be served in a given professional position before one is eligible for tenure in that position. Moreover, tenure may attach to a single position (*e.g.*, teacher, or principal, or counselor), in a particular school system within a state, and does not transfer from one position to another, or from one school system to another, or from one state to another. Also, probationary periods of teachers can be extended by local school boards,[52] and additional periods of probation can be required by state law in order for one to acquire continuing contract status in an administrative or supervisory position.[53]

The length of time that new teachers in public school systems must serve in a "probationary" classification varies from state-to-state, sometimes from school system to school system within a state, and sometimes from professional position to professional position within a particular school system. Generally, the period of probation required ranges from three to five years.

Once a teacher has successfully served the probationary period in a given school district, tenure (continuing contract) status is acquired in that school district.[54] Prior to the completion of the probationary period, however, there is no "expectancy of continued employment." Thus, courts have held that *Roth* and *Sindermann* do not apply, and the probationary teacher is only entitled to notice that his or her contract will or will not be renewed for the next year,[55] unless state statutes specify otherwise.

Teachers do not possess legal entitlement to probationary employment, theirs is a year-to-year appointment. As an Arizona court has put it, ". . . a probationary teacher's right to remain in public service is dependent upon whether the appointing officers are satisfied with the teacher's conduct and capacity, and they are, in law, the sole judges . . ." [56]

---

52. Graham v. Board of Educ., 15 Ill. App. 3d 1092, 305 N.E.2d 310 (1973).

53. VA. CODE, § 22-217.3.

54. Jacob v. Board of Regents, 365 A.2d 430 (R.I. 1976).

55. Abbott v. Board of Educ., 558 P.2d 1307 (Utah 1976). *See also,* Ryan v. Aurora City Board of Educ., 540 F.2d 222 (6th Cir. 1976).

56. School Dist. v. Superior Ct., 102 Ariz. 478, 433 P.2d 28 (Ariz. 1967).

Termination of a probationary teacher during a contract year is different from nonrenewal of that teacher at the end of a contract year. As such, it is considered a dismissal from employment. The Supreme Court of Missouri, for example, (relying on *Roth*) held that a nontenured teacher dismissed during a contractual period is entitled to procedural due process.[57] Similarly, the Rhode Island Supreme Court held (in interpreting that State's tenure law),

> Any committee which dismisses a nontenured teacher during the school year is required to afford the teacher a hearing at which just cause for the committee's action must be shown.[58]

Some states mandate, by statute, that all teachers (including probationary teachers) must be notified of nonrenewal by a specific date. For example, Section 22-217.4 of the CODE OF VIRGINIA mandates:

> If a teacher who has not achieved continuing contract status receives notice of reemployment, he must accept or reject in writing within fifteen days of receipt of such notice. Written notice of nonrenewal of the contract must be given by the school board on or before April fifteenth of each year.[59]

Thus, in Virginia, if a probationary teacher is not notified of nonrenewal on or before April 15, that teacher may reasonably expect another year of employment in the same position.

b. *Tenure Guarantees.* As contrasted with a teacher's *constitutional* rights, "tenure is a statutory right imposed upon a teacher's contractual employment status ...."[60] Even though tenure guarantees differ from state-to-state, there are usually *three* basic elements contained in tenure statutes: *notice* (by a specific date), *cause* (specific statement of reasons), and *hearing* (a chance for the reasons to be discussed). All three elements have been and continue to be the subject of legal challenge.

Since procedures to be followed in the dismissal of tenured teachers are prescribed by state statute, the wording of each

---

57. Valter v. Orchard Farm School Dist., 511 S.W.2d 550 (Mo. 1976).
58. *Jacob, supra,* at 433.
59. VA. CODE, § 22-217.4.
60. 68 AM. JUR. 2d 484 (1973).

statute is critical. In 1977, an Arizona court overturned a local school board's dismissal of a tenured teacher, finding fault with the board's notice to that teacher. Interpreting the Arizona *Code,* the court held that where state law mandates that a tenured teacher be dismissed prior to April 15, that action must be made official prior to that date; mere notice of intention to dismiss is not enough.[61] Two years earlier, in a Washington case (in 1975), a tenured teacher challenged a school board's action to terminate because the school board had placed a statement of its official action to dismiss within the initial notice statement sent to the teacher, rather than the notice simply containing probable cause for dismissal. The Supreme Court of Washington upheld the board, ruling that the action did not create an unfair advantage for the board.[62]

Tenured teachers can be terminated solely for cause specified in a given state statute. Cause for dismissal differs from state-to-state; yet, there are similarities. For example, in *Pennsylvania,* tenured professional employees can be dismissed only for immorality, incompetency, intemperance, cruelty, persistent negligence, mental disarrangement, or violation of school laws of the Commonwealth.[63] In *Connecticut,* cause for dismissal is specified as inefficiency, incompetency, insubordination, moral misconduct, disability as shown by competent medical evidence, elimination of position, or for other due and sufficient cause.[64] In *Illinois,* cause is enumerated as incompetency, cruelty, negligence, immorality, and whenever in the board's opinion a teacher is not qualified to teach, or the best interests of the school require it.[65]

As stated earlier in this Chapter, state statutes do not define the causes listed for dismissal of tenured employees. Definition of cause is a matter left to the courts to determine. Courts, therefore, have been placed in a position of ensuring that tenured employees are dismissed for cause only. Similarly, courts seek to ensure that teachers are not dismissed for reasons violative of their rights

---

61. Board of Trustees v. Carter, 559 P.2d 216 (Ariz. 1977).
62. Martin v. Dayton School Dist., 536 P.2d 169 (Wash. 1975).
63. PA. STAT. ANN., tit. 24, § 11-1102 (1962).
64. CONN. GEN. STAT. ANN., tit. 5A § 10-151 (1977).
65. ILL. ANN. STAT. (Smith-Hurd), Ch. 122 § 10-22.4 (1977).

guaranteed under the United States Constitution. When the change is made, the *burden of proof* is placed upon the complaining employee to show that: 1. the behavior was constitutionally protected, and 2. the exercise of that protected behavior was the "motivating factor" in the board's action to dismiss him.[66]

State law may provide tenured employees with an opportunity to have a *hearing* prior to formal *dismissal.* In some states, however, a *hearing* before the school board is not mandatory and is often not held in public. Virginia offers an example of a state statute that offers the possibility of an interview with the superintendent in lieu of a hearing and places the onus upon the complaining teacher to decide (if a hearing is held) on whether that hearing should be private or public.[67]

In *Morelli v. Board of Education,* a former principal sought reversal of his dismissal claiming that his superintendent's presenting a *bill of particulars* to the school board prior to his hearing before that same board rendered the board biased to his case. He claimed that he was therefore not granted a fair, impartial hearing.[68] The Appellate Court of Illinois, Third District, disagreed with him and bolstered its opinion with the following quotation from the United States Supreme Court's decision in *Hortonville District v. Hortonville Education Association*: [69]

> [T]he initial charge or determination of probable cause and the ultimate adjudication have different bases and purposes. The fact that the same agency makes them in tandem and that they relate to the same issue does not result in a procedural violation.[70]

c. *Teacher Reassignment, Transfer, and Demotion.* State law typically grants local school boards the legal prerogatives to reassign and transfer professional personnel to any single position or combination of positions for which they are qualified.[71] Tenure laws are interpreted as not precluding the exercise of these board prerogatives. As a United States District Court said in an Illinois

---

66. Mt. Healthy City School Dist. v. Doyle, *supra.*
67. Va. Code, § 22-217.7.
68. Morelli v. Bd. of Educ., *supra.*
69. 426 U.S. 482, 96 S. Ct. 2308, 49 L. Ed. 2d 1 (1976).
70. *Morelli, supra.*
71. Lester v. Board of Educ., 230 N.E.2d 893 (Ill. 1967).

case involving the reassignment of a principal to regular teaching duties, the "job security envisioned by the teacher tenure law (Illinois) is a guarantee of employment but not a guarantee of continued employment in any single capacity when the educational employee is qualified to serve in more than one capacity." [72] The court added that the Tenure Act of Illinois permits boards to make such reassignments (administrators to teaching positions) without a prior hearing, provided the board has acted in good faith. [73]

In addition to upholding the reassignment (or transfer of teachers and other professionals) to positions for which they are qualified, so too have courts insisted that the former position and the new position be "coequal"; otherwise, the reassignment might be considered a demotion. For example, in *Frank v. Arapahoe County School District,*[74] a Colorado Court opined that since a school counselor was basically a teacher under state law and not an "administrator," counselor and teacher are (for transfer purposes) coequal positions. [75] A United States District Court added, in deciding a similar case in Missouri, that there can be no demotion so long as an individual is transferred between two coequal positions. [76]

In 1977, however, a California appellate court demonstrated the tenuous nature of the above legal point. The court was convinced that the transfer of a school counselor to a teaching position "was not a reassignment to a position of a rank and grade equal to the position of counselor. . . ." [77] Thus, the transfer was improper.

In the past, courts of law have heard cases of several teachers who claimed that their *reassignments* to other positions were actually *demotions.* In 1970, the Court of Appeals for the Fifth Circuit decided *Singleton v. Jackson.*[78] In that case the court constructed the following definition of the term demotion, a definition used by subsequent courts to adjudicate such matters:

> . . . demotion includes any reassignment (1) under which
> the staff member receives less pay or has less

---

72. Danno v. Peterson, 421 F.Supp. 950 (N.D. Ill. 1976), at 953.
73. *Id.*
74. 506 P.2d 373 (Colo. 1972).
75. *Id.*
76. Birdwell v. Hazelwood School Dist., 352 F.Supp. 613 (Mo. 1972).
77. Thompson v. Modesto City H.S. Dist., 134 Cal. Rptr. 496 (1977).
78. 419 F.2d 1211 (5th Cir. 1970). *See also,* 43 MISS. L. J. 368 (1972).

responsibility than under the assignment he held previously, (2) which requires a lesser degree of skill than did the assignment he held previously, or (3) under which the staff member was asked to teach a subject and grade other than one for which he is certified or for which he has had substantial experience within a reasonably current period. In general and depending upon the subject matter involved, five years is such a reasonable period.[79]

The court added that all reassignments and discharges must be made through the application of *objective, reasonable,* and *nondiscriminatory* criteria.[80]

Regarding assignments of teachers to extracurricular duties, courts have granted discretion to local boards of education. In a recent New Jersey case it was held that a local board show only that the extracurricular assignments are reasonable, nondiscriminatory, are related to a teacher's interests and expertise, and do not require excessive hours.[81] And, a teacher need not be compensated for such assignments.

d. *Procedural Safeguards: Bishop v. Wood.* On June 10, 1976, the United States Supreme Court (by a vote of 5-4) rendered a decision in *Bishop v. Wood,*[82] a nonschool case with direct bearing on teachers' tenure protections as well as on Constitutional guarantees of job security.

In *Bishop,* the city manager of Marion, North Carolina, terminated the employment of a policeman who claimed he had "permanent employment" as defined by city ordinance. The policeman brought suit in federal district court seeking reinstatement and back pay, claiming that he had been terminated without a "pretermination hearing" — a constitutional guarantee afforded permanent employees.[83]

The United States District Court granted a motion for summary

---

79. *Id.*

80. *Id.* at 1218.

81. Board of Educ. of Asbury Park v. Asbury Park Educ. Ass'n, 145 N.J. Super. 495, 368 A.2d 396 (N.J. 1976).

82. 426 U.S. 341, 96 S. Ct. 2074, 48 L. Ed. 2d 684 (1976).

83. *Id.* at 1076. In his petition, the policeman claimed that he was told *privately,* by the city manager, that his dismissal was based upon his failure to follow orders, poor attendance at police training classes, causing low morale, and for conduct unsuited to an officer.

judgment holding that, on the basis of state law (North Carolina), the policeman held his position at the "will and pleasure of the city." [84] A three-judge panel of the Court of Appeals for the Fourth Circuit affirmed that decision,[85] and the Supreme Court of the United States granted certiorari.[86] The two questions before the high court were: (1) Was the policeman's employment status a *property* interest protected by the Due Process Clause of the Fourteenth Amendment? (2) If the reasons given for his discharge were false, was that false explanation a violation of *liberty* as protected by that same clause?

In answering the first question, the Supreme Court majority looked to North Carolina State law, the Marion City Ordinance under which the policeman worked, and the United States District Court's interpretation of these two. Said Mr. Justice Stevens:

> A property interest in employment can, of course, be created by ordinance, or by an implied contract. In either case, however, the sufficiency of the claim of entitlement must be decided by reference to state law. The North Carolina Supreme Court had held that an enforceable expectation of continued employment in that State can exist only if the employer, by statute or contract, has actually granted some form of guarantee.... Whether such a guarantee has been given can be determined only by an examination of the particular statute or ordinance in question.[87]

Thus, looking to the United States District Court's interpretation as controlling, the majority accepted the view that the policeman "held his position at the will and pleasure of the city," and that his only guarantees in removal were procedural.[88]

Regarding the *liberty* question, the Supreme Court was of the opinion that since the city manager's determination of the grounds for discharge were communicated orally to the policeman (in private), it cannot be assumed that the policeman's " 'good name, reputation, honesty, or integrity' was injured." [89] And, even if the

---

84. 377 F.Supp. 501 (W.D. N.C. 1973).

85. 498 F.2d 134 (4th Cir. 1974).

86. 423 U.S. 890, 96 S. Ct. 185, 46 L. Ed. 2d 121 (1975).

87. *Bishop, supra,* note 82 at 426 U.S. 345.

88. *Id.*

89. *Id.* at 2079.

reasons for discharge stated to the policeman were false, "... the reasons stated to him in private had no different impact on his reputation than if they had been true." [90]

In rendering the majority opinion, Mr. Justice Stevens concluded:

> The federal court is not the appropriate forum in which to review the multitude of personnel decisions that are made daily by public agencies. We must accept the harsh fact that numerous individual mistakes are inevitable in the day-to-day administration of our affairs. The United States Constitution cannot feasibly be construed to require federal judicial review for every such error. In the absence of any claim that the public employer was motivated by a desire to curtail or to penalize the exercise of an employee's constitutionally protected rights, we must presume that official action was regular and, if erroneous, can best be corrected in other ways. The Due Process Clause of the Fourteenth Amendment is not a guarantee against incorrect or illadvised personnel decisions. [91]

There have been several public school personnel cases heard by courts (since the Supreme Court's decision) wherein the judges saw *Bishop* as controlling. [92] An analysis of these recent cases reveals the emergence of a definite pattern of court attitudes toward public school personnel decision-making and teachers' rights. Some of these attitudes are: 1. a return of federal courts to a "hands off" attitude toward public school personnel decisions, 2. a renewed insistence by federal courts that aggrieved individuals seek remedies provided in state law before taking their complaint to a federal court, 3. non-intervention by a federal court in public school personnel decisions unless there is clearly present a gross violation of either constitutional law or federal statutory law, 4. the application of a more *flexible* standard of due process when school personnel decisions are heard in federal court, and 5. a look to appropriate state law and local school board policy by federal judges as controlling their decisions in school personnel cases.

---

90. *Id.*

91. *Id.* at 2080.

92. *See* for example, Danno v. Peterson, *supra,* note 46; and Chamberlain v. Wichita Falls Ind. School Dist., 539 F.2d 566 (5th Cir. 1976).

§ 7.6. Antidiscrimination in Employment: *Griggs v. Duke Power Company.*

Beginning in the early 1970's, several cases were heard by federal courts challenging alleged discrimination in employment practices. A mandate emerged from these decisions requiring all employers to establish a relationship between the *purpose* of differential treatment of job applicants and employees, and the *criteria* used for identification and classification of individuals who are to be placed in various categories for purposes of hiring, promotion, salary, and retention. The Supreme Court's landmark decision in *Griggs v. Duke Power Company* [93] firmly established this element of Equal Protection.

Griggs was the first case to present the nation's highest court with the question of whether *Title VII of the Civil Rights Act of 1964* prohibited an employer from instituting, as a condition of employment, a high school education or achieving a passing grade on a standardized test.[94] In deciding this issue, the Supreme Court considered several related questions among which were the following: 1. What relationship, if any, exists between employment requirements and "job performance?" 2. What methods of evaluation are used by employers to judge the *effectiveness* of "job criteria" as they relate to job success? 3. Can employers demonstrate the "job relatedness" of "job requirements?"

A primary effect of *Griggs* was to force employers to remove arbitrary, irrational criteria of applicant and employee selection. Also, they were to immediately publish detailed job descriptions — including not only statements describing job functions, but also including sets of qualifications necessary to obtain that job and to perform those functions.

---

93. 401 U.S. 424, 91 S. Ct. 849, 28 L. Ed. 2d 158 (1971).

94. *Id.* According to the Supreme Court, "What is required by Congress is the removal of artificial, arbitrary, and unnecessary barriers to employment when the barriers operate invidiously to discriminate on the basis of racial or other impermissible classification." *See also,* Washington v. Davis, 426 U.S. 229, 96 S. Ct. 2040, 48 L. Ed. 2d 597 (1976). In deciding this Title VII case involving black applicants for the District of Columbia police training program who were rejected because of scores on a verbal skills test, Mr. Justice White said: "In order to violate the Constitution, an employment criterion must be used with racially discriminatory intent; racial impact alone is not sufficient."

Thus, the *Griggs* decision and a host of previous and subsequent federal laws and regulations offered civil rights lawyers the legal leverage necessary to force *Equal Employment Opportunity* into action, and to bring a halt to discrimination in employment. It became the law of the land that job applicants and employees were not to be treated arbitrarily, irrationally, or capriciously. As the Court commanded in *Griggs,* a person must be measured for the job and not measured in the abstract.

Griggs has had a profound impact on public school personnel decision-making. Shortly after *Griggs* several decisions emanated from lower federal courts striking down the use of the *Graduate Record Examination* (GRE) and *National Teachers Examination* (NTE) as means of selecting, promoting, and retaining professional personnel.

In *Armstead v. Starkville,* the Board of Education of Starkville, Mississippi, had a policy that all applicants for teaching positions and in-service teachers take the GRE, General Aptitude Test, and subject area test. Attainment of specified minimum scores on these exams as a precondition of employment and retention was the board's requirement.

A group of teachers filed suit in federal court alleging they had been denied employment because of the board's GRE requirement, and that such a criterion was unreasonable and arbitrary. The court ruled in the plaintiffs' favor, holding that the GRE requirement was arbitrary and unreasonable for the following reasons:

> (1) GRE tests evaluate an individual's capacity for advanced studies at the master's and doctoral levels; they are not "job related" to teacher competencies; and
> (2) The school system had never conducted any empirical studies to see if the exams and required scores (combined 640 on the General Aptitude, and 50th percentile on the Advanced Test) were predictive of teacher success in that system.[95]

---

95. 325 F.Supp. 560 (D.C. Miss. 1971). More recently, in National Educ. Ass'n v. South Carolina, 434 U.S. 1026, 98 S. Ct. 756, 54 L. Ed. 2d 775 (1978), the United States Supreme Court upheld use of the National Teachers' Examination (NTE) to hire and classify teachers in South Carolina's public schools, where plaintiffs failed to prove a racially discriminatory purpose in the state's use of that examination.

Chance v. Board of Examiners offers another example of a post-*Griggs* case. In *Chance,* New York City, through its board of examiners, prescribed and administered exams to candidates seeking licenses for permanent appointment to supervisory positions in the City's public school system.

A class action suit was brought challenging the constitutionality of the examination program by parties claiming a conspicuous disparity between the numbers of qualified blacks and whites who failed to pass the exams — thus the whole program was "constitutionally suspect."

A United States District Court found the examination "too subjective" and not sufficiently "job related." The exams, said the court, simply called for a "regurgitation" of memorized material, "not related" to showing necessary skills and qualifications for obtaining a principal's or supervisor's position. Also, the City School System made no attempt to establish the reliability or validity of the exams through empirical studies.[96]

A review of more recent cases indicates that classroom teachers in public school systems, as well as all other professional personnel, must not be discriminated against in hiring, assignment, promotion, reassignment, and retention. These cases demonstrate that an evaluation of each teacher's professional qualifications and performance, evaluated on objective criteria and compared to all other similar teachers is a key to practicing fairness and to avoiding discrimination.

There is evidence, however, that some federal judges have sought, as their first priority, to achieve racial and sexual balance within a given school system's population of professionals. A benchmark case regarding racial balance is *Porcelli v. Titus,*[97] wherein the Court of Appeals for the Third Circuit widened the scope of faculty desegregation, making it possible to consider *race* as a factor in the selection, assignment, promotion, and retention of professionals in schools. Said the court, the integration of faculties "is as important as proper integration of schools themselves...."[98] As such, "State action based partly on consideration of color, when color is not used per se, and in the

---

96. 330 F.Supp. 203 (S.D. N.Y. 1971), 534 F.2d 993 (2nd Cir. 1976).
97. 431 F.2d 1254 (3rd Cir. 1970).
98. *Id.,* at 1257.

furtherance of a proper governmental objective, is not necessarily a violation of the Fourteenth Amendment." [99]

Thus, out of this era of affirmative action has come an attempt by both administrative directive and judicial decree to "balance" faculties by race and by sex. Precedent was established in the early 1970's for having numerical goals in the furtherance of a proper governmental objective; namely, to move with all deliberate speed toward removal of discrimination from every sector of employment, including public school systems.

Cramer v. Virginia Commonwealth University [100] is an example of a recent case, (among several), wherein "reverse discrimination" in employment is the plaintiff's claim. Heard by a United States District Court in Richmond, Virginia, this case involved a white, male applicant for a university teaching position who "brought an action for a declaratory judgment that the university, by hiring two women to the faculty despite his own equal or better qualifications, had engaged in illegal reverse . . . discrimination." [101] In holding for the male, Judge Warriner ruled that Title VII of the Civil Rights Act of 1964, forbids the use of sex quotas or goals in employment even to overcome an existing imbalance.[102] He further opined that the University's "admittedly discriminatory hirings, having been based on sex, were unconstitutional and illegal even though they represented an attempt by the University to comply with a federally ordered affirmative action program to recruit women for faculty positions in order to compensate for alleged past deficiencies in minority hiring." [103]

To Judge Warriner, "Reliance upon such discriminatory practices to achieve 'quotas' or 'goals' is the use of an unconstitutional means to achieve an unconstitutional end." [104] The university's plan of affirmative action had been approved by federal officials under Executive Order 11246, governing all

---

99. *Id. See also* Patterson v. American Tobacco Co., 535 F.2d 257 (4th Cir. 1976), wherein it was said ". . . . racial quotas and preferential hiring may be an appropriate remedy where a long-standing practice of unlawful discrimination has been shown to exist."

100. 415 F.Supp. 673 (1976), *remanded.*

101. *Id.*

102. *Id.* at 679.

103. *Id.* at 673.

104. *Id.* at 680.

federal contractors. *Cramer* was before the United States Court of Appeals, for the Fourth Circuit, as of 1977.

Total ramifications of such cases as *Cramer* certainly have yet to be realized and it is too early to forecast their impact. Gluckman, however, sees three directions for educators as they look to possible future litigation. These are:

> (1) If the adverse effect of "affirmative action" programs on *whites* or *males* is severe enough to be regarded as actual *discrimination,* courts will likely find such affirmative action programs unacceptable.
>
> (2) If the *quality* of a program or organization is adversely affected by "affirmative action," such efforts to compensate for past discrimination will be unacceptable.
>
> (3) When preferential treatment of a race or sex approaches a level of "fixed percentages," it will likely be judged a quota system, and thus courts will deem such efforts unacceptable.[105]

§ 7.7. Teacher Evaluation and Job Security.

As public education moved into the second half of the decade of the 1970's, school systems across the nation found themselves increasingly facing serious budgetary problems. In recent years declines in enrollment and decreases in revenues have forced school boards to reduce budgets and expenditures and since a major portion of a school system budget is for professional services (salaries), reductions in professional force (RIF) were a certainty.

Currently, there exists a growing competition between new teachers for a shrinking number of job openings, and an increased feeling of insecurity among experienced teachers as programs are cut from school system budgets. Local boards of education have been called upon to devise employment and retention policies and procedures to accommodate these budgetary conditions while still striving to provide job security for employees and quality education for their students.

Phillippi v. School District of Springfield [106] is a recent RIF-type case. Speaking to the issue of staff reductions based upon "decreases in student enrollment," the Commonwealth Court of

---

105. I. Gluckman, "Affirmative Action: Is It Really Discrimination in Reverse?" (Blacksburg, Va.: an unpublished paper, 1976), at 11.

106. 367 A.2d 1133 (Pa. 1977).

Pennsylvania held that local school boards have the discretion to determine what is a "substantial decrease in enrollment" to justify reductions in force, absent abuse of discretion, arbitrariness, or a misconception of law.[107]

The Pennsylvania court further opined that there is a difference between an RIF of nontenured staff and an RIF of tenured staff. To the court, nontenured employees ". . . have no rights of retention based either on efficiency rating or seniority as against tenured employees or as among themselves." [108]

a. *Fairness in Evaluation: The Ultimate Remedy.* In 1972, United States District Court Judge Hoffman made the following statement in deciding a case involving Nansemond County, Virginia: ". . . school board members are charged with the crucial task of providing the best quality education possible for all children and this duty may be discharged only if teachers are employed by ability and no other criteria."[109] In the opinion of Judge Hoffman, quality personnel produce quality instruction.

In preceding discussions of recruitment, hiring, assignment, transfer, and retention of personnel a common thread runs through each; namely, the need to establish a standard of fairness and fair treatment in evaluation. Fair evaluation procedures and fair treatment will likely yield a sense of job security. And, the more secure the competent teacher, the greater the likelihood of quality instruction.

It is imperative that procedural safeguards be built into the substantive protections of teachers. Four basic elements necessary to establish procedural rights to fair treatment in teacher evaluation have emerged from case law in point. A teacher evaluation must 1. be directly related to the measurement of teacher effectiveness in job performance, 2. include valid, reliable, and defensible criteria as a basis for making all evaluative judgments of job effectiveness, 3. involve those individuals to be evaluated from formation of criteria to implementation of process, and 4. be developmental and not punitive in nature.[110]

---

107. *Id.*

108. *Id.* at 1141.

109. United States v. Nansemond County School Bd., 351 F.Supp. 196 (1972), *rev'd* at 492 F.2d 919 (4th Cir. 1974).

110. 1 COLLECT. BARG. QUART. 1 (1976), at 3.

A California court ruled, in 1976, that just because state law established a uniform system of evaluation and assessment of performance for all certified employees, it does not mean that local boards can no longer reassign administrators to teaching positions. Administrators serve at the pleasure of the board and can be reassigned at any time, no matter what the ratings are.[111]

b. *The Doctrine of Business Necessity and Teacher Evaluation.* The doctrine of business necessity (or purpose) may prove to be a viable defense for school boards whose personnel decisions are challenged in court; and, at the same time, might prove to be the tool needed to ensure both *substantive* and procedural fair treatment of teachers. Not an absolute defense of practices affecting minority employment, business necessity implies that the employment practice "is necessary to the safe and efficient operation of the business. . . ." [112] According to Urbach,

> Business purpose is defined as having three criteria. First, it must be sufficiently compelling to override any racial impact. Secondly, no other available alternative having a less discriminatory impact can exist. Finally, the business practice must accomplish its stated purpose.[113]

Ideally, states Divine, business necessity as developed in *Griggs* and subsequent cases encompasses "a careful balance between merit, on the one hand, and equality, on the other." [114] Divine then cautions school personnel officials that "judgments of teacher quality are at best a very crude tool . . . ." [115] And, "when measurement of merit is not reliable, or when qualitative distinctions between candidates are not significant, the scales tip in favor of equality, requiring an appropriate representation of minority and women employees." [116]

Local school boards must retain the best qualified and most

---

111. Anaclerio v. Skinner, 134 Cal. Rptr. 303 (Calif. 1976), at 304.

112. RR. Urbach, *"Color-Conscious Quota Relief: A Constitutional Remedy for Racial Employment Discrimination,"* 11 URB. LAW ANN. 333 (1976).

113. *Id.*

114. T. Divine, *"Women in the Academy: Sex-Discrimination in University Faculty Hiring and Promotion,"* 5 J. OF LAW AND ED. 429, 443 (October, 1976).

115. *Id.* at 442.

116. *Id.* at 443.

competent teachers (with proven records of competence in job performance) in an effort to provide quality education for students.

c. *Seniority: Last-Hired, First-Fired and Job Security.* The possibility of mass teacher layoffs has raised a legal question concerning the effects of seniority rules on minority employees. The question is usually phrased as follows: Is *seniority* (last-hired, first-fired doctrine) a system that perpetuates and renews the effects of racial discrimination in the guise of job security?

For an analysis of the seniority practice as a legal issue one must first turn to court decisions involving business and industry, (*e.g., Quarles v. Philip Morris,*[117] *Franks v. Bowman Transportation Company,*[118] and several others). A review of the substance of plaintiff arguments reveals that

> Minority and women employees are seeking legal protection from layoffs. They contend that layoffs based on length of service perpetuate past discrimination by threatening newly won jobs of groups long denied equal opportunity. These groups have been unable to accrue the necessary seniority to withstand layoffs.[119]

Seniority ("last-hired, first-fired"), says Depuy, discriminates between employees solely on the basis of "length of service." And, a system that favors older employees to new ones does not constitute a Title VII violation. Congress, states Depuy, "did *not* outlaw discrimination based on length of service. In fact, it sought to preserve it." [120]

Recognizing that opponents of seniority systems argue that the addition of Section 703 (h) to Title VII nullifies the "last-hired, first-fired" procedure, Depuy reaches a contrary conclusion, based on an analysis of *three* recent decisions from the Third, Fifth, and Seventh Circuits, wherein it was held that "use of seniority to determine the order of layoffs does not violate Title VII." [121] He

---

117. 279 F.Supp. 505 (E.D. Va. 1968).

118. 424 U.S. 747, 96 S. Ct. 1251, 47 L. Ed. 2d 444 (1976).

119. W.K. Depuy, *"Last-Hired, First-Fired: Discrimination or Sacrosanct?"* 80 DICK. LAW REV. 747 (Summer, 1976), at 748.

120. *Id.* at 750.

121. Jersey Central Power and Light Co. v. Local 327, Int'l Brotherhood of Electrical Workers, 508 F.2d 687 (3rd Cir. 1975), *vacated,* at 421 U.S. 987 (1976); Watkins v. Local 2369, United Steelworkers of America, 516 F.2d 41 (5th Cir. 1975); and Waters v. Wisconsin Steel Workers, 502 F.2d 1309 (7th Cir. 1974).

warns, however, that courts will look closely at a seniority plan to be certain that it is absent any discriminatory intent.

Depuy's analysis of the current legal scene reveals that

> The last-hired, first-fired doctrine governing work force reductions is not discriminatory and not prohibited by law. To conclude otherwise would authorize preferential treatment of groups who have not suffered from perpetuation of past discrimination. Preferential treatment is prohibited by Title VII because the act does not require integration, but only an end to employment discrimination. It requires "the elimination of racial barriers, not their creation in order to satisfy our theory as to how society ought to be organized." [122]

The seniority system in employment remains intact. To reach a contrary conclusion "would lead to an unwarranted remedy of a non-legal wrong that plagues one class by imposing a legal disadvantage on another." [123]

The importance of local school boards taking seniority into consideration when facing a reduction in professional force (RIF) situation was stressed in a recent case decided in Pennsylvania. The court made it clear that boards must be free to take RIF actions at any time; however, boards ". . . must also respect the seniority rights of tenured employees." [124] Citing a 1943 case in point, the court included the following quotation from that case:

> Seniority rights exist for the dual purposes of assuring continuity of service for faithful labor and providing efficient service to the state gained by experience.
>
> Seniority is a matter not to be treated lightly. The very stability of our schools depends on retaining those teachers who because of long years of experience and devotion have earned the obedience of pupils, the admiration of the parents, and the respect of the community. [125]

Seniority must be recognized by a school board as an important factor to consider when making personnel decisions, prior to

---

122. *Depuy, supra,* at 758.
123. *Id.* at 766.
124. *Phillippi, supra,* at 1143.
125. Appeal of Wesenberg, 346 Pa. 438, 31 A.2d 151 (Pa. 1943).

implementation of any reduction plans that rely on a "last-hired, first-fired doctrine." Faced with evaluating a school system's reduction in force plan, a Washington court held that a school board may consider *seniority* only when it is a *previously* adopted criterion.[126]

§ 7.8. Summary.

In recent years personnel administration in public school systems has been an active area of school law. The passage of statutes (federal and state), the enactment of policy at all levels of government, and the increasing number of court decisions (federal and state), on matters of personnel have had profound impact on the daily operation of school systems.

The importance of studying the legal status of public school personnel and the decision-making prerogatives of local school boards in matters of personnel administration have grown over the past decade with the proliferation of litigation involving such matters. Each year the number of court cases involving employment increased over that of the previous year.

Today's personnel decisions in public school systems must be the direct result of carefully planned strategies and legally defensible policies. Thus, the need to study the legal dimensions of certification, recruitment, assignment, transfer, evaluation, nonrenewal, and dismissal of school personnel is a must for school boards and school administrators.

There is little doubt that across this nation job security is the top priority concern of contemporary public school teachers. As developed in previous sections of this Chapter, budgetary conditions and the flooded job market are forcing school systems to make radical reductions in instructional costs resulting in mass teacher layoffs. As Levin points out, "Whether or not a teacher has acquired tenure, as well as his or her relative degree of seniority if tenured, has become an increasingly important and more frequently litigated issue. . . ."[127]

School boards and administrators continue to find themselves in a position of having to reduce the number of teachers and other

126. Black v. Joint School Dist., 13 Wash. App. 444, 535 P.2d 135 (1975).
127. B. Levin, *supra*, at 151.

professionals employed, as public school systems try to live within shrinking budgets. Their task is no easy one as attempts are made to improve the quality of programs while pressures are felt to maintain an equitable balance among faculty in matters of sex, age, and race.

Unless contemporary local school boards implement carefully devised plans and procedures for evaluating the competence of the professional force, they will find themselves open to legal challenge from several vantage points. Evaluation systems must therefore be able to withstand strict legal scrutiny by both government agencies and courts of law.

It behooves local school boards to establish, as their primary reason for *retaining* certain teachers, (while dismissing or not reappointing others), the need to keep and reward the best *qualified* and most *competent* teachers (with proven records of competence in job performance), in an effort to provide *quality* education. Thus, the need to implement a sound, reliable, and valid program of teacher evaluation becomes vital and provides a context for promoting feelings of job security.

Chapter Eight

ACADEMIC FREEDOM

§ 8.0. In General.

In this country, the concept of academic freedom grew from the influence of German colleges and universities to the effect that scholars should be free to search for and to teach the truth, free of constraints of their immediate superordinate or by government. Anything else would be interference with their scholarly pursuits. They have resisted efforts by others attempting to influence their teaching, its content and methodology.

The Germanic notion of academic freedom has had considerable influence on the institutions of higher learning in this country. To a lesser degree, it has had an impact on elementary and secondary schools. Unlike college students, public school pupils are subject to a compulsory attendance law and are viewed as having impressionable minds. These two distinctions justify more restraints on public school teachers than on college professors.

Academic freedom has two dimensions. It has a dimension of substantive freedom of a teacher to determine, within reasonable bounds, content and methodology which serve an educationally

167

defensible purpose; it also has a dimension of procedure which protects one from dismissal except for violation of a law, policy, or regulation clearly known.

As citizens, teachers have the same rights as anyone else. As teachers, individuals may have to forego some of those rights at given times or places. One is not entitled to exercise all his citizenship rights in a public school classroom. In 1952, the Supreme Court of the United States declared that a teacher had a choice of teaching or exercising his rights as a citizen:

> It is clear that such persons have the right under law to assemble, speak, think, and believe as they will. It is equally clear that they have no right to work for the state in a school system on their own terms. They may work for the school system under reasonable terms laid down by proper authorities. . . . If they do not choose to work under such terms, they are at liberty to retain their beliefs and associations and go elsewhere. Has the state thus deprived them of any right to free speech and assembly? We think not.[1]

The prevailing view at the time of the above decision was that, since the Constitution does not guarantee employment to anyone, a teacher agrees to work under conditions laid down for him. Yet, these conditions can transcend legality. In recent years, teachers have asserted rights of academic freedom, in particular, under the First and Fourteenth Amendments. Increasingly, a number of these rights have been given protection by the courts. Academic freedom was first recognized as receiving constitutional protection by the Supreme Court of the United States in *Adler v. Board of Education* when, in dissent, Justice Douglas stated:

> I cannot for example find in our constitutional scheme the power of a state to place its employees in the category of second-class citizens by denying them freedom of thought and expression. The Constitution guarantees freedom of thought and expression to everyone in our society. All are entitled to it; and none needs it more than the teacher.[2]

The Court's majority affirmed Justice Douglas's position

---

1. Adler v. Board of Educ., 342 U.S. 485, 492, 72 S. Ct. 380, 96 L. Ed. 2d 517 (1952).
2. *Id.* at 508.

seventeen years later in the *Tinker v. Des Moines Independent School District* decision:

> First Amendment rights applied in light of the special characteristics of the school environment are available to teachers and students. It can hardly be argued that either students or teachers shed their constitutional rights to freedom of speech or expression at the schoolhouse gate.[3]

The Court cautioned in *Tinker* that the rights of speech and association may be limited, because of the unique nature of a school. One cannot exercise this right to the extent that it creates disruption; however, the right cannot be limited because of "a mere desire to avoid the discomfort and unpleasantness that always accompany an unpopular viewpoint." [4]

The problem is one of balance: the rights of a teacher as opposed to what is best for the student and the school community. That is the central focus of this Chapter, to ascertain what courts have ruled as being academic freedom rights of teachers and under what conditions their rights can be curtailed for some greater good. Since procedural rights were treated in the previous Chapter, only substantive rights will be considered here.

§ 8.1. Freedom in the Classroom.

a. *Teaching Controversial Subjects.* Teachers have considerable freedom in organizing their classes and teaching their students. This freedom is subject, however, to some restraints. State laws may require or forbid the teaching of specific subjects or topics; similarly, local school board policy may require or forbid the teaching of specific subjects and topics. Beyond that, a teacher often can determine what specific subject matter may be incorporated into a syllabus, and one often treats subjects that arise spontaneously. Criteria in determining the efficacy or wisdom of teaching such material often rest with its relevancy to the course and the restraint and objectivity in which the material is presented. When courts have difficulty in determining the appropriateness of the subject matter and the way in which it is presented, they often

---

3. 393 U.S. 503, 506, 89 S. Ct. 723, 21 L. Ed. 2d 731 (1969).
4. *Id.* at 509.

rely on the testimony of educational experts in determining if the matter in dispute has the general approval of the preponderance of the teaching profession.

Three cases illustrate that teaching controversial, irrelevant material can result in dismissal. In *Goldwasser v. Brown,* an air force officer taught basic English to foreign officers. Although his class assignment was to cover "At the Dentist" and "How to Test a Used Car" he discoursed on Vietnam and made anti-Semitic remarks. The court held that his comments bore no relevancy to his subject matter.[5]

In the second case, the dismissal of a high school social studies teacher was upheld.[6] He had used the classroom for discussions of a number of questionable topics, including his personal opinion about union activities, approval of polygamy, criticism of marriage, castigation of fellow teachers, and proselytizing students.

A teacher who was also a minister was dismissed for insubordination, for carrying his civil rights activities into the classroom. He conducted organizational meetings in class which disrupted the instructional program. Despite warnings by the administration, he persisted in this activity. The dismissal was upheld.[7]

Beyond the classroom, but still within the school itself, a teacher's restraint is still necessary. Two cases involving assembly programs point out that teachers' freedom of speech has its limits. In a 1970 case, a teacher interrupted an assembly and stated he was walking out until a mural of Dr. Martin Luther King, Jr. was hung. The school board had decided earlier not to hang the mural in the school. The court ruled that since the teacher's speech was disruptive, it was not protected. "The interest of the State in maintaining an educational system is a compelling one. Order is necessary to accomplish this, and the First Amendment cannot be used as a device to defeat such necessity."[8]

Three years later, in a Missouri case, a court upheld the dismissal of two teachers who presented an assembly program that was

5. Goldwasser v. Brown, 417 F.2d 1169 (D.C. Cir. 1969).

6. Knarr v. Board of School Trustees, 317 F. Supp. 832 (N.D. Ind. 1970). *Aff'd* 452 F.2d 649 (7th Cir. 1971).

7. Cooley v. Board of Educ., 327 F. Supp. 454 (E.D. Ark. 1971).

8. State v. Beeson, 266 A.2d 175, 178 (N.J. 1970).

profane, obscene, and which inflamed racial discord. Although the teachers were warned after one presentation, they presented the program a second time, and it created disorder, injured people, and caused a fire. The teachers were suspended immediately and later dismissed.[9]

1. SEX EDUCATION. Few issues in education create more volatile reaction than sex education. States vary considerably with respect to legislation on teaching it in the public schools. Some states permit and encourage such teaching, others specifically forbid it; in between those two positions others allow it, provided exacting conditions are met. The position of boards of education also varies; it often, but not always, reflects community opinion. People in favor of teaching sex education view the topic as being a natural one to treat; opponents often cite two reasons in opposition to it: it violates one's rights under the First Amendment and it is beyond the authority of the school board to offer such courses.

Much controversy over sex education centers on a person's religious and moral views. The controversy is frequently concerned with the context within which such subject matter is taught. Far less criticism would likely grow out of a lesson on the human reproductive system in a biology class than to the same subject being treated in a mathematics class. For example, in a 1961 case in Wisconsin, a tenured teacher was dismissed for discussing sex with a senior boys' class in speech. The court ruled that the bounds of propriety had been exceeded in that the teacher had described procedures of houses of prostitution and the sex act involving the "breaking of the hymen" as if he were recalling his personal experiences, had condoned premarital relations, and told vulgar stories.[10]

The principle of sex education having a relationship to the course was affirmed more recently when a high school band director was dismissed for his remarks in class about sex, virginity, and premarital relations.[11]

---

9. Harrod v. Board of Educ., 500 S.W.2d 1 (Mo. 1973).

10. State v. Board of School Directors of Milwaukee, 14 Wis. 2d 243, 111 N.W.2d 198 (1961).

11. Pyle v. Washington County School Bd., 238 So. 2d 121 (Fla. 1970).

The court saw a need for a teacher's restraint in talking about so sensitive an issue when it stated:

> It may be that topless waitresses and entertainers are in vogue in certain areas of our country and our federal courts may try to enjoin our state courts from stopping the sale of lewd and obscene literature and the showing of obscene films, but we are still of the opinion that instructors in our schools should not be permitted to so risqué ly discuss sex problems in our teenage mixed classes as to cause embarrassment to the children or to invoke in them other feelings not incident to the courses of study being pursued.[12]

When a course on sex education is made optional, courts tend to uphold its legality. Two cases illustrate this. In *Medeiros v. Kijosaki,* the Supreme Court of Hawaii ruled in 1970 that the constitutional rights of the complaining students were not violated by sex education courses so long as the parents had the option of not permitting their children to attend. The court was also of the opinion that to forbid the showing of a sex education film in that class would be an infringement on the free speech rights of others.[13] In a New Jersey case, decided one year later, the court held that a school board violated the constitutional rights of students in that it required attendance of children at a course, "Human Sexuality." The court held that the course could be offered; however, attendance could not be required. The court noted that if the course teaches a student how to plan a future life and what conduct in life is acceptable, and if these two topics conflict with one's religious beliefs, his free exercise rights are violated.[14]

Courts have handed down conflicting opinions on allowing spontaneous discussions about sexual matters. A teacher was not rehired for making offensive sexual references in class,[15] and for relating personal sexual experiences and describing houses of prostitution and masturbation to a class of fifteen-year-olds.[16]

---

12. *Id.* at 123.
13. Medeiros v. Kijosaki, 478 P.2d 314 (Hawaii 1970).
14. Valent v. New Jersey State Bd. of Educ., 274 A.2d 832 (N.J. 1971).
15. Robbins v. Bd. of Educ., 313 F. Supp. 642 (Ill. 1970).
16. Moore v. School Bd., 364 F. Supp. 355 (N.D. Fla. 1973).

A court decided for a teacher who, during spelling class, was asked by students, eighth graders, to define homosexuality. After persistence by the students, she discussed the subject in objective terms.[17]

2. EVOLUTION. As an exercise of academic freedom, the teaching of evolution is less volatile than the subject of sex education. By the mid-1960's only Arkansas, Tennessee, and Mississippi had statutes that forbade such teaching. Where the issue has been raised, it has grown out of a belief that the Darwinian theory of evolution runs counter to the teaching of sacred scriptures.

The earliest court test of the legality of teaching evolution occurred in the state of Tennessee where the real issue was often overshadowed by the stature and personalities of the opposing attorneys, William Jennings Bryan and Clarence Darrow. On trial was John Scopes, a teacher who taught that man descended from lower forms of animals. The state court held that he had no right to teach such a doctrine, although outside school he could believe it as well as oppose the law. "He had no right or privilege to serve the state except upon such terms as the state prescribed. His liberty, his privilege, his immunity to teach and proclaim the theory of evolution elsewhere than in the service of the state, was in no way touched by this law." [18]

The Supreme Court of the United States ruled on the constitutionality of an Arkansas statute in 1968. Passed one year after the *Scopes* trial, the act reflected a time when fundamental thinking was prevalent and when many people relied on a literal interpretation of the Bible, including the origin of man as reported in the book of Genesis. The test of the act came after a teacher taught from a text approved by the school system and which contained the Darwinian theory. The Supreme Court ruled that the First Amendment does not permit the states to require that teaching and learning must be tailored to the principles and prohibitions of any religious sect or dogma. Speaking for the

---

17. Brown v. Coffeeville Consolidated School Dist., 365 F. Supp. 990 (N.D. Miss. 1973).

18. Scopes v. Tennessee, 154 Tenn. 105, 289 S.W. 363, 364 (1927).

majority, Justice Fortas ruled that the statute conflicts with a given religious doctrine in the book of Genesis. He concluded:

> The State's undoubted right to prescribe the curriculum for its public schools does not carry with it the right to prohibit, on pain of criminal penalty, the teaching of a scientific theory or doctrine where that prohibition is based upon reasons that violate the First Amendment. It is much too late to argue that the State may impose upon the teachers in its schools any conditions that it chooses, however restrictive they may be of constitutional guarantees.[19]

Two years later, the Mississippi anti-evolution statute was overturned. The state's supreme court ruled that the statute violated the free exercise clause of the First Amendment.[20] Finally, in 1972, a federal circuit court in Texas ruled that the teaching of evolution does not violate the religion clauses of the First Amendment. Although an anti-evolution statute was not the issue, a state law did permit students to leave the classroom during presentations that offended their religion.[21]

3. ASSIGNMENTS. In their claim to exercise of academic freedom, teachers often make assignments that offend someone: their superordinates, students, or parents. This section will treat some such issues. It does not treat the question of procedural rights of teachers for alleged violations of law or policy; the substantive rights of teachers treated here involve only the academic freedom of teachers to make questionable assignments. In *Parducci v. Rutland,* a court enunciated two distinct principles in determining if a questionable assignment merited a teacher's dismissal.[22] It looked at the relevancy of the material to the subject being taught and examined the fairness and balance of the teacher's presentation. Using these criteria, the court ordered the teacher's reinstatement. She had assigned *Welcome to the Monkey House* by Vonnegut as outside reading material to her eleventh grade English class. The story contained slang, vulgarity, and

---

19. Epperson v. State of Arkansas, 393 U.S. 97, 107, 89 S. Ct. 266, 21 L. Ed. 2d 228 (1968).

20. Smith v. State, 242 So. 2d 692 (Miss. 1970).

21. Wright v. Houston Ind. School Dist., 486 F.2d 137 (5th Cir. 1973).

22. 316 F. Supp. 352 (M.D. Ala. 1970).

references to involuntary sexual intercourse. Although she was asked not to teach the story, she did anyway. The court noted that it was considered as being appropriate for the students when compared to other accepted works of literature and that school was not disrupted.

When the teacher is the primary source of vulgarity rather than students being exposed to it through another means, courts look more closely to the extent of one's academic freedom. Unlike the above case, an English teacher's dismissal was upheld. He maintained that it was an exercise in academic freedom to read to his tenth grade class a short story he had written and which contained vulgar language. No one complained, but the board of education advised him that he would not be retained because of this and other charges. The court ruled that the teacher's academic freedom had not been violated, and the one vulgarity charge was sufficient cause for not rehiring him.[23]

A number of circumstances, taken together, rather than one isolated incident, may render a teacher unfit for teaching. A teacher allowed an alleged vulgar poem, written by a pupil, to remain on the blackboard for two weeks, approved a picture of a row of urinals for the school newspaper, and used the word "rape" before a group of girls in class. The court held that his philosophy and practices were detrimental to secondary school students.[24]

Sponseller summarized the position of the courts concerning the freedom that teachers have in making controversial assignments.

> These rights are not absolute, but have usually been extended to teachers in these areas provided the utterance or assignment was not deemed to be inappropriate for the age and maturity of the students, irrelevant to the course's objectives or such that they do not materially and substantially disrupt or threaten to disrupt the discipline of the school.[25]

4. DISCUSSIONS. This section treats briefly the matter of the extent to which teachers can engage in class discussions which may

---

23. Lindros v. Governing Bd. of Torrance, 108 Cal. Rptr. 188 (1972).

24. Jergeson v. School Bd., 364 F. Supp. 355 (N.D. Fla. 1973).

25. Edwin H. Sponseller, Jr., *Freedom of Expression for Teachers in the Public School Classroom,* in CURRENT LEGAL ISSUES IN EDUCATION 50 (M. A. McGhehey, ed. Topeka: National Organization on Legal Problems of Education, 1977).

or may not be related to the subject the teacher is assigned to teach. Only recent cases will be considered. They cover a variety of issues and reflect a degree of consistency on the part of judges' decisions. Unprofessional discussions in class about one's colleagues are not protected under the guise of academic freedom. Discussions of sex that offend one's sensibilities may not be protected. Discussions irrelevant to the subject may or may not be protected. When students initiate the topic, courts look more favorably than when teachers introduce questionable topics. Courts do not look favorably on a teacher discussing and exploiting his personal lifestyle, particularly when it deviates from conventional living. Finally, sensitive issues bearing on the topic may be protected, even though parents object.

A teacher was discharged, and she alleged that it was because of her civil rights activities. The administration disagreed, pointing out that she had been encouraged to become involved in them. She was actually discharged for using offensive sexual references and for discussing in class the action taken against a teacher for growing a beard.[26]

In spite of objections by parents, a civics teacher was ordered reinstated. He had been warned not to discuss controversies and to teach from the text. Instead, he taught a unit on race relations and made comments on race and prejudice that parents found objectionable. The court held that his teaching was acceptable in that there had been no disruption and students had not been indoctrinated.[27]

In a case previously treated in the section on sex education, a female teacher was protected for having discussed homosexuality in an eighth grade spelling class. The subject was raised by students, and the teacher treated it carefully. This, the court found, was acceptable.[28]

A federal district court agreed with the school board in *Moore,* where that teacher strayed from the subject in discussing a variety of topics: teachers' salaries, the school board and administration, his personal sexual experiences, Japanese houses of prostitution, and masturbation. The court and the school board agreed that it

---

26. Robbins v. Board of Educ., 313 F. Supp. 642 (N.D. Fla. 1970).
27. Sterzing v. Fort Bend, 376 F. Supp. 657 (S.D. Tex. 1972).
28. *Brown, supra,* note 17.

is in order for a teacher to stray occasionally from the subject, although in this instance the teacher had gone too far.[29]

The Tenth Circuit held, in 1975, that the liberty to structure one's courses is not unlimited; rather, community standards may dictate the extent of academic freedom. In this particular case the small community had a right to insist on an orthodox approach to teaching. Three teachers were dismissed, and they contended it was because they had played questionable records in class ("Alice's Restaurant", "Hair"), discussed Vietnam, political matters, drugs, and hippies. The board alleged that their dismissals resulted from their creating dissension among the faculty, for being tardy, insubordinate, failing to cover material and to discipline students, and for disturbing other classes. The dismissals stood.[30]

b. *Teaching Forbidden Subjects.* Although some state constitutions have provisions with respect to teaching specific subjects, state statutes are more explicit as to what shall be taught. Statutes may even provide for how a subject shall be taught. Similarly, statutes may forbid the teaching of a specific subject, as for example, evolution which was treated in a previous section.

Local school boards are also clothed with considerable autonomy in determining curriculum, so long as their decisions are not in conflict with state rulings. More often than not, state statutes and local school board policies require rather than restrict what is taught. In general, where a statute *requires* that a subject be taught, a complainer has less chance to win than under a statute that *forbids* the teaching of a specific subject. An elective course will usually be protected in a suit, for it is clear that an individual has the option of enrolling or not enrolling in it.

In recent years there has been more sensitivity to the portrayal of people in curriculum materials. Many states have passed laws that forbid racial stereotyping or making one class look inferior to another; they have also required that all groups of people be viewed as being equal. They have mandated programs for bi-lingual and bi-cultural students.

More than legislatures, courts have spoken on the degree to which religion can be taught in public schools. This subject will be treated more fully in Chapter Twelve. However, the Supreme

---

29. *Moore, supra,* note 16.
30. Adams v. Campbell City School Dist., 511 F.2d 1242 (10th Cir. 1975).

Court of the United States has ruled that the Bible cannot be taught as a religion in school,[31] prayer and Bible reading as devotional exercises cannot be held in school,[32] and evolution can be taught as a theory.[33] The Court has stated that it is permissible to teach religion as literature or as history so long as it is handled objectively and without any attempt to indoctrinate one's religious thinking.

The Supreme Court ruled, in 1923, that a state law that forbade the teaching of any language other than English to elementary school students was unconstitutional.[34] A violator would be subject to a fine of $25 to $100 or 30 days in jail. The stated purpose of the act was to prevent foreigners from rearing their children in their native language and to delay the teaching of foreign language to non-foreigners until secondary school. In striking down the statute as an infringement of the rights of teachers and students, the Court stated:

> His right to teach and the right of parents to engage him so to instruct their children, we think, are within the liberty of the (Fourteenth) Amendment.
> That the State may do much, go very far indeed, in order to improve the quality of its citizens, physically, mentally and morally, is clear; but the individual has certain fundamental rights which must be respected. The protection of the Constitution extends to all, to those who speak other languages as well as to those born with English on the tongue.[35]

c. *Refusing to Salute the Flag.* The controversy over requiring a flag salute as a part of school activities is old. Most of the flag salute litigation has involved students; however, a few recent cases have also involved teachers, all decided since 1970. The courts have consistently ruled that teachers are protected in their refusal to join in the flag salute exercises.

---

31. Illinois *ex rel.* McCollum v. Board of Educ. of School Dist. No. 71, 333 U.S. 203, 68 S. Ct. 461, 92 L. Ed. 2d 649 (1948).

32. Engel v. Vitale, 370 U.S. 421, 82 S. Ct. 1261, 8 L. Ed. 2d 601 (1962); School Dist. of Abington Township v. Schempp, 374 U.S. 203, 83 S. Ct. 1560, 10 L. Ed. 2d 844 (1963).

33. *Epperson, supra,* note 19.

34. Meyer v. Nebraska, 262 U.S. 390, 43 S. Ct. 625, 67 L. Ed. 2d 1042 (1923).

35. *Id.* at 400, 401.

In *Hanover v. Northrup,* a teacher notified her principal that she would not participate in the salute. Instead, a student led the exercises while the teacher remained seated with her head bowed. There was no disruption. The court overturned her dismissal for insubordination and ruled that her refusal was protected by the First Amendment.[36]

A different factual situation existed in *Maryland v. Lindquist,* where a teacher objected philosophically and politically to the pledge. He felt that he could not force patriotism on his classes, and he believed that the requirement interfered with his individual right to express his loyalty to his country. The court upheld him, citing the statute as being an abridgement to his freedom of speech.[37]

The third case involved a school board policy that required all teachers recite the flag salute at the opening of the school day. The teacher refused and instead had a second teacher, assigned to her, lead the pledge. Although the teacher had refused to participate all year, that fact was not discovered by school officials until April. Her students were not disrupted by her behavior. Although the court saw some value in the salute, it recognized that the teacher's individual rights, however obnoxious, outweighed the state's interests.[38]

The courts here have tended to look to the substantive rights that a teacher possesses as well as to the effect of the exercise of that right. Where no disruption occurs and where students are not otherwise harmed or adversely influenced, there is a real burden on the school board to justify a curtailment of that teacher's freedom not to salute the flag. That justification must also be more than a mere speculation that disruption may occur.

d. *Selection of Methods of Instruction.* It is unquestioned that a state has a right to prescribe specific methods of instruction. Courts are very reluctant to substitute their judgment for that of state legislatures or local school boards. This was expressed over half a century ago by a Massachusetts court: "The determination of the procedure and the management and direction of pupils and studies in this Commonwealth rests in the wise discretion and

---

36. 325 F. Supp. 170 (D. Conn. 1970).
37. 278 A.2d 263 (Md. 1971).
38. Russo v. Central School Dist., 469 F.2d 623 (2nd Cir. 1972).

179

sound judgment of teachers and school committees, whose action in these respects is not subject to the supervision of this court." [39]

Similarly, by virtue of their training and experience, teachers have considerable freedom in determining their methods of instruction. The freedom is limited, however, by state requirements and by their local school board.

Older cases confirm that methodology rests with the wisdom of local school personnel when not in conflict with state laws. Thus, a taxpayer could not require that bookkeeping be taught by the double entry rather than the single entry method.[40] Courts have reasoned that, to try to accommodate all parents who have their own notion about the best way to teach a subject would be to place teachers in an untenable position.

Recent cases on record deal with narrow issues such as teaching a specific lesson rather than a course. In *Mailloux v. Kiley,* an English class was discussing taboo words. Mailloux wrote a four-letter word on the board and asked the students to define it. Without repeating the word, he then asked students why some words were objectionable and others were not. He was later dismissed for "conduct unbecoming a teacher." The circuit court treated the question of the relevancy of the method; it did not consider the necessity of the method. It recognized that for a method to be constitutionally protected, it must have the support of the preponderant opinion of the teaching profession. Further, there was no regulation prohibiting the method he had used. He was reinstated and recovered his lost salary.[41]

An elementary school teacher with twenty-five years experience, dismissed for insubordination, also recovered lost wages and was reinstated. Her class of second-graders had written letters to the cafeteria supervisor, asking that raw carrots be served, had drawn cartoons showing inoperative water fountains, and had complained to the superintendent about an incinerator on the school yard. The court held that such action did not constitute protest but was relevant to the children's study.[42]

---

39. Wulff v. Inhabitants of Wakefield, 221 Mass. 427, 109 N.E. 358, 359 (1915).
40. Neilan v. Board of Directors of Ind. School Dist., 200 Iowa 860, 205 N.W. 506 (1925).
41. 448 F.2d 1242 (1st Cir. 1971).
42. Downs v. Conway, 328 F. Supp. 338 (E.D. Ark. 1971).

A teacher was dismissed for allowing her students to write essays on anything they wished. Most of them treated the subjects of sex and drugs. Instead of rejecting the articles, the teacher used them as teaching devices by duplicating and distributing them to the students. The court upheld her, recognizing that her method was questionable but not unacceptable.[43]

A case that was decided against teachers was handed down in 1974. Three teachers distributed brochures of the "Woodstock" experience of 1969 that contained materials related to drugs, sex, and vulgarity. These teachers claimed that the material was relevant to their teaching. The court ruled that they had failed to make such a case for their use as exemplary teaching tools.[44]

§ 8.2. Freedom Outside the Classroom.

a. *Association.* The right of association is not directly mentioned in the First Amendment; it is implied by two clauses: assembly and petition. It has been constitutionally protected from invasion by both the federal and state governments. However, like most freedoms, it is not absolute. Government may condition the exercise of that right in protecting others and in ensuring public order and safety. The question often arises as to the extent that government may set conditions that affect a teacher's right of association. That question involves two issues: the organizations with which one affiliates and the company one keeps.

1. AFFILIATIONS. School boards are not as disposed, as a few decades ago, to restrict teachers in their affiliation with organizations outside school. The decade of the 1950's was a period in which school boards attempted to regulate teachers' behavior by curbing subversive influences in the schools. In the 1960's some school districts attempted to discourage teachers from engaging in civil rights activities. The 1970's have involved issues of sexual associations. A few cases in each of the first two areas will illustrate the predominant thinking of the courts on these three subjects. The third area will be treated in the section on living arrangements.

The Supreme Court of the United States has handed down

43. Oakland Unified School Dist. v. Olicker, 102 Cal. Rptr. 421 (1972).
44. Brubaker v. Board of Educ., 502 F.2d 973 (7th Cir. 1974).

several decisions involving the associational freedom of teachers. One concerned a teacher who refused to answer questions about his political affiliations. His superintendent asked him to answer questions about his alleged affiliation with the Communist Party, and he refused to respond. He was discharged, not for disloyalty, but for incompetency on the basis of his refusal to cooperate with the superintendent. By a 5-4 vote the Court upheld the dismissal. The majority held:

> By engaging in teaching in the public schools, petitioner did not give up his right to freedom of belief, speech, or association. He did, however, undertake obligations of frankness, candor, and cooperation in answering inquiries made of him by his employing Board examining into his fitness to serve as a public school teacher.[45]

One year later, the Supreme Court held that investigations about teachers and students concerning Communist associations serves the public interest to a greater extent than it intrudes on one's personal liberties. In *Barenblatt v. United States,* the Court upheld the legitimacy of an inquiry into the field of education. The case did not involve the issue of what one teaches but rather the matter of one's associations.[46]

The *Shelton v. Tucker* decision reflected a shift from subversive influences to an overriding concern of the 1960's: civil rights. It involved an Arkansas statute that required all public school teachers to disclose annually the names of all organizations to which they belonged or contributed within the previous five years. A teacher in the Little Rock schools for twenty-five years refused to comply. In the meantime, he testified that he was not a Communist but that he did belong to the National Association for the Advancement of Colored People. The Supreme Court reaffirmed that school boards may properly investigate the competence of people it employs. However, requiring a teacher to disclose all his affiliations restricts one's right of association. A school board may require the disclosure of some, but not all,

---

45. Beilan v. Board of Pub. Educ., 357 U.S. 399, 405 (1958).
46. 360 U.S. 109, 79 S. Ct. 1081, 3 L. Ed. 2d 115 (1959).

associations, for every association does not necessarily have any relevance to one's teaching.[47]

There were a number of other cases decided in the 1960's that had bearing on a teacher's civil rights activities. Where those activities were carried on outside school and did not interfere with one's teaching, the courts consistently sustained them as being constitutionally protected by the First Amendment. A leading case is *Johnson v. Branch*,[48] in which a black teacher was very active in civil rights in a community experiencing racial tension. The teacher was dismissed for such matters as being fifteen minutes late in supervising an athletic contest, arriving a few minutes late to school, failing to stand outside her door in supervising students as classes changed, and failing to see that cabinets in her room were clean. The court agreed that the combined offenses were insufficient to merit dismissal, particularly in view of her twelve years of successful teaching. It agreed that those infractions had relevance to her teaching but none related specifically to what transpires in the classroom.

2. LOYALTY OATHS. Government has often attempted to establish loyalty for teachers during wartime. New York State, for instance, passed a law after World War I which provided for the dismissal of any teacher for "the utterance of any treasonable or seditious act." Two years later the statute was repealed. During and after World War II many states enacted loyalty oath laws, many of which were aimed specifically at teachers.[49] In order to keep subversives out of the schools, these people had to execute an oath usually providing for one or two conditions: supporting the Constitution and defending the country against all enemies, and swearing that one is not, nor has been, a member of a subversive organization designed to overthrow the government. It is the latter category to which teachers have objected. They are wary over the potential misuse of the oath by having to speculate what is acceptable and what is forbidden.

---

47. 364 U.S. 479, 81 S. Ct. 247, 5 L. Ed. 2d 231 (1960).

48. 364 F.2d 177 (4th Cir. 1966).

49. For a study of loyalty oath laws during the period of their greatest influence, *see* Joseph E. Bryson, LEGALITY OF LOYALTY OATH AND NON-OATH REQUIREMENTS FOR PUBLIC SCHOOL TEACHERS. (Asheville, North Carolina: Miller Printing Company, 1963).

From 1951 to 1971, the Supreme Court of the United States handed down nine decisions involving the legality of loyalty oath laws. In 1951 it upheld the legality of a requirement that one list past or present membership in the Communist Party and that one swear non-affiliation with an organization advocating overthrow of the government.[50] The next year it handed down two decisions. It overturned an Oklahoma statute requiring all state employees to subscribe a loyalty oath. The justices distinguished between innocent and knowing membership in a subversive organization.[51] In the second case, the Court upheld New York's Feinberg Law that authorized dismissal for membership in a subversive organization advocating overthrow of the government.[52] The justices ruled, in effect, that a teacher could decide between membership and employment. They recognized the crucial role that teachers play in our society:

> A teacher works in a sensitive area in a schoolroom. There he shapes the attitude of young minds towards the society in which they live. In this, the state has a vital concern. It must preserve the integrity of the schools. That the school authorities have the right and the duty to screen the officials, teachers, and employees as to their fitness to maintain the integrity of the schools as a part of ordered society, cannot be doubted. One's associates, past and present, as well as one's conduct, may properly be considered in determining fitness and loyalty.[53]

After the *Adler v. Board of Education* decision, the Court took a different turn and began to rule that a teacher's First Amendment rights were paramount over any interest the state has in protecting students from possible subversive teachers. It held in 1961 that a statute requiring teachers to swear that they had not given "aid, support, advice, counsel, or influence" to the Communist Party is overly vague and cannot be enforced.[54] A loyalty oath providing dismissal for enrollment in a subversive

---

50. Garner v. Board of Pub. Works, 341 U.S. 716, 71 S. Ct. 909, 95 L. Ed. 1317 (1951).

51. Wieman v. Updegraff, 344 U.S. 183 (1952).

52. Adler v. Board of Educ., 342 U.S. 485 (1952).

53. *Id.* at 493.

54. Cramp v. Board of Pub. Instr., 368 U.S. 278, 82 S. Ct. 275, 7 L. Ed. 2d 285 (1961).

organization or for advocating overthrow of the government is too ambiguous.[55] A loyalty oath making anyone ineligible for state employment who took an oath while knowingly a member of the Communist Party or a subversive organization is unconstitutional.[56] An oath law requiring one to swear "I am not engaged in one way or another in the attempt to overthrow the Government of the United States, or the State of Maryland, or any political subdivision of either of them, by force or violence" was declared illegal in that it placed too much surveillance on teachers and did not clearly distinguish between permissible and impermissible conduct.[57] In 1967, the Court overturned the Feinberg Law of New York which it had upheld in 1952. The specific provisions it overturned were: advocating overthrow of the government, uttering treasonable or seditious words or committing treasonable or seditious acts. The Court invalidated the oath on the bases of vagueness, *i.e.,* a teacher not knowing what was acceptable and nonacceptable and on overbreadth, *i.e.,* it did not distinguish between knowing membership and membership actively engaged in unlawful overthrow.[58]

In the last two cases decided by the Supreme Court as of 1977, the Court upheld loyalty oaths with a positive affirmation, in each instance with a *per curiam* opinion. The Colorado oath provided the teacher to:

> solemnly swear (affirm) that I will uphold the Constitution of the United States and the constitution of the State of Colorado, and I will faithfully perform the duties of the position upon which I am about to enter.[59]

In the other case, the Court upheld one section and overturned another of a Florida loyalty oath law. It held that one could be required to "support the Constitution of the United States and of the State of Florida." It ruled as being unconstitutional a provision that one swear that he does not "believe in the overthrow of the

---

55. Baggett v. Bullitt, 377 U.S 360, 84 S. Ct. 1316, 12 L. Ed. 2d 377 (1964).

56. Elfbrandt v. Russell, 384 U.S. 360, 86 S. Ct. 1238, 16 L. Ed. 2d 321 (1964).

57. Whitehill v. Elkins, 389 U.S. 54, 88 S. Ct. 184, 19 L. Ed. 2d 228 (1967).

58. Keyishian v. Board of Regents, 385 U.S. 589, 87 S. Ct. 675, 17 L. Ed. 2d 629 (1967).

59. Ohlson v. Phillips, 397 U.S. 317, 90 S. Ct. 1124, 25 L. Ed. 337, *reh. denied,* 397 U.S. 1081 (1970).

government of the United States or the State of Florida by force or violence." [60]

When one examines the oath law cases more carefully, he is aware that the Supreme Court recognizes that states have a responsibility for protecting pupils from subversive influences. However, like other citizens, teachers have a right to examine or be exposed to a variety of ideas, and membership in an unpopular or even subversive organization may not be grounds for dismissal. The right of association is basic to everyone, including teachers.

For a loyalty oath law to be upheld, it must have some standard of objective measurement. The justices have indicated that this is exceedingly difficult for negatively-stated oaths. They have looked instead to the need for protecting teachers in their practice of academic freedom.

3. LIVING ARRANGEMENTS. A more recent challenge to the right of association has involved domestic lifestyles of teachers. In particular, the issue has focused on teachers having living arrangements at variance with wishes of the administration or with community thinking. These arrangements have sexual connotations in that cases have often involved unmarried adults of the opposite sex living together. When discovered, teachers have been charged with immorality. Courts have interpreted immorality in different ways and thus offer no clear-cut standard for condoning or resisting nonconventional living arrangements. Moreover, one's notion of what constitutes immorality is not the same as four or five decades ago when, for example, a female teacher was subject to dismissal only because she married. In 1973, the Eighth Circuit overturned the dismissal of a teacher who permitted young men, friends of her son, to spend the night in her one-bedroom apartment. One such occupant was a young man engaged in student-teaching in the district. The court held that, because of the living arrangement, one could speculate as to what might have happened, but one could not infer that any immoral behavior had transpired.[61]

In contrast to the above case, the same Circuit two years later upheld the dismissal of a female teacher for living with a male

---

60. Connell v. Higginbotham, 403 U.S. 207, 91 S. Ct. 1772, 29 L. Ed. 2d 418 (1971).
61. Fisher v. Snyder, 476 F.2d 375 (8th Cir. 1973).

teacher not her husband. She claimed a right of privacy and freedom of association; the court recognized that a greater interest than her claimed freedom was the protection of the integrity of the schools. Although sexual immorality was not specifically established, the court held that the school board could reasonably believe that, because of the negative community reaction, her behavior could have an adverse effect on her elementary school pupils. Her conduct was seen as a violation of local community mores and was inconsistent with the community's interest in maintaining a properly moral scholastic environment.[62]

A different question on the right of association arose in the Fifth Circuit in 1975.[63] Three teachers were dismissed because they sent their children to a racially discriminatory private school. The school board argued that, because of this, the teachers would be less effective since the district was under desegregation order. "[T]eachers who send their own children to a segregated school manifest a belief that segregation is desirable in education and a distrust in desegregated schools." [64]

b. *Residency Requirements.* At the turn of the century, it was not unusual for teachers to live in homes in the community in which they taught. Later, as they established their own homes, it was also not unusual for them to have an understanding with the school board that they would live within the school district.

The 1970's have witnessed a number of court suits attacking the legitimacy of requiring one to live in the district in which he teaches. Teachers claim that this policy is in violation of the Equal Protection Clause.

In considering the legality of residency requirements, courts have applied the "rational interest" test. If it can be shown that there are a set of facts which support the state's interest and purposes, the statute will be upheld. Using that standard, courts have consistently upheld residency laws and policies. They have cited the fact that teachers would have a better understanding of the community in which they work, they would tend to become more involved in community activities, and they would tend to support increased tax levies in support of education.

---

62. Sullivan v. Meade City Ind. School Dist., 530 F.2d 799 (8th Cir. 1975).

63. Cook v. Hudson, 511 F.2d 744 (5th Cir. 1975).

64. Citing the district court opinion at 365 F. Supp. 855, 860 (N.D. Miss. 1973).

In a 1975 court decision, a Michigan state court held that a residency regulation for administrators only was not unreasonable, neither was it arbitrary, in exempting those employed before the policy was established.[65]

Five cases on this subject were decided in 1976, and they uniformly uphold the requirement; they also reflect a consistency of reasoning.

The Cincinnati school board was free to distinguish in a residency policy between new teachers and teachers with experience.[66] Similarly, a prospective residency requirement was upheld in Pittsburgh. The policy did not affect one's right to travel.[67] A school district's policy was not in violation of the Equal Protection Clause; the plaintiff could still properly perform his duties as a teacher.[68]

A residency policy for teachers in the School District of Philadelphia was upheld, with conditions. When adopted, it was to be applied only to teachers hired after the policy was approved; however, it was not enforced for nearly four years. The court held that, although the residency requirement was legal, it could not be enforced against those teachers employed between February 1, 1972, and May 16, 1976 (the time the policy was in effect but inoperative).[69]

The Supreme Court of the United States has also spoken on this issue. In 1976, it upheld the constitutionality of a Philadelphia ordinance requiring city employees to be residents of the city. It was challenged by a fireman who moved outside the city. The Court held the ordinance to be rational and not in violation of his Fourteenth Amendment rights.[70]

c. *Public Statements.* Many teachers have been reluctant to speak out on public or controversial issues for fear that their jobs may be in jeopardy. The Constitution protects them to a

---

65. Park v. Lansing School Dist., 62 Mich. App. 397, 233 N.W.2d 592 (1975).

66. Wardwell v. Board of Educ., 529 F.2d 625 (6th Cir. 1976).

67. Pittsburgh Fed'n of Teachers v. Aaron, 471 F. Supp. 94 (W.D. Pa. 1976).

68. Mogel v. Sevier County School Dist., 540 F.2d 478 (10th Cir. 1976).

69. Philadelphia Fed'n of Teachers, Local No. 3, AFL-CIO v. Board of Educ., No. 3583 (Ct. Common Pleas, Oct. 4, 1976).

70. McCarthy v. Philadelphia Civil Service Comm'n, 424 U.S. 645, 96 S. Ct. 1154, 47 L. Ed. 2d 366 (1976).

considerable degree; however, the right of free speech is not unlimited. Conversely, the condition of being a teacher does not mean that one has to forego his First Amendment rights as a citizen. Courts look to what is said, the forum in which it is presented, and its relationship to or effect on the school environment.

The leading case in this area is *Pickering v. Board of Education,* a 1968 decision by the Supreme Court of the United States.[71] It involved the dismissal of a teacher for making critical statements about his local board of education. He criticized the board and its emphasis on athletics, expressing his dismay over the fact that three of four bond elections had been defeated between 1961 and 1964. Pickering's letter to the newspaper criticized the manner in which the board handled those elections, criticized the board for its priorities in allocating school funds, and criticized the superintendent for allegedly influencing teachers not to vote in the bond election.

In dismissing Pickering, the board charged that his letter contained false statements, impugned the motives of the administration, and damaged the school system.

The Court held that Pickering's speech was protected by the First Amendment. It saw value in teachers speaking out on public issues, particularly as they affect them. The errors in the letter were minor, the court pointed out, and the data were already a matter of public record. The justices also attached no malice to the teacher's motives.

In a 1977 case, a teacher was dismissed for openly criticizing the school board and administration at a board meeting. The school board alleged that her dismissal was on the basis of her classroom performance, not as a result of her statements. The court held that the public statements were protected by the First Amendment.[72] The First Amendment was no protection to a teacher who called his superintendent a "liar" and "an autocratic administrator." [73] A teacher was ordered reinstated with lost salary after he had been dismissed for public remarks to a city council and board of trustees

---

71. Pickering v. Board of Educ., 391 U.S. 563, 88 S. Ct. 1731, 20 L. Ed. 2d 811 (1968).

72. Branch v. School Dist., 432 F. Supp. 608 (D. Mont. 1977).

73. Spano v. School Dist., 12 Pa. Cmwlth. 170, 316 A.2d 657 (1974).

about his concern over community and economic problems affecting teachers and students in the district.[74]

On the subject of teacher-school board negotiations, courts have distinguished between a teacher's right to talk at school and in an open forum. A school board policy was overturned which prohibited teachers from circulating petitions concerning disputed budget proposals during off-duty hours.[75] A school board policy was upheld which forbade teachers from discussing in class any aspect of a local strike. In upholding the policy, the court noted its effects on the district and the fact that fifth graders were a captive audience of children, subject to compulsory attendance laws.[76] In contrast, a nonunion teacher who spoke out at an open meeting of the school board, in opposition to an agency shop provision of a proposed collective bargaining agreement, was protected. The Court found that the teacher's statement did not constitute negotiations. The meeting was open to the public and the teacher had the same right as any other citizen under the First Amendment to speak out.[77]

d. *Political Activity.* Like other citizens, teachers have the right to engage in political activity. They have the right to vote, to speak out on public issues, to participate in political campaigns, and to run for office. The two sections that follow will treat two basic rights of engaging in political activity: campaigning for office and holding office.

1. CAMPAIGNING FOR OFFICE. Statutes of the various states and local school board policies may restrict the rights of teachers in campaigning. They do not allow a teacher to engage in such activity at school or within the classroom. On the other hand, statutes and policies prohibiting teachers from engaging in political activity outside the school premises and outside school time have not been upheld.

An old case illustrates the prohibition of a teacher's campaigning in the school setting.[78] A teacher openly solicited students in class

74. Lusk v. Estes, 361 F. Supp. 653 (N.D. Tex. 1973).

75. Los Angeles Teachers' Union v. Los Angeles City Bd. of Educ., 78 Cal. Rptr. 723 (1969).

76. Nigosian v. Weiss, 343 F. Supp. 757 (E.D. Mich. 1971).

77. City of Madison Joint School Dist. v. Wisconsin Empl. Rel. Comm'n, 429 U.S. 167, 97 S. Ct. 421, 50 L. Ed. 2d 376 (1976).

78. Goldsmith v. Board of Educ., 66 Cal. App. 157, 225 P. 783 (1924).

to inform their parents to vote for a specific candidate for superintendent. He was dismissed. Here, the court recognized that the crucial element was the place of the campaign.

> ... [T]he attempt thus to influence support of such candidate by the pupils and through them by their parents — introduces into the school questions wholly foreign to its purposes and objects; that such conduct can have no other effect than to stir up strife among the students over a contest for a political office, and the result of this would inevitably be to disrupt the required discipline of a public school.[79]

It is a different matter when a school classroom is not used as a forum for teacher campaigning. In 1932, a school board policy was overturned that prohibited a teacher from engaging in a political campaign. In challenging the restriction, she campaigned against the election of a school trustee. In retaliation, the board refused her a teaching position for which she had been recommended. The court overturned the policy and held that, like any other citizen, a teacher has a right to support a candidate of one's choice.[80]

More recently, a Kentucky court upheld this principle. Several teachers and administrators supported a candidate for school board who was opposed by the superintendent. Their candidate lost. Later, the superintendent recommended, and the school board authorized, transfer and demotion of the administrators and teachers for "the betterment of the schools." The court disallowed the action which it interpreted as being punitive.[81]

2. HOLDING OFFICE. By virtue of the fact that one is a teacher, he or she is not restricted in running for office. That right may be subject to conditions provided for in state statutes which may specify the kinds of offices which would be incompatible with teaching. Incompatibility exists where a superordinate-subordinate relationship exists. Where the superordinate makes decisions that affect a teacher, one could not hold both positions. No problem exists if the teacher resigns his position.

State statutes also vary with respect to the point that one

79. *Id.* at 789.
80. Board of Educ. v. Ayers, 234 Ky. 177, 47 S.W.2d 1046 (1932).
81. Calhoun v. Cassidy, 534 S.W.2d 806 (Ky. 1976).

becomes ineligible to teach while running for or holding an office. States may require a teacher to resign upon announcing candidacy for the office, upon being elected, or upon assuming office.

Court decisions over teachers' rights in office-holding may seem contradictory until one remembers that this litigation is based on a given state statute. Several states have held to the view of a California court decision that a teacher is not a public officer and thus can also hold a position as legislator.[82] In contrast, both a trial court and the Supreme Court of Alaska held that a superintendent and two teachers could not also serve as legislators.[83] A like ruling was handed down in Oregon where it was charged that the separation of powers was violated by a teacher serving in the state's House of Representatives. The state's supreme court agreed:

> Our concern is not with what has been done but rather with what might be done, directly or indirectly, if one person is permitted to serve two different departments at the same time. The constitutional prohibition is designed to avoid the opportunities for abuse arising out of such dual service whether it exists or not.[84]

For the right of teachers to serve on local boards of education, see Chapter Three.

---

82. Leymel v. Johnson, 105 Cal. App. 694, 288 P. 858 (1930).
83. Begich v. Jefferson, 441 P.2d 27 (Alaska 1968).
84. Monaghan v. School Dist. No. 1, 211 Ore. 360, 315 P.2d 797, 805 (1957).

PART IV

LAW AND STUDENTS

Chapter Nine

ASSIGNMENT AND PLACEMENT

§ 9.0. Introduction.

As the nation moved through the closing years of the nineteenth century, public education experienced rapid growth. Public school enrollments (kindergarten through Grade 12) doubled, the school year was extended from 135 to 173 days, total expenditures per child increased, and attendance in public schools was made more regular.[1] At the turn of the century, state governments began to assume a much more active role in providing education of their citizens.

In these early days, the prevalent judicial attitude regarding state authority over public education was that said authority was legislative. State legislatures, said the courts, possessed unrestricted prerogatives of control over educational matters, and judges would not interfere with the exercise of these prerogatives.[2]

During the first three decades of the new century, several cases regarding public school decision-making reached the courts of the various states. These early cases involved such specific matters as textbook selection, courses of study offered, and the selection of

---

1. Edwards and Richey, THE SCHOOL IN THE AMERICAN SOCIAL ORDER, 2d ed. (Boston: Houghton Mifflin Company, 1963.)

2. Leeper v. State, 53 S.W. 962 (Tenn. 1899).

instructional materials. Throughout the early decisions, courts consistently upheld the right of state legislatures to do all necessary to establish and control public school systems, with certain limitations.[3] As the United States Supreme Court stated in *Meyer v. Nebraska,*

> ... that the state may do much, go very far, indeed, in order to improve the quality of its citizens, physically, mentally, and morally, is clear; but the individual has certain fundamental rights which must be respected.[4]

As indicated in previous sections of this book, the omission of any explicit mention of education in the United States Constitution, and the absence of any specific provisions directing the federal government to exercise control over schools, left the primary responsibility of providing education and schools to each state. Today, state constitutions and statutes generally charge the legislature with plenary authority to establish, control, and continually maintain a system of public education for all children of school age.

In most states, evidence of legal authority over public education is found in various statutes that: 1. create compulsory attendance for children of school age, 2. establish and define student classifications (*e.g.,* exceptional children), 3. mandate vaccination of school-age children as a precondition of their entrance to school, and 4. set a minimum length for the school year. Exercising their police power, states seek to bring about intellectual enlightenment and to promote the safety, welfare, and prosperity of their citizenry through enactment and implementation of such regulations.[5]

§ 9.1. Compulsory Attendance.

Over the years, courts of law have supported the notion that

---

3. *See,* for example, Hardwick v. Board of School Trustees, 205 P. 49 (Cal. 1921), and Smith v. State Bd., 10 P. 2d 736 (Cal. 1932).

4. 262 U.S. 390, 43 S. Ct. 625, 67 L. Ed. 2d 1042 (1923), at 627. *See also,* Flory v. Smith, 134 S.E. 360 (Va. 1926).

5. "The police power of a State today embraces regulations designed to promote the public convenience or the general prosperity as well as those to promote public safety, health, morals, and is not confined to the suppression of what is offensive, disorderly, or unsanitary, but extends to what is for the greatest welfare of the state. In N.T. Small (Editor), *The Constitution of the United States of America: Analysis and Interpretations* (Washington, D.C.: U.S. Government Printing Office, 1964), at 1089.

compulsory school attendance laws represent a valid exercise of state police power. That an enlightened citizenry is vital to ensuring the progress and stability of this nation, is an established tenet of school law. Between 1918 and 1954, all states had statutes of mandatory compulsory school attendance.

An Illinois case, decided in 1901, demonstrates the historical underpinnings of compulsory school attendance laws in court precedent. In upholding the state's authority to compel school attendance (even where parents oppose said attendance), the court said:

> The welfare of the child and the best interests of society require that the state shall exert its sovereign authority to secure to the child the opportunity to acquire an education. Statutes making it compulsory upon the parent, guardian, or other person having the custody and control of children to send them to public or private schools for longer or shorter periods during certain years of the life of such children have not only been upheld as strictly with the constitutional power of the legislature, but have generally been regarded necessary to carry out the express purposes of the constitution itself.[6]

More than fifty years ago, the United States Supreme Court handed down a decision having a narrowing effect on the scope of legal authority of states to establish compulsory school attendance. A case involving the property rights and business interests of a group of private schools and the right of teachers to engage in their profession, *Pierce v. Society of Sisters,* was decided in 1925.

At issue in *Pierce* was an Oregon statute (Compulsory Education Act) requiring that every child (aged eight to sixteen years) attend public school only. Parents found in violation of the law would be guilty of a misdemeanor.

In declaring the Oregon statute unconstitutional (violating both the property rights of the schools and liberty interests of parents, protected by the Fourteenth Amendment), the high court declared: ". . . the fundamental theory of liberty upon which all governments in this Union repose excluded any general power of the state to standardize its children by forcing them to accept instruction from public teachers only." [7]

---

6. State v. Bailey, 61 N.E. 730 (Ill. 1901), at 731-32.
7. 268 U.S. 510, 45 S. Ct. 510, 69 L. Ed. 1070 (1925).

a. *Yoder and Exceptions to Compulsory Attendance.* A number of court cases involving compulsory school attendance laws as being in conflict with one's religious beliefs have involved the Amish. In 1972, the United States Supreme Court heard the first case specifically challenging a state's compulsory attendance requirements. The case, *Wisconsin v. Yoder,*[8] involved a challenge by some Amish parents to the State's compulsory school attendance law which required that all children, seven to sixteen years old, attend a public or private school. According to their petition, the Free Exercise Clause of the First Amendment to the United States Constitution caused their children to be exempt from compulsory school attendance beyond the eighth grade, because high school attendance was contrary to Amish religious beliefs.

Initially, Jonas Yoder and Adin Yutzy, Old Order Amish members, were convicted for violating Wisconsin's compulsory attendance law. Yoder and Yutzy refused to send their children to any school, after the children completed eighth grade. Both the trial court and a Wisconsin Circuit Court ruled against the parents. Each court considered the law a reasonable and constitutional exercise of governmental power.

On appeal to the Wisconsin Supreme Court, the lower court rulings were reversed. The state's highest court was convinced that the compulsory school attendance law unnecessarily infringed upon the parent's free exercise of their religion.[9]

The United States Supreme Court affirmed the Wisconsin Supreme Court. Convinced that the Amish parents' objection to the compulsory school attendance requirement was "firmly grounded" in Amish religious doctrine, that the Amish community does provide for the continued education and training of its children (after the eighth grade) through vocational-agricultural experiences, and seemingly impressed with the reputation of the Amish community as a "productive, self-supporting" society, the nation's highest Court upheld the Wisconsin Supreme Court's decision favoring the parents' claim.[10]

Precedent was thus established in *Yoder* for possible future

---

8. 406 U.S. 205, 92 S. Ct. 1526, 32 L. Ed. 2d 15 (1972).

9. State v. Yoder, 182 N.W.2d 539 (Wis. 1971).

10. *Yoder, supra,* 406 U.S. 212, 214.

exemptions from compulsory school attendance laws being granted for children whose parents can establish a bona fide religious objection to such attendance. The onus in such law suits before today's courts is on the objecting parents to establish their reasons (whether for religious reasons or other reasons) for noncompliance with compulsory attendance statutes, with failure to do so subjecting the parents to possible prosecution by the state.[11]

Other religious groups or individuals have on occasion sought some modification of a state's compulsory attendance law. They have usually attempted to set up their own educational system and with varying degrees of success. Courts tend to look strictly to the way in which a nonpublic school is organized and maintained to ascertain if it has standards comparable to those of the public schools. It is not necessary that a nonpublic school meet all the standards and requirements of a public school, so long as the state is satisfied that a student is receiving a comparable education. A New York court ruled in 1951, that a school in which the conventional subjects were not taught was not comparable. The teacher lacked minimum qualifications and no attendance records were kept. The court ruled that the parents' stated religious beliefs that forbade formal education were not violated by the compulsory attendance statutes.[12]

In another case, a court held that it was insufficient for parents to withdraw their children from school because they felt that racial mixing was sinful.[13]

In a case based on state regulations rather than standards, the Ohio Supreme Court ruled in 1976, that the regulations covering nonpublic schools were such as to eliminate all differences between them and public schools.[14] It overturned an indictment of twelve parents whose children attended a religious school. In another 1976 case, the North Carolina Court of Appeals decided a matter in-

---

11. *See,* for example, Matter of Franz, 378 N.Y.S. 2d 317 (1976) involving home tutoring, and Matter of Baum, 382 N.Y.S. 2d 672 (1976), wherein parents couldn't support their charge of "racism" of their child's teacher, as their reason for not sending their daughter to school. *See also,* State v. LaBarge, 357 A.2d 121 (Vt. 1976).

12. People v. Donner, 302 N.Y. 833, 100 N.E.2d 57 (1951).

13. F. and F. v. Duval City, 273 So. 2d 15 (Fla. Ct. App. 1973).

14. State v. Whisner, 351 N.E.2d 750 (Ohio 1976).

volving Indian parents who refused to send their children to school because the school did not teach Indian heritage and culture. As a result of their parents' actions, the children had been declared "neglected" and were thus made wards of the juvenile court.[15]

On appeal the parents claimed that the First Amendment protected their prerogatives "as parents" to keep their children home from school for what they believed were legitimate reasons. In rejecting the parents' claim, the North Carolina court saw this case as being different from *Yoder*. First, the court did not treat instruction in Indian heritage or culture as a "religious" matter; thus, the First Amendment protection of free exercise was not applicable. Secondly, unlike the parents in *Yoder*, there was no showing by the Indian parents that their children were being provided with sufficient "alternative" education opportunities.

b. *State Law and Exceptions to Compulsory Attendance.* In recent years the compulsory attendance statutes of several states have been amended to allow for alternative education and for exemptions, while maintaining the state's authority to require education for its children. The Florida School Code, for example, mandates regular attendance at school of all children between the ages of seven and sixteen. What is more, the Code provides that parents or guardians are responsible for their child's attendance and are subject to prosecution if they are found in violation of the law.[16] The Code allows, however, that regular school attendance may be achieved through one of the following means: 1. public school, 2. parochial or denominational school, 3. private school, or 4. a private tutor who meets all requirements of state law and state board regulations.[17]

In Florida, a child may be granted a "certificate of exemption" from compulsory school attendance. The bona fide reasons specified by law are: 1. physical or mental disability, 2. distance a child would be compelled to walk to the nearest school or to the nearest publicly maintained school bus route, 3. lawful employment, and 4. upon recommendation of the juvenile and

---

15. *In re* McMillan, 226 S.E.2d 693 (N.C. 1976).
16. 29 *Florida Jurisprudence,* at 162-163.
17. *Id.* at 162.

domestic relations court (accompanied by the agreement of the county superintendent of schools).[18]

§ 9.2. Vaccination.

In addition to the legality of compulsory attendance statutes, states may set conditions for children to enroll in schools. One of these conditions is the requirement that one be inoculated against specified contagious diseases. This requirement grows out of the state's police power in looking after the health and welfare of its citizens.

The major objection to compulsory vaccination laws is that they conflict with one's religious beliefs. These objectors often cite scriptural passages as a basis for their beliefs. Their problem was less acute prior to the enactment of compulsory attendance statutes, for parents simply had a choice of submitting their children to be inoculated or withholding them from school. However, at the end of World War I (when all states had compulsory attendance laws), courts tended to hold parents in violation of both the vaccination and compulsory attendance statutes.

When parents first challenged the vaccination laws, their objection was premised on the Due Process Clause. Later, it was based on the First Amendment. The Supreme Court ruled in 1923, that a San Antonio, Texas, ordinance requiring vaccination was not in violation of one's due process.[19] The ordinance was held not to be arbitrary but designed to protect public health.

Parents have objected to compulsory vaccination statutes for a variety of reasons. Non-vaccinated children of parents who objected on the basis that they believed in Divine healing through faith were denied admission to public schools and then held in contempt of the compulsory attendance law. The court held that health and safety take precedence over one's religious convictions.[20]

An Arkansas court went one step further in 1964 when it ruled that parents who objected to vaccination statutes and who kept

---

18. *Id.* at 163. *See also* the VA. CODE, § 22-275.4.

19. Zucht v. King, 260 U.S. 174, 43 S. Ct. 24, 67 L. Ed. 2d 194 (1923).

20. Anderson v. State, 84 Ga. App. 259, 65 S.E.2d 848 (1951).

their children out of school were in violation of the state's attendance laws and ordered their children removed from their custody and placed with juvenile authorities until foster homes could be found for them.[21]

Some states have allowed a child to be exempt from the compulsory vaccination requirement if he presents supporting evidence based on his religious convictions. The Supreme Court of North Carolina ruled in favor of a parent on this matter.[22] A Texas statute was upheld. It provided for an exemption based on two criteria: possession of a doctor's certificate and the filing of an affidavit that the law conflicted with one's religious beliefs.[23] A Kentucky statute allowing exemptions for members of a nationally recognized and established church or religious denomination was upheld.[24]

Courts have also looked very strictly at statutes providing for exemption to vaccination. They have attempted to prevent an abuse of the intent of the legislation. That was an issue in a New York court which held against a parent because he was not a member of a bona fide religious organization.[25] The law exempted only children whose parents were members of a bona fide religious sect.

A Massachusetts court went beyond that and declared a statute unconstitutional.[26] It held that the law providing for exemptions favored those who belonged to recognized religious bodies over those who might profess sincere religious beliefs outside a formally recognized church.

§ 9.3. Admission to Public School.

Children do not possess an absolute right to attend a public school. They are *entitled* to attend if they possess the qualifications specified in state law (*e.g.,* age, residence, vaccination for certain communicable diseases, etc.). Typically, matters of deciding admissibility of children to public school are left to local school boards.

---

21. Cude v. State, 237 Ark. 927, 377 S.W.2d 816 (1964).
22. State v. Miday, 263 N.C. 747, 140 S.E.2d 325 (1965).
23. Itz v. Penick, 493 S.W.2d 506 (Tex. 1973).
24. Kleid v. Board of Educ., 406 F. Supp. 902 (W.D. Ky. 1976).
25. Maier v. Beeser, 73 Misc.2d 241, 341 N.Y.S.2d 411 (1972).
26. Dalli v. Board of Educ., 358 Mass. 753, 267 N.E.2d 219 (1971).

Admission to a public school is one area of board authority over the pupil that has been clearly defined in judicial precedent. According to Bolmeier:

> Generally a child has a right, or at least the privilege to attend a public school. The right of a child to be admitted to the public school, however, is not absolute. It is subject to reasonable restrictions and regulations. If the statutes do not state specifically what the restrictions and regulations are which limit admission, the board is clothed with the discretionary authority to so determine within reasonable bounds.[27]

That local boards of education possess considerable *discretionary* authority to determine the admissibility of pupils to local public schools, has been consistently upheld by courts of law.

Watson v. Cambridge[28] was an early case establishing the discretionary authority of local boards of education to determine the admissibility of children to public schools. In *Watson* it was held that a board of education has a right to deny admission to a child, when the child is subject to physical defects.

In 1913, a Massachusetts court reinforced the prerogative of a local board to refuse admission to a student, and expanded the board's discretionary authority to include retention and promotion. The court said, in part:

> The care and management of schools which is vested in the school committee includes the establishment and maintenance of standards for the promotion of pupils from one grade to another for their continuance as members of any particular class. So long as the school committees act in good faith their conduct in formulating and applying standards and making decisions touching this matter is not subject to review by any other tribunal.[29]

In *Barnard v. Shelbourne,* the legal authority of a school board to assign a pupil to a particular class and a board's legal prerogative to maintain standards of student continuance were clearly established.

---

27. BOLMEIER, THE SCHOOL IN THE LEGAL STRUCTURE, 2d ed. 225 (Cincinnati, Ohio: The W.H. Anderson Company, 1973).

28. Watson v. Cambridge, 32 N.E. 864 (Mass. 1893).

29. 102 N.E. 1095 (Mass. 1913), at 1096.

201

Courts of law were most reluctant to interfere with decision-making when deciding the early cases brought by parents who challenged board admission prerogatives. Beginning in the mid-1950's, however, a move to secure equal educational opportunities for "all children" had its beginning in *Brown v. Board of Education of Topeka*.[30] Decided by the United States Supreme Court, *Brown* established the principle of extending equal educational opportunities to all children of school age as a matter of constitutional entitlement. Education, said the court, "where the state has undertaken to provide it, is a right which must be made available to all on equal terms." [31] Courts, in the years following *Brown*, consistently viewed public education as a matter of entitlement.

In the early 1970's, admission of children with handicaps to public schools and subsequent placement of these children into appropriate educational programs became issues taken by parents to federal and state courts.[32] This was also the era of massive racial integration of public schools and the ongoing battle to remove *race* as a condition of admission to or rejection from attendance in a public school.

The impact of the avalanche of court decisions from the past twenty-five years was to "open the doors" of public schools to all children, no matter what their race, socio-economic status, marital status or form of handicap. That no child of school age shall be arbitrarily or capriciously denied admission to a public school became the law of the land. Some recent cases in point illustrate this principle in action.

In *Cuyahoga County Association for Retarded Children and Adults v. Essex,* a federal district court held that I.Q. score alone can not be the determiner of whether or not a child is incapable of profiting from education. Certainly, a state may consider I.Q. scores when classifying students; however, to deny children admission to school solely on the basis of I.Q. is a violation of equal protection.[33]

---

30. 347 U.S. 483, 74 S. Ct. 686, 98 L. Ed. 873 (1954).

31. *Id.* at 691.

32. *See,* for example, P.A.R.C. v. Commonwealth of Pennsylvania, 334 F. Supp. 1257 (1971). Final consent agreement at 343 F. Supp. 279 (E.D. Pa. 1972).

33. 411 F. Supp. 46 (N.D. Ohio 1976).

A 1975 Oklahoma case offers another example of limitations being placed by federal district courts on local school board admissions prerogatives. According to the court, a school board cannot prevent black students moving into the school district from attending school because the board believes that the school's educational level would decrease.[34]

§ 9.4. Bases of Pupil Assignment to Classes and Schools.

The discretionary authority of local boards of education has been upheld, relative to the assignment of pupils to special schools and to particular classrooms within those schools. For example, as early as 1936, an Iowa court upheld the authority of a school board, over parental objections, to assign a pupil with infantile paralysis, who suffered continually from pain, to a special school. In the court's opinion said assignment was a reasonable determination and did not exceed board authority.[35]

In the recent past, however, student assessment and placement within public schools have received much attention and criticism. According to Ross, DeYoung, and Cohen, public school systems were told by courts of law that they must cease to use evaluation and placement procedures that discriminate against children on racial or socio-economic bases.[36]

The principle that pupil assignments to particular schools and classes be made on reasonable and substantial bases was of vital concern in a 1954 New York case. In *Isquith v. Levitt*[37] a New York State court ruled that the board of education could legally place children in any grade within a school based upon the "mental attainment of the child" and upon "training, knowledge, and ability."[38]

The landmark decision in the area of classification and assignment of public school pupils, however, came in 1967. In

---

34. Board of Educ. of Ind. School Dist. No. 53 v. Board of Educ. of Ind. School Dist. No. 52, 413 F. Supp. 342 (W.D. Okla. 1975).

35. State v. Christ, 270 N.W. 376 (Iowa 1936), at 379.

36. Sterling L. Ross, Jr., Henry G. DeYoung, and Julius S. Cohen, *Confrontation: Special Education and the Law,* EXCEPTIONAL CHILDREN 38 (September, 1971). *See* in particular, their discussions of the relationships between standardized test results, socio-economic background, and student grouping.

37. 137 N.Y.S.2d 493 (1954).

38. *Id.* at 496 and 498.

Hobson v. Hansen [39] the method of testing utilized at that time by Washington, D.C., public schools to place students in "ability groups" was questioned in federal district court.

Upon completion of hearing arguments in *Hobson,* District Judge J. Skelley Wright held that the tests and methods of student placement utilized by the Washington, D.C., schools were unconstitutional, since they discriminated against certain children. Judge Wright was convinced that a student's chance of being enrolled in a track was directly related to his socio-economic background; and, as Reutter and Hamilton have pointed out, the court found the Washington, D.C., Public School System's "tracking" method of ability-grouping not rationally explainable. [40] Thus, the system denied students equal access to educational opportunity. (On later appeal, the United States Court of Appeals for the District of Columbia, upheld, among other things, the lower district court's order to abolish the "ability grouping" plan in the District of Columbia public schools). [41]

The United States Court of Appeals for the District of Columbia, offering the subsequent ruling in *Smuck v. Hobson,* did not remove or negate the District of Columbia school board's legal prerogative to make decisions concerning educational programming. In presenting a rationale for its decision the court said, "We conclude that this directive does not limit the discretion of the school board with full recognition of the need to permit the school board latitude in fashioning and effectuating the remedies for the ills of the District school system." [42]

a. *Race as a Factor.* Public school segregation has undergone

---

39. 269 F. Supp. 401 (D.C.D.C. 1967). The Washington, D.C. School System placed students into either the *Honors, General,* or *Special* (educable mentally retarded) tracks based upon results from the following battery of standardized tests: *Sequential Tests of Educational Progress* (STEP) and the *School and College Ability Test* (SCAT) administered in the fourth grade, the *Stanford Achievement Test* (SAT) and *Otis Quick-Scoring Mental Ability Test* administered in the sixth grade. Since *Hobson,* other cases have reached the courts in which the uses of other standardized tests (*e.g., Stanford-Binet* and *Wechsler* intelligence tests) as bases of student grouping have been challenged.

40. *See* REUTTER, JR., AND HAMILTON, THE LAW OF PUBLIC EDUCATION 142 (2d ed. Mineola, New York: The Foundation Press, Inc., 1976).

41. *See* Smuck v. Hobson, 408 F.2d 175 (D.C. Cir. 1969).

42. *Id.* at 189.

a number of legal phases: application of the *Plessy* decision of 1896; modification of *Plessy* in cases involving higher education from 1938-1950; two decades of the *Brown* era, 1954-1974; and the retrenchment era, 1974 to the present.

Justification for segregation in schools was initially found in economic, political, and social policy, not to gainsay court decisions. It received great impetus from the *Plessy* decisions.[43] There, the Supreme Court ruled that a Louisiana law requiring that races be segregated in public transportation facilities was reasonable, within the meaning of the Fourteenth Amendment. The Court held that such laws did not necessarily impute a feeling of inferiority to the black man. "If this be so," the Court observed, "it is not by reason of anything found in the act, but solely because the colored race chooses to put that construction upon it." [44] Only Justice Harlan dissented, holding that "Our Constitution is color-blind, and neither knows nor tolerates classes among citizens. In respect of civil rights, all citizens are equal before the law." [45]

The origin of the phrase "separate but equal," can be found in the *Plessy* decision. The Justices cited many instances wherein the races were kept separate, schools being one such institution. Through its language, the Court looked with favor on this practice. At any rate, the Justices indicated that they would not upset laws and long-established customs governing segregation. The Court's stance became the accepted justification for segregation of almost all public school districts in the South. Further, for almost five decades after *Plessy,* there were very few challenges in court to segregated schools.

It was higher education that first began to desegregate, and this was achieved by court order. A series of four key decisions, beginning in 1938, set the tone for the *Brown* decision that was to follow sixteen years later.[46] *Brown* was a jointure of four cases

---

43. Plessy v. Ferguson, 163 U.S. 537, 16 S. Ct. 1138, 41 L. Ed. 256 (1896).

44. *Id.* at 551.

45. *Id.* at 559.

46. *See* Missouri *ex rel.* Gaines v. Canada, 305 U.S. 337, 59 S. Ct. 65, 83 L. Ed. 233 (1938); Sipuel v. Board of Regents, 332 U.S. 631, 68 S. Ct. 299, 92 L. Ed. 2d 247 (1948); McLaurin v. Oklahoma State Regents, 339 U.S. 637, 70 S. Ct. 139, 94 L. Ed. 1149 (1950); Sweatt v. Painter, 339 U.S. 629, 70 S. Ct. 848, 94 L. Ed. 1115 (1950). In each of these decisions, the Supreme Court ruled in favor of the black plaintiffs.

from Kansas, South Carolina, Virginia, and Delaware.[47] Each case had similar factual situations in that students had been assigned to racially segregated schools either through state constitutional mandate or legislative action. In its unanimous opinion, the Court concluded that "in the field of public education the doctrine of 'separate but equal' has no place. Separate educational facilities are inherently unequal." [48] That one decision overturned constitutional provisions or state laws in twenty-one of the then forty-eight states.[49] The same day the Court overturned segregation in schools in the District of Columbia.[50]

When the Court handed down the *Brown* decision, it asked for reargument on the question of how best to implement it. What followed those hearings was the second *Brown* decision, handed down in 1955.[51] In recognizing the complexity of dismantling dual school systems, the Court cited the following considerations: problems related to school plants, transportation systems, and personnel; revision of school districts and attendance areas; and revision of local laws and regulations. The Court then charged local school officials as being the best instruments for implementing the desegregation decrees "with all deliberate speed." Should a school district be charged with noncompliance, a person could seek relief in federal district courts.

What has followed since the two *Brown* decisions are almost two and a half decades of litigation over a variety of desegregation issues. That litigation and the courts' opinions have brought forth various kinds of criteria for desegregation, the major criteria being treated below. Since hundreds of desegregation cases have been handed down since 1954, only decisions by the Supreme Court of the United States will be considered initially, followed by some lower court decisions.

---

47. The following 17 states required segregation by state constitutional or statutory law prior to 1954: Alabama, Arkansas, Delaware, Florida, Georgia, Kentucky, Louisiana, Maryland, Mississippi, Missouri, North Carolina, Oklahoma, South Carolina, Tennessee, Texas, Virginia, and West Virginia. Segregation was allowed under permissive legislation in Arizona, Kansas, New Mexico, and Wyoming.

48. Brown v. Board of Educ., 347 U.S. 483, 74 S. Ct. 686, 98 L. Ed. 873 (1954).

49. *Id.*

50. Bolling v. Sharpe, 347 U.S. 497, 74 S. Ct. 693, 98 L. Ed. 884 (1954).

51. Brown v. Bd. of Educ., 349 U.S. 294, 75 S. Ct. 753, 99 L. Ed. 1083 (1955).

In its first decision following *Brown,* the Supreme Court extended its holding to bring essentially private schools subject to the Equal Protection Clause.[52] The Justices held that Girard College, an elementary and secondary school for "poor white male orphans," according to the will establishing the school, was subject to state action because its board of trustees were agents of the city of Philadelphia.

On a broader scale, the Court ruled in 1958 that violence or the threat of violence was insufficient cause for delaying desegregation.[53] The case involved desegregation of the Little Rock, Arkansas, schools. The desegregation process was achieved only with the assistance of and protection by the National Guard stationed at the school for one year.

In ruling that evasive plans for delaying desegregation would not be upheld, the unanimous Court saw that the legislature and the governor had been the major elements in thwarting the desegregative process.

Desegregation proceeded cautiously and slowly for a decade after *Brown,* during which time the federal courts acted with restraint and patience while, at the same time, consistently ruled that school districts must proceed with dismantling dual school systems. The Court seemed to be less concerned with the speed of desegregation than with its actually being done. It gave some indication of its patience wearing thin, however, in 1964, in a case from Virginia.[54] There, the state had shut down its public schools in Prince Edward County and set up a system of private schools for both races. At first, those schools were supported entirely by private donations; later the state subsidized them and granted tax concessions for persons who made financial contributions to the schools.

Black parents rejected the plan and sought relief in the courts. In rejecting the state's action, the Court reasoned that "Whatever nonracial grounds might support a State's allowing a county to abandon public schools, the object must be a constitutional one, and

---

52. Pennsylvania v. Board of Directors, 353 U.S. 230, 77 S. Ct. 806, 1 L. Ed. 2d 792, *reh. denied,* 353 U.S. 989 (1957).

53. Cooper v. Aaron, 358 U.S. 1, 78 S. Ct. 1401, 3 L. Ed. 2d 5 (1958).

54. Griffin v. County School Bd., 377 U.S. 218, 84 S. Ct. 1226, 12 L. Ed. 2d 256 (1964).

grounds of race and opposition to desegregation do not qualify as constitutional." [55] The Court observed further that the "all deliberate speed" criterion of *Brown II* had elapsed. One year later, the Court ruled that a grade-a-year plan could not be sustained in that it would require too long to desegregate the schools. [56]

The mid-1960's was a transitional period in the desegregation movement. There were increased federal funds available to the schools and, with those funds were guidelines requiring desegregation. With the passage of the Civil Rights Act of 1964, the federal government began to take a harder line on desegregating the schools. That stance was also reflected in the judiciary. While these changes were taking place, school districts began to use various plans and ploys to comply with federal rulings and orders and desegregate at a pace less rapidly than some people wanted. One such plan was freedom of choice wherein a student would actually decide which school he wished to attend. In three separate opinions, the Supreme Court in 1968 ruled that freedom of choice is constitutional, provided it works. [57] Thus, the Court began to look, not at the legality of a plan in the abstract but to the effect that the plan had in accomplishing the intended purpose of creating a unitary school system. In each of the three cases, that effect had not been met. In *Green v. County School Board of New Kent County,* the lead case, the Court noted that the plan, in operation for three years, had resulted in no white children being reassigned to the all-black school and only 15 percent of the black children being assigned to the former all-white school.

Busing became a legal issue in the early 1970's when the Supreme Court entertained the question of its being required to achieve a racial balance. Several lower court opinions had produced conflicting and inconclusive legal standards prior to 1971. In the *Swann v. Charlotte-Mecklenburg Board of Education* decision, the Court ruled that busing is a legitimate tool for desegregating schools and courts are within their power in requiring it. [58] The

---

55. *Id.* at 231.

56. Rogers v. Paul, 382 U.S. 198, 86 S. Ct. 358, 15 L. Ed. 2d 265 (1965).

57. Green v. County School Bd., 391 U.S. 430, 88 S. Ct. 1689, 20 L. Ed. 2d 716 (1968); Raney v. Bd. of Educ., 391 U.S. 443, 88 S. Ct. 1697, 20 L. Ed. 2d 727 (1968); Monroe v. Board of Comm'rs, 391 U.S. 450, 88 S. Ct. 1700, 20 L. Ed. 2d 733 (1968).

58. Swann v. Charlotte-Mecklenburg Bd. of Educ., 402 U.S. 1, 91 S. Ct. 1267, 28 L. Ed. 2d 554, *reh. denied,* 403 U.S. 912 (1971).

Court observed that state-imposed segregation must be eliminated "root and branch." However, the Justices acknowledged the complexity of desegregating schools and made three concessions: 1. Not every school in every community must reflect the racial composition of the entire district. 2. A small number of one-race or virtually one-race schools within a district does not necessarily imply a dual school system. 3. There are no rigid, fixed guidelines as to how far a court can go in ordering desegregation. The Court recognized that school officials are not required to make year-by-year adjustments in racial composition once a district has been desegregated. Within the context of those guidelines, the Court ordered the school district to bus students, for the state had been guilty of *de jure* segregation.

In *Swann* the Court implied that the difference between *de facto* and *de jure* segregation is minimal. Had it ruled specifically that there was no difference, then *Brown I* would have been applicable to all states where *de facto* segregation existed. The Court did not go that far, however, as was evident in the first real school desegregation case outside the South.[59] The case arose in Denver, Colorado, which had no law requiring segregation. The school board there adhered to a neighborhood school plan, although there was some evidence of gerrymandered attendance zones which had resulted in one section of the city being essentially all-white. The Court did not hand down a substantive ruling on the constitutionality of *de facto* segregation; rather it remanded the case and asked the local school board to establish that it was actually not responsible for the racial imbalance. Since the board was unable to do this, the district court ordered further desegregation.

The Court dealt more directly with *de facto-de jure* segregation in 1974 in a case in Detroit.[60] In deciding the case, the Justices used as a criterion the intent of a condition that establishes segregation rather than the actual existence of it. At issue was the legality of court-imposed merger of the city schools of Detroit with fifty-three suburban school districts. The Supreme Court overturned the lower court's order and held that the suburban districts were not

---

59. Keyes v. School Dist. No. 1, 413 U.S. 189, 93 S. Ct. 2686, 37 L. Ed. 2d 548 (1971).

60. Milliken v. Bradley, 418 U.S. 717, 94 S. Ct. 3112, 41 L. Ed. 2d 1069 (1974).

responsible for the segregative condition existing in the city. Further, although there was evidence of *de jure* segregation in Detroit, there was no evidence of it in the surrounding school districts. The Justices then ruled that "Before the boundaries of separate and autonomous school districts may be set aside by consolidating the separate units for remedial purposes or by imposing a cross-district remedy, it must first be shown that there has been a constitutional violation within one district that produces a significant segregative effect in another district. That is, "it must be shown that 'racially discriminatory acts of the state or its local school districts have been a substantial cause of inter-district segregation. Thus, an inter-district remedy might be in order where the racially discriminatory acts of one or more school districts caused racial segregation in an adjacent district, or where district lines have been deliberately drawn on the basis of race." Consequently, "without an inter-district violation and inter-district effect, there is no constitutional wrong calling for an inter-district remedy." [61]

In a later ruling involving the Detroit schools, the Court held that federal courts can order compensatory programs for children who have been victims of *de jure* segregation.[62] Further, the agency responsible for the segregation can be ordered to bear the costs of the program.

In 1974, the Court also held that special programs could be offered to Chinese students whose native language was not English.[63]

In relying on its earlier *Swann* decision, the Supreme Court held that the Pasadena, California, schools did not have to adjust their black-white pupil ratio which had become more disparate after an initial program balancing the schools.[64] There was no evidence that school officials were in any way responsible for the desegregation which had resulted in five of 32 schools having a black population of over 50 percent, a condition at variance with the lower court's order.

---

61. *Id.* at 744-745.

62. Milliken v. Bradley, 433 U.S. 267, 97 S. Ct. 2749, 53 L. Ed. 2d 745 (1977).

63. Lau v. Nichols, 414 U.S. 563, 94 S. Ct. 786, 39 L. Ed. 2d 1 (1974).

64. Pasadena City Board of Educ. v. Spangler, 427 U.S. 424, 96 S. Ct. 2697, 49 L. Ed. 2d 599 (1976).

In a 1976 decision in Virginia, the Court was faced with a case similar to the private school issue of its 1957 decision. Here, the Justices ruled that a commercially operated, nonsectarian private school discriminated under Section 1981 of 42 U.S.C. when it refused to admit black students.[65] The Court reasoned that a contractual agreement was involved wherein the school offered instructional services in exchange for tuition. The state's interest and control over these schools stem from its having to exact assurance that constitutional and statutory regulations are followed.

The Supreme Court ruled that the Dayton, Ohio, schools did not have to reflect, within 15 percent, the city's black-white population.[66] In affirming its position in the Detroit case, the Court held that the existence of segregation is not so acute as the source or intent of it. Where no intentional action of the board to segregate exists, there is no compelling reason to order that the board desegregate.

In a much-publicized ruling concluding the Court's work in its 1977-78 term, the Justices ruled for the first time on reverse discrimination.[67] The case involved a suit by a white student who was rejected by the medical school at the University of California at Davis. The applicant was bypassed under a program in which 16 of 100 first-year slots were designated for minority students, a number of them less qualified than Bakke, a Caucasian, who did not qualify. The Court divided 5-4 on two key rulings. In one, the Justices ruled that race was the key reason by which Bakke had been rejected, thus the admissions program operated on unconstitutional grounds. Bakke was ordered admitted to the medical school. In the other ruling, the Court approved the concept

65. Runyon v. McCrary, 427 U.S. 160, 96 S. Ct. 2586, 49 L. Ed. 2d 415 (1976). Section 1981 of The United States Constitution provides: All persons within the jurisdiction of the United States shall have the same right in every State and Territory to make and enforce contracts, to sue, be parties, give evidence, and to the full and equal benefit of all laws and proceedings for the security of persons and property as is enjoyed by white citizens, and shall be subject to like punishment, pains, penalties, taxes, licenses, and exactions of every kind, and to no other.

66. Dayton Board of Educ. v. Brinkman, 433 U.S. 406, 97 S. Ct. 2766, 53 L. Ed. 2d 851 (1977).

67. Regents of the University of California v. Bakke, — U.S. —, 98 S. Ct. 257, 57 L. Ed. 2d 750 (1978).

of affirmative action in which a variety of criteria involving both objective and subjective data, including race, can be employed in admissions. The Court did not approve of rigid quotas based on race. It remains to be seen what effect this decision will have on public school desegretation, on faculty employment, and on admissions in higher education.

The above cases catalog briefly a chronology of desegregation in the nation's highest court. Beginning in 1964, the Court was unequivocally resolute in affirming a plaintiff's complaint of discrimination in school assignments by race. The Court consistently and unanimously upheld a student seeking admission to a desegregated school A decade later, it became even firmer in ordering immediate desegregation, It showed a lack of patience with plans that did not desegregate and which attempted to evade or forestall desegregation. Beginning in 1974, the Court began to retreat when it realized that there are limits beyond which courts cannot go in desegregating schools. It has recognized that other avenues may be as successful as court edicts.

Numerous cases have also been resolved in lower courts in which the bases of classification and assignment of pupils were challenged on racial grounds. In such cases, as in those previously cited, courts have neither denied nor negated the legal prerogatives of school officials. However, they have insisted that all subsequent classifications and assignments of pupils be based on objective, non-racial standards. A Florida case and a Mississippi case (decided in 1970) both illustrate this point. Significantly, each case involved assignment of public school students to special educational settings.

In the first case, *Wright v. Board,* the Court of Appeals for the Fifth Circuit directed that assignment of students to schools offering compensatory or remedial training be made on objective and non-racial grounds.[68] In the second case, *U. S. v. Hinds,* the Fifth Circuit approved assignment of students to a reading clinic where those assignments were made on "sound education and administratively feasible grounds." [69]

---

68. Wright v. Board of Pub. Instr., 431 F.2d 1200 (5th Cir. 1970), at 1202.

69. United States v. Hinds County School Bd., 433 F.2d 602 (5th Cir. 1970), at 605.

Spangler v. Board[70] is another important decision involving special grouping of students, from a federal district court out of California. It offers a similar ruling to those cited above in *Wright* and *Hinds*. The court in *Spangler* found for the plaintiffs, for it was convinced that the degree of racial segregation present within the integrated public schools of Pasadena, California, was "a result of interclass grouping...."[71] Three factors influenced the court's decision. They were: 1. The school system's achievement test and intelligence test scores were acknowledged as "racially discriminatory" by the Assistant Superintendent of Schools. 2. Teachers and counselors, whose recommendations were considered in evaluating student placement, admitted assuming that blacks, particularly those from lower socio-economic backgrounds, would achieve lower than others if placed in upper groups. 3. Parents were allowed to make requests for placement of their children in higher groups; thus children of more assertive parents would have an advantage of placement.[72] In the opinion of Judge Real, the racial effect of these grouping procedures was to increase segregation in the schools.

The Fifth Circuit, ruling in a 1971 Louisiana case, held that a public school district which operated as a unitary system for only one semester could not assign students to schools within that district on the basis of achievement test scores.[73] Relying heavily on *Singleton v. Jackson Municipal Separate School District,*[74] the court made it clear that "regardless of the innate validity of testing, it could not be used until a school district had been established as a unitary system."[75]

Precedent does exist, however, allowing local boards of education to assign special students (specifically, handicapped children) to particular schools "without respect to unitary zones."

---

70. Spangler v. Board of Educ., 311 F. Supp. 501 (C.D. Cal. 1970).

71. *Id.* at 519. Two systems of grouping students were in general use in the Pasadena schools. At the elementary school level, students were grouped as *gifted* or *below-average*; at the secondary level as *fast, regular,* or *slow.*

72. *Id., see* the discussion of "Interclass Grouping" at pages 519-520.

73. Lemon v. Bossier Parish School Bd., 444 F.2d 1400 (5th Cir. 1971). *See also* United States v. Sunflower County School Dist., 430 F.2d 839 (5th Cir. 1970).

74. Singleton v. Jackson Municipal Separate School Dist., 419 F.2d 1211, 396 U.S. 290 (1970).

75. See *Lemon, supra* at 1401.

A case in point, decided by a federal district court in Tennessee, is *Robinson v. Shelby County Board of Education.*[76]

In recent years, court-ordered desegregation plans (generally calling for the massive busing of public school students) have dominated the legal scene in all sections of the nation — Wilmington, Louisville, Indianapolis, Boston and Los Angeles, among other cities. The net effect of such plans has seriously diminished the once plenary power of local school boards to assign pupils to schools within their school districts. With the primary emphasis placed on achieving acceptable racial and ethnic mixes of student populations, federal judges and federal governmental agencies (*e.g.*, HEW) maintained constant checks on school system enrollments, by individual schools, and overruled any school board assignment plan that fell below the court's or agency's standard.[77]

Some federal judges have taken the prerogative away from local boards and have placed the entire student assignment plan under the supervision of court appointed experts.[78] While in other jurisdictions, state courts have sanctioned state boards of education to mandate the implementation of "magnet school programs" to attract non-white students back to public schools.[79]

b. *Sex as a Factor.* In the past, there have been situations wherein sex has been considered as a criterion for determining a student's eligibility to public school, and in making assignment to given schools. As with other admissions' criteria previously discussed, local school boards, until recent years, were generally presumed correct in their judgment as to the qualifications of a student for said admission or assignment, and courts of law were reluctant to review these matters. The passage and implementation of new federal statutes [80] regarding discrimination based upon sex, however, have forced several cases into the courts.

---

76. 311 F. Supp. 97 (C.D. Cal. 1970), at 105.

77. For some recent cases on point *see,* for example, Northside Ind. School Dist. of Bexar v. Texas Educ. Agency, 410 F. Supp. 360 (D.C. Tex. 1975); United States v. Texas Educ. Agency, 532 F.2d 380 (5th Cir. 1976); Morgan v. Kerrigan, 530 F.2d 401 (1st Cir. 1976); and Acree v. County Bd. of Educ., 533 F.2d 131 (5th Cir. 1976).

78. Morgan v. Kerrigan, *supra.*

79. Board of Educ. v. School Comm'n, 345 N.E.2d 345 (Mass. 1976).

80. *See* for example: tit. 6, C.R.A. 1964, 42 U.S.C. 2000 (d); and tit. 9, Education Amendments 1972, 20 U.S.C. 1681, *et. seq.*

Vorchheimer v. School District of Philadelphia involved a challenge brought by a female high school student (Susan Vorchheimer) who had been denied admission to an all-male academic high school. In a class action suit originally brought in the federal district court for the Eastern District of Pennsylvania, the plaintiff, who had graduated with honors from a junior high school, sought relief, under 42 U.S.C. section 1983, from alleged unconstitutional discrimination. Upon completion of the trial, the district court granted her an injunction, ordering that plaintiff and other qualified female students be admitted to the all-male (Central) academic high school.[81]

In November, 1973, while completing her ninth grade year, Susan Vorchheimer's parents received a communication from the junior high school principal listing the four types of senior high schools available to their daughter. These types were: *comprehensive* (providing a wide range of courses and courses of study, with the criterion for enrollment being residency within a designated area of the City), *technical, magnet,* and *academic.* For the academic high schools (all-male Central High and all female Girls High), certain admissions requirements were specified. These requirements were: *tests* (a minimum score in the 82 percentile, national composite score in the most recent Iowa Tests), and *achievement* (a record of all A's and B's with not more than one C in any major subject taken). Only 7% of the students in the entire Philadelphia School District were able to attend either high school.

After visiting a number of senior high schools in the City, Susan decided that she wished to attend Central High School. Subsequently, her father submitted her application for admission and it was rejected, solely on the basis of her sex.[82]

Finding no Congressional enactments which authoritatively addressed the problem before the court, the district court reviewed the line of recent sex discrimination cases from the other federal courts. As a result of his analysis, district Judge Newcomer held that the result of the school board policy excluding young women from attending Central High School "is to deny them the opportunity to attend a coeducational, academically superior, high

---

81. 532 F.2d 880 (3rd Cir. 1976), *aff'd,* 430 U.S. 703 (1977).
82. Vorchheimer v. School Dist., 400 F. Supp. 326 (E.D. Pa. 1975).

school." [83] To Judge Newcomer, the denial was significant enough to have an "adverse impact on her and on other women." [84]

On appeal, the United States Court of Appeals, Third Circuit, reversed Judge Newcomer. The high court held that where attendance at either of the two single-sex high schools was voluntary, and where the educational opportunities at both schools were basically equal, the regulations which established admission based on gender classification did not offend the Equal Protection Clause. As circuit Judge Weis said for the majority:

> It is not for us to pass upon the wisdom of segregating boys and girls in high school. We are concerned not with the desirability of the practice but only its constitutionality. Once that threshold has been passed, it is the school board's responsibility to determine the best methods of accomplishing its mission.[85]

Judge Weis' attitude toward maintaining school board decision-making in this matter is quite clear.

The United State Court of Appeals for the Fifth Circuit had an opportunity, in 1977, to hear an appeal from a federal district court in Mississippi involving a county school district's sex-segregated student assignment plan.[86] The district court had recommended that the Amite County School District be permitted to maintain a sex-segregated student assignment plan among the four schools which comprise the district.

County school officials argued that their sex-segregated assignment plan was not racially motivated. Further, they stated that sex segregation within schools is not a denial of federal statutory rights.[87] Finally, school officials maintained that the

---

83. *Id.* at 328. *Central High School* was founded in 1836 as the first public high school in Philadelphia and was the second public high school in the United States. *Girls High School* was organized as an academic high school for females, in 1893. These two were not the only single-sex schools in Philadelphia. Edison High School and Benjamin Franklin High School admitted only males, and Kensington High School admitted only females.

84. *Id.* at 342.

85. *Id.* at 888.

86. United States v. Hinds County School Bd., 560 F.2d 619 (5th Cir. 1977). *See also* United States v. Georgia, 466 F.2d 197 (5th Cir. 1972), and Moore v. Tangipahoa Parish School Bd., 421 F.2d 1407 (5th Cir. 1969).

87. *Id.* United States v. Hinds, at 623.

continued operation of sex-segregated schools would aid in keeping whites in the racially desegregated public school system.[88]

Regardless of Amite County's educational reasons using gender as a basis for assigning students to schools within the district, the Fifth Circuit Court considered the assignment plan as prohibited by federal statutory law. They remanded the case back to district court where a remedy was to be fashioned, ". . . in light of the best educational interests of the children and parents involved." [89]

c. *Marriage or Pregnancy as a Factor.* Over the years, public school systems have generally discouraged, and in some instances excluded, married or pregnant students from attending school. Some past reasons specified by school officials for such decisions are: 1) marriage emancipates children from their parents, therefore married students are exempt from compulsory attendance statutes,[90] 2) married students may cause turmoil and therefore their presence is detrimental to the other students,[91] 3) pregnancy and parenthood at school-age are socially unacceptable, and 4) unwed pregnancy is an example of "immoral" behavior.[92]

In *Carrollton-Farmers Branch Independent School District v. Knight,* students were suspended from high school because of their marriage. They filed suit in county court seeking reinstatement and were successful. The school board then appealed to the Court of Civil Appeals of Texas.

In upholding the lower court ruling for the students' reinstatement, the appellate court based its decision on three points. First, the presence of the married students had not caused disorder in the high school. Second, there was no evidence that marriage had impaired the study habits of the couple. Finally, that the suspension policy for marriage had not been uniformly applied to other students.[93]

More recently, a federal district court in Georgia heard a complaint filed by a fifteen-year-old girl who was seeking readmission to regular (day) school. School officials had denied her

---

88. *Id.* at 624.
89. *Id.* at 625.
90. State v. Priest, 270 So. 2d 173 (La. 1946).
91. McLeod v. State, 122 So. 2d 737 (Miss. 1929).
92. Nutt v. Board of Educ., 278 P.2d 1065 (Kan. 1928).
93. 418 S.W.2d 535 (Tex. 1967).

admission to regular school, invoking a school board policy that required students who married or became parents to attend night school.

Even though the court found a rational basis for the school board's "night school" policy, it nevertheless opined that the plaintiff student had been denied equal protection of the law, thus she should be readmitted. The major determining factor for the court's decision was that night school students were required to pay tuition and buy their own textbooks, but regular day school students were not required to do the same.[94]

In 1969, a federal district court in Mississippi heard *Perry v. Grenada Municipal Separate School District.* At issue was a school board policy automatically excluding unwed mothers from high school admission. Ruling in the students' favor, the court held that unwed mothers could not be excluded solely because they were "unwed mothers." Moreover, that a charge of "lack of moral character" would have to be clearly established and substantiated through a fair hearing process. The court was also of the opinion that before any such exclusion could be upheld, a link must be established between the unwed pregnancy and a harmful effect on other students.[95]

Ordway v. Hargraves [96] is a similar case, and was heard by a federal district court in Massachusetts. The matter involved an unmarried senior (Fay Ordway) at Middlesex Regional High School. In 1971, Fay became pregnant and was told by her principal that she must cease attending regular classes at the high school, citing a school regulation that stated "whenever an unmarried girl ... shall be known to be pregnant, her membership shall be immediately terminated." [97]

Deciding in the student's favor, and ordering her reinstatement to classes, the court reasoned:

> ... no danger to petitioner's physical or mental health resultant from her attending classes during regular hours has been shown; no likelihood that her presence will cause any disruption of or interference with school

---

94. Houston v. Prosser, 361 F. Supp. 295 (N.D. Ga. 1973).

95. 300 F. Supp. 748 (N.D. Miss. 1969).

96. 323 F. Supp. 1155 (D. Mass. 1971).

97. *Id.* at 1156.

activities or pose a threat of harm to others has been shown; and no valid educational or other reason to justify her segregation and require her to receive a type of educational treatment which is not the equal of that given to all others in her class has been shown.[98]

The Court went on to say:

It would seem beyond argument that the right to receive a public school education is a basic personal right or liberty. Consequently, the burden of justifying any school rule or regulation limiting or terminating that right is on the school authorities.[99]

Apparent in the above cases is the legal principle that students of school age possess an entitlement to public school attendance. As such, they shall not be denied admission or placement in appropriate classes and schools *solely* because of their marital status or because they are pregnant.

d. *Exceptionality as a Factor.* Court decisions and legislative enactments (federal and state) of the past ten years have mandated that *all* children, including exceptional children, are entitled to admission to and placement in an appropriate, meaningful, and quality education. As one writer has summarized the results of the past decade,

... the "right to education" means that the school systems must provide all children equal opportunities to develop their own capabilities; the school systems thus are required to provide different programs and facilities for pupils with different needs, according to their needs.[100]

Certainly implied in the above statement is the mandate that students of legal age of attendance in public school systems shall not be denied admission or appropriate school and classroom placement solely because they are in some way exceptional or different. They must be provided for.

Beginning with *P.A.R.C. v. Commonwealth of Pennsylvania*

---

98. *Id.* at 1158.
99. *Id.*
100. Turnbull, *Legal Aspects of Educating the Developmentally Disabled* in CONTEMPORARY LEGAL PROBLEMS IN EDUCATION 183 (Topeka, Kansas: NOLPE, 1975).

(1972),[101] the federal courts have firmly brought the Due Process and Equal Protection guarantees of the Fourteenth Amendment into the field of special education. Even though the final consent agreement in P.A.R.C. was only binding on the parties involved, the case served to generate several subsequent class actions, brought on behalf of all types of exceptional children (*e.g.,* mentally retarded, autistic, gifted, language impaired, etc.), each of which ensured them access to an appropriate, meaningful, and effective public education, whatever their unique needs.

Lau v. Nichols was decided by the United States Supreme Court in 1974. A class action, *Lau* was originally brought in a United States District Court by parents of non-English speaking Chinese students in the San Francisco public schools. The plaintiffs sought relief claiming that officials operating the public schools were responsible for their children's "unequal educational opportunities" by failing to provide courses in the English language, which parents alleged violated the equal protection of the Fourteenth Amendment. The district court denied relief, and the circuit court of appeals affirmed that holding, finding no violation of equal protection.[102]

In a decision overturning the circuit court's holding, the United States Supreme Court (Mr. Justice Douglas, speaking for the majority) focused upon the necessity of a public school system providing equal access to a meaningful educational opportunity. In Douglas' words, ". . . there is no equality of treatment merely by providing students with the same facilities, textbooks, teachers, and curriculum." . . .[103]

With Chief Justice Burger, and Justices White, Stewart, and Blackmun concurring, Mr. Justice Douglas rendered the following opinion regarding the notion of an "effective educational program:"

Basic English skills are at the very core of what these

---

101. 334 F. Supp. 1257 (E.D. Pa. 1971); final consent agreement at 343 F. Supp. 279 (E.D. Pa. 1972).

102. 483 F.2d 791 (9th Cir. 1974). The case law discussions beginning with this footnote and ending with footnote 119, are adopted from a lengthier discussion prepared by the author of this Chapter and appearing in Stephen B. Thomas, ed., *Financing Public Schools in Virginia,* 1976.

103. 414 U.S. 565, 94 S. Ct. 786, 39 L. Ed. 2d 1 (1974), at 565.

public schools teach. Imposition of a requirement that, before a child can effectively participate in the educational program, he must already have acquired those basic skills is to make a mockery of public education. We know that those who do not understand English are certain to find their classroom experiences wholly incomprehensible and in no way meaningful.[104]

Serna v. Portales Municipal Schools [105] involved a 1974 class action for declaratory and injunctive relief against a school district in New Mexico, alleging that school officials discriminated against Spanish surnamed students. A United States District Court held for the plaintiff parents and created a bilingual-bicultural school program as relief. The school board appealed this action to the United States Circuit Court of Appeals for the Tenth Circuit.

In their behalf appellee parents claimed and showed that: 1) very little English was spoken by many Spanish surnamed children when they entered school; 2) these children also grew up in a culture totally alien to the one thrust on them in public school; 3) these children were subjected to intelligence tests and achievement tests given totally in English; 4) no bilingual instruction was available in the schools; 5) there were no Spanish surnamed teachers or administrators in any of the individual schools; 6) nothing in the curriculum reflected the historical contributions of people of Mexican and Spanish descent and, as a direct result; 7) there was a higher rate of failure and drop-out among Spanish surnamed children as compared to the other children.[105]

In affirming the lower court decision granting relief to the parents and children, Circuit Judge Hill saw *Serna* as "strikingly similar" to *Lau,* and the emphasis of the Supreme Court on "meaningful educational opportunity." Said Judge Hill,

> . . . we believe the trial court, under its inherent equitable power, can properly fashion a bilingual-bicultural program which will assure the Spanish surnamed children receive a meaningful education.[106]

Berkelman v. San Francisco Unified School District was a 1974 civil rights action taken in a district court, challenging the San

---

104. *Id.*
105. 499 F.2d 1147 (10th Cir. 1974), *aff'g,* 351 F. Supp. 1279 (D.N.M. 1972).
106. *Id.* at 1154.

Francisco Unified School District's standards for admitting students to Lowell High School (an academic, college preparatory high school). A school system policy existed that stated that only applicants whose prior academic achievement placed them in the top fifteen percent of all junior high school graduates in San Francisco would be accepted to Lowell High School. The district court denied relief, and plaintiffs appealed.[107]

In upholding the district court's decision (denying relief), circuit Judge Goodwin was of the opinion that a disproportion of black and Spanish-American students attending Lowell High School did not create a suspect classification, and did not render the system's admissions standards unconstitutional. The school system's legitimate interest in establishing an academic, college preparatory high school outweighed any harm "imagined" or "suffered" by "students whose achievement had not qualified them for admission to that school." [108]

Judge Goodwin then focused on the circuit court's need to ensure that the end product of the admission standards created a meaningful educational setting at Lowell High School when he said:

> The task is to examine the school district's assertion that the standard of past academic achievement substantially furthers the purpose of providing the best education for the public school students in the district. If the past achievement standard does substantially further that purpose, then the district has not unconstitutionally discriminated in its . . . admission policy.[109]

Significantly, Judge Goodwin's notion of meaningful educational opportunity did not equate equality to sameness; rather, he emphasized the need to effectively provide for individual differences in students, as evidenced by the following quotation from his opinion:

> The student whose best performance has demonstrated ability to move at an advanced program will receive a

---

107. Appealed at 501 F.2d 1264 (9th Cir. 1974).

108. *Id.* at 1264. It should be noted, however, that the circuit court struck down as unconstitutional the requiring of higher admission standards for girls than for boys.

109. *Id.* at 1267.

"better" education than he or she would receive if required to work in subject matter and at a pace which does not provide as great an educational challenge. Likewise, a student with an interest in vocational training receives a "better" education if permitted to take vocational courses than if required to continue against his wishes with the "traditional" high school program.[110]

Davis v. Page was a civil rights action (not a class action) brought in a district court in New Hampshire, in 1974. In *Davis,* a father brought action on behalf of his elementary school children on grounds that a local board policy requiring that his children remain in school classrooms where religiously offensive activities and discussions were taking place was unconstitutional. The district court denied relief.[111]

Ruling against plaintiff's claim of exclusive control of his children, District Judge Bownes stated most emphatically that the interests of children "are not coterminous with that of their parents." Nor, he said, are children's rights and interests "limited to those which their parents assert." [112] In Judge Bownes' opinion:

> The balance is a most precarious one. The parents' right to freely exercise their religion and their inherent right to control the upbringing of their children must be weighed against the state's interest in providing its youth with a proper and enabling education and the children's right to receive it.[113]

In summary, Judge Bownes said that parents do not possess a constitutional right to stand between their children and an "effective" education.[114] What is more, "The state has an interest in maintaining and sustaining a coherent and comprehensive educational program." [115]

In re G.H. was a 1974 decision of the Supreme Court of North Dakota. This was an appeal from a juvenile court involving obligations to pay for the education of a school-aged, handicapped girl. Several references to *Rodriguez* and its implications for the

---

110. *Id.*
111. 385 F. Supp. 395 (D. N.H. 1974).
112. *Id.* at 398.
113. *Id.* at 399.
114. *Id.* at 400-401.
115. *Id.* at 404.

rights of children to equal access to a meaningful educational program are contained in the North Dakota court's decision. Examples of such references follow.[116]

"We are satisfied," said Judge Vogel, "that all children in North Dakota have the right, under the State Constitution, to a public school education. Nothing in *Rodriguez* . . . holds to the contrary." [117] Therefore, failure to provide educational opportunity for handicapped children (except those, if there are any, who cannot benefit at all from it) is a constitutional violation.[118] As such, depriving the handicapped girl of a "meaningful educational opportunity would be just the sort of denial of equal protection which has been held unconstitutional in cases involving discrimination based on race and illegitimacy and sex." [119]

There is no doubt that court decisions similar to those cited above, coupled with emerging federal[120] and state statutes, have given birth to a movement in public school systems across this nation. The intent of this movement is for states and their schools to provide an appropriate educational opportunity for all children of school age (whatever their unique needs) — an educational opportunity that ensures basic, minimal quality for each child. As a New York court said recently, where the New York State Constitution mandates a right for *all* children to obtain a free public education, that mandate includes handicapped children.[121]

§ 9.5. Summary.

The legal authority to determine the admissibility of children to public school systems and to place them in appropriate schools and classes is, within the bounds of state law, the local school board's to exercise. Provided the board acts in good faith and does not

---

116. 218 N.W.2d 441 (N.D. 1974).

117. *Id.* at 446.

118. *Id.*

119. *Id.* at 447.

120. *See,* for example, Public Law 94-142, The Education for all Handicapped Children Act (a revision to Part B, Education for all Handicapped Act), enacted in November, 1976. *See also,* P.L. 93-112, 29 U.S.C. 794, § 504, Rehabilitation Act of 1973.

121. Matter of Wagner, 383 N.Y.S.2d 849 (N.Y. 1976).

violate either state or federal law, courts of law will not interfere with board decisions on admission and placement of students.

As demonstrated in this Chapter, court decisions and legislative enactments (federal and state) of the past ten years have mandated that all children, whatever their race, religious belief, socio-economic background, or handicap, are entitled to a meaningful, appropriate, and quality educational opportunity. Contemporary public school boards, administrators, and professional staff members must therefore accept their legal responsibilities to carry out these mandates.

There are also many responsibilities that must be accepted by parents. This Chapter also demonstrates that parents are not completely free to stand between their child and a meaningful educational opportunity. Parents too must possess a bona fide reason for refusing to send their child to school and, they have a legal responsibility to see to it that acceptable educational alternatives are offered when their child is kept out of school.

Chapter Ten

CONTROL AND PUNISHMENT

§ 10.0. In Loco Parentis.

When students are at school, they are expected to submit to school authority. This is necessary in order that teachers may teach and students may learn. In establishing and maintaining a climate conducive to teaching and learning, educators have considerable discretion in controlling student conduct. The legal term for the relationship of educator to pupil is *in loco parentis* (in place of the parent). It was explained by Blackstone in his *Commentaries:*

A parent may also delegate part of his parental

226

> authority, during his life, to the tutor or schoolmaster of his child; who is then *in loco parentis,* and has such a portion of the power of the parents *viz.* that of restraint, and correction as may be necessary to answer the purposes for which he is employed.[1]

As originally conceived, the doctrine of *in loco parentis* was intended to treat discipline matters; however, it was later expanded to include other areas of the school program.

In its original state, *in loco parentis* clothed school personnel with almost unlimited authority in disciplining children. The right extended, not only to the time that students were in school, but also while they were en route to and from school and at school-sponsored activities away from school. Teachers and administrators were consistently upheld in using questionable methods of exacting student obedience, and courts only interfered when it was clearly shown that educators had acted arbitrarily, capriciously, or unreasonably. As a result of this almost unlimited authority, school officials sometimes acted imprudently but with reasonable assurance that their actions would be upheld.

The concept of *in loco parentis* has undergone considerable modification since the Blackstone statement. As a result of court decisions, school authorities now cannot make arbitrary decisions regarding student discipline without being challenged. Further, courts have set conditions that must be met if boards, administrators, and teachers are to be upheld.

This chapter will include an examination of the doctrine of *in loco parentis* as it applies to two basic areas of school control: discipline and search and seizure. Both substantive and procedural aspects of discipline will be studied, and the more recent issue of the application of *in loco parentis* in searching students will also be examined.

§ 10.1. Corporal Punishment.

Corporal punishment denotes the infliction of physical pain upon a student for misconduct. The legal justification for it is found in state statutes. Some states specifically authorize it, some states

---

1. BLACKSTONE, COMMENTARIES OF THE LAWS OF ENGLAND, 453 (T. Cooley, ed. 1884).

specifically forbid it, other states do not mention it but by implication authorize or allow it. New Jersey and Massachusetts forbid it by statute, and Maryland forbids it by a policy of its State Board of Education. The policy of the Pennsylvania Board of Education forbids it unless a local school board elects to authorize it.

Where corporal punishment is allowed, it must conform with the law of reasonableness. That law has been derived from lower court decisions through the years.

a. *Supreme Court Decisions.* In 1975 and 1977 the Supreme Court of the United States spoke for the first time on the legality of corporal punishment. Each time it upheld the practice. In the first case, *Baker v. Owen,*[2] the Court affirmed without comment a decision of a federal district court out of North Carolina that allowed teachers to administer corporal punishment. Further, it was allowable, in spite of an objection by the child's parents. However, for a teacher to be protected, four guidelines must be observed: 1. Students must be warned in advance as to the kinds of behavior punishable by paddling. 2. It must not be used as a first-line of punishment for misbehavior. 3. A second school official must be present to witness the paddling. 4. Parents, on request, must be furnished a written statement of the paddling, including the reasons for it and the names of the witnesses.

This opinion should not be construed as meaning that it is applicable to all states when, in fact, it applied only to North Carolina.

In the second case out of Florida, the Supreme Court in 1977 ruled that since the Eighth Amendment is applicable only in criminal matters, it does not protect one who has been corporally punished, even when it is severe.[3] The Court held further that a student is not entitled to notice and a hearing prior to corporal punishment in that both require time, personnel, and a diversion of attention from normal school pursuits.

b. *Legal Guidelines.* Where corporal punishment is allowed, it must conform to the laws of a state as well as to the law of reasonableness. Through the years, courts have spelled out some

---

2. Baker v. Owen, 395 F. Supp. 294 (M.D.N.C. 1975), *aff'd mem.,* 423 U.S. 907 (1975).

3. Ingraham v. Wright, 430 U.S. 651, 97 S. Ct. 1401, 51 L. Ed. 2d 711 (1977).

general guideliness as to what constitutes reasonable corporal punishment. A few cases will be given to illustrate each guideline, and they will be drawn from recent opinions.

1. IT IS CONSISTENT WITH STATUTORY LAW.[4] Where statutes authorize or allow corporal punishment, a student has little chance of overturning the legislation. Where it is forbidden, a teacher will not be protected unless it was used in self-defense or in protecting the lives and property of others.

In a 1973 case out of Vermont, a student was charged with sending a vulgar note to a fellow classmate, and for that he was spanked. He challenged the law as being vague, overbroad, and in violation of his Fourteenth Amendment rights. The court upheld the law and rejected each of the student's contentions.[5] In contrast, a 1976 decision out of Missouri upheld the dismissal of a teacher for repeatedly resorting to corporal punishment outside the scope of school board policy. Specifically, and in spite of warnings, she had slapped students on the face, a violation of the local policy. The state's Supreme Court upheld the dismissal.[6]

2. IT IS FOR CORRECTION. Like a parent, a teacher may occasionally need to resort to corporal punishment as the best means of bringing a child to obedience. When one acts with the same kind of authority and in the same manner that a parent would, the teacher will be upheld. An example is a 1975 case out of Louisiana.[7] It initially involved a fight by two eighth grade students and, although the teacher separated them, they resumed fighting. The teacher then grabbed the boys and threatened to send them to the principal, whereupon one of the boys cursed him and threatened reprisal by his father. The teacher then paddled the boy with a wooden paddle, the boy cursed him again, and the teacher turned him over his knees and paddled him again. The court held for the teacher, recognizing that, like parents, teachers have the right to administer corporal punishment for good cause.

3. IT IS NOT CRUEL OR EXCESSIVE. If educators used excessive

---

4. This guideline and the six others that follow are adapted, in part, from EDWARD C. BOLMEIER, LEGALITY OF STUDENT DISCIPLINARY PRACTICES, 63 (Charlottesville: The Michie Company, 1976).

5. Gonyaw v. Gray, 361 F. Supp. 366 (D. Vt. 1973).

6. Board of Educ. v. Shank, 542 S.W.2d 779 (Mo. 1976).

7. Roy v. Continental Ins. Co., 313 So. 2d 349 (La. App. 1975).

force in disciplining students, they will not be upheld. Further, they may be sued for criminal liability. The determination of what constitutes cruel or excessive punishment is determined by the factual situation. A classic example is a 1967 court decision which did not uphold a teacher.[8] The teacher who stood 6'2" and weighed 230 pounds, subdued a student in his physical education class who was 4'9" and weighed 101 pounds. In squeezing the boy's chest and shaking him, the teacher broke the boy's arm. The court did not accept the teacher's actions as being necessary to his self-defense but rather saw him as exerting excessive force on his pupils.

Recent allegations have involved, not so much charges of excessive punishment but rather unusual punishment. Persons bringing such complaints have attempted to protect students from paddling by elevating students' rights to protection under the Eighth Amendment. Although there have been a few decisions to the contrary, lower courts have, for the most part, been reluctant to give students this protection. A 1974 decision out of the Eighth Circuit held that excessive corporal punishment may be cruel and unusual.[9] That same year the Seventh Circuit held that pupils who were administered corporal punishment in a state correctional institution were subjected to cruel and unusual punishment in violation of the Eighth Amendment.[10]

The specific question was answered by the Supreme Court of the United States in 1977 [11] when it ruled 5-4 that two junior high school students, spanked for misconduct, were not subject to Eighth Amendment protection. Although there was evidence that the students had been badly whipped, corporal punishment, no matter how severe, was insufficient to create a violation of the Eighth Amendment. The Court ruled that it was the intent of the Eighth Amendment to apply only to situations involving criminal punishment. Regarding the issue of excessive punishment, the Court stated:

> If the punishment inflicted is later found to have been excessive — not reasonably believed at the time to be

---

8. Frank v. Orleans Parish School Bd., 195 So. 2d 451 (La. 1967).
9. Bramlet v. Wilson, 495 F.2d 174 (8th Cir. 1974).
10. Nelson v. Heyne, 491 F.2d 352 (7th Cir. 1974).
11. Ingraham, *supra*.

necessary for the child's discipline or training — the school authorities inflicting it may be held liable in damages to the child and, if malice is shown, they may be subject to criminal penalties.[12]

The four dissenting Justices felt that the Eighth Amendment should apply. Speaking for the minority, Justice White observed that if the same beatings had been inflicted on a criminal, they likely would not have passed constitutional muster.

4. IT LEAVES NO PERMANENT OR LASTING INJURY. This standard implies that a student may have a temporary injury and still have no case against a teacher or administrator who disciplined him. Courts have consistently ruled this way. However, where the reverse is true and lasting injuries do occur, one may be liable. The testimony of experts is often called on for analysis and verification of one's injuries. In one case, a doctor who examined a boy testified that the spanking was excessive, and he prescribed tranquilizers for him. The teacher had paddled the child, age eleven, for defiance on the playground. The court agreed that the punishment was excessive.[13] In another case, a student charged a teacher with assault and battery when, while being removed from class, the boy shoved his hand in a glass window and sustained severe cuts. Here the court ruled in favor of the teacher, whose actions had been reasonable in attempting to correct the obstreperous pupil.[14] A Pennsylvania court decided for a student who was struck on the head, knocked against the blackboard and furniture, and subjected to ridicule during class.[15]

5. IT INVOLVES NO MALICE. If a teacher is angry when administering corporal punishment, that individual's actions will not be upheld. The object of corporal punishment is correction of the child, not revenge on the part of the teacher. A court ruled in 1961 that a teacher's discipline was in anger.[16] A student was told to remove gloves belonging to another student. Before he could do so, the teacher struck him on the ear, bursting an eardrum.

---

12. *Id.* at 1415.
13. People v. Ball, 58 Ill. 2d 96, 317 N.E.2d 54 (1974).
14. Simms v. School Dist., 508 P.2d 236 (Ore. App. 1973).
15. Landi v. West Chester Area School Dist., 353 A.2d 895 (Pa. 1976); Caffas v. Board of School Directors, 353 A.2d 898 (Pa. 1976).
16. Tinkham v. Kole, 110 N.W.2d 258 (Iowa 1961).

6. It Suits the Age and Sex of the Child. The law of reasonableness applies here. It would be unreasonable to paddle an eighteen year old senior, for other forms of discipline may serve better. It would also be unreasonable for a female teacher to paddle a high school male; likewise, for a male teacher to paddle a high school female. However, in a 1963 case, a male teacher slapped a fifteen-year-old girl twice — lightly and without anger — and was protected. He did this after persuasion had been unsuccessful. Although he had been given orders not to spank students at the school, a psychiatric hospital, the court upheld him, ruling that his authority can be no more questioned than that of parents.[17]

A Texas court considered a student's weight, among other factors, in upholding school officials who had spanked a boy for unexcused absences.[18]

7. It Involves an Appropriate Instrument. Various kinds of implements have been used to paddle students, and the efficacy of them has been considered by the courts. The use of a wooden paddle has been upheld.[19] A twelve-inch ruler has been held to be a reasonable instrument.[20] A paddle three inches wide and twenty inches long, used excessively, creating psychological trauma involving medication, was not upheld.[21] Striking a student on his ear was not upheld.[22] Slapping a student on his face has not been upheld.[23] For the most part, it has not been the instrument itself that is questionable, but rather the part of the person to which it is applied, the degree to which it is used, and the end result of the spanking. If the punishment results in more than temporary pain or injury, the teacher will not be upheld.

Through the years courts have upheld corporal punishment as a legitimate means of disciplining students. That position has not changed in recent years.[24] Attempts to give constitutional

---

17. Indiana State Personnel Bd. v. Jackson, 192 N.E.2d 740 (Ind. 1963).
18. Coffman v. Kuehler, 409 F. Supp. 546 (N. D. Tex. 1976).
19. Roy, *supra.*
20. People v. DeCaro, 17 Ill. App. 3d 553, 308 N.E.2d 196 (1974).
21. People v. Ball, *supra.*
22. Tinkham, *supra.*
23. Landi, *supra.*
24. In the 1970's the courts have upheld and protected teachers and administrators in the use of corporal punishment in the following cases: Ware v. Estes, 458 F.2d 1360 (5th Cir. 1972); Sims v. Board of Educ., 329 F. Supp. 678

protection to students against its use have failed. Students do, however, have recourse against its excessive use, and those avenues have always been available. Otherwise, the *in loco parentis* doctrine still applies with respect to the use of corporal punishment.

§ 10.2. Sanctions.

Employed less frequently as a disciplinary tool than corporal punishment, "sanctions" is another method that some school officials have used in punishing students. It is designed to deny a student a privilege or to penalize an individual for what he has otherwise earned. Although there are unofficial reports of its use in a number of schools, there are very few cases that have been litigated in the courts. These cases have involved denying a person the right to participate in graduation exercises and lowering a student's grade. For the most part, school officials have not been upheld in applying such sanctions. A major justification is that, what a student has already earned, he is entitled to.

The earliest case involved three girls who refused to wear graduation caps and gowns because of their alleged odors.[25] The girls were punished by not being allowed to participate in graduation exercises and their diplomas were withheld. The court ruled that the students could be prohibited from participating in graduation exercises but the diplomas could not be withheld since all requirements for graduation had been completed.

In a more recent case involving graduation, a New York court

(D. N.M. 1971); Gonyaw v. Gray, 361 F. Supp. 366 (D. Vt. 1973); People v. DeCaro, 17 Ill. App. 3d 553, 308 N.E.2d 196 (1974); Gordon v. Oak Park School Dist., 24 Ill. App. 3d 131, 320 N.E.2d 389 (1974); Roy v. Continental Ins. Co., 313 So. 2d 349 (La. App. 1975); Baker v. Owen, 395 F. Supp. 294 (M.D.N.C. 1975), *aff'd mem.*, 423 U.S. 907 (1975); Coffman v. Kuehler, 409 F. Supp. 546 (N.D. Tex. 1976); Sims v. Waln, 536 F.2d 686 (6th Cir. 1976); Jones v. Parmer, 421 F. Supp. 738 (S. D. Ala. 1976); Ingraham v. Wright, 430 U.S. 651, 97 S. Ct. 1401, 51 L. Ed. 2d 711 (1977). During the same time the courts have not upheld teachers and administrators in their use of corporal punishment in the following cases: Johnson v. Horace Mann Mut. Ins. Co., 241 So. 2d 588 (La. 1970); Nelson v. Heyne, 491 F.2d 352 (7th Cir. 1974); Bramlet v. Wilson, 495 F.2d 714 (8th Cir. 1974); People v. Ball, 58 Ill. 2d 36, 317 N.E.2d 54 (1974); Hogenson v. Williams, 542 S.W.2d 456 (Tex. App. 1976); Board of Educ. v. Shank, 542 S.W.2d 779 (Mo. 1976).

25. Valentine v. Ind. School Dist., 191 Iowa 1100, 183 N.W. 434 (1921).

ruled that a girl should be allowed to participate in graduation exercises.[26] She had been punished for having allegedly assaulted the principal. The court viewed the punishment as unrelated to the offense and not suited for attaining desirable educational results of the school system.

Two cases in the 1970's have treated the subject of lowering of grades as a sanction. One was decided in favor of the student, the other in favor of the school board. The Illinois case upheld a school board policy that provided for the reduction of a student's grades as punishment for unexcused absences.[27] The specific penalty involved a drop of one letter grade for each class missed. The court reasoned that the sanction was helpful in discouraging truancy which is itself an indication of a lack of effort. Conversely, good grades are dependent on effort, including class attendance.

A Kentucky court decision is in conflict with the above opinion. The case grew out of a policy providing for a five-point reduction of a grade for each unexcused absence during a nine-month period. In declaring the regulation invalid, the court held that the school was justified in suspending the student but not in lowering the grade.[28] The court refused to decide the constitutionality of such a rule, but it held that the board was without power to authorize the punishment since it was not provided for in the statutes governing student conduct.

A different issue concerned a student who wore a black armband to graduation exercises. A letter of recommendation to a college contained that information, and the student sought to have it restricted from his permanent record. The court allowed the information to stay, for the data had been recorded objectively and no punitive intent could be ascertained from the school having recorded it.[29]

§ 10.3. Exclusion from School.

a. *Substantive Due Process.* It is well established that school authorities may exclude from school students whose conduct

---

26. Ladson v. Board of Educ., 323 N.Y.S.2d 545 (N.Y. 1971).
27. Knight v. Board of Educ., 38 Ill. App. 3d 603, 348 N.E.2d 299 (1976).
28. Dorsey v. Bale, 521 S.W.2d 76 (C. A. Ky. 1975).
29. Einhorn v. Maus, 300 F. Supp. 1169 (E.D. Pa. 1969).

interferes with the operation of the schools and who defy school regulations. Like the doctrine of *in loco parentis,* the authority to exclude students rests in statutory law.

The two terms which characterize exclusion are suspension and expulsion. Suspension denotes the temporary exclusion from school and is the prerogative of a teacher or administrator, according to a given state's statutes. Explusion denotes a longer term of exclusion, varying from a specified number of days to the end of a school term. A board of education is vested with the authority of expulsion.

Through the years courts have not interfered with the substantive right of school officials to exclude students. Although in recent years many courts have increasingly recognized the value of children remaining in school and in acquiring an education, they also accept the necessity of suspending or expelling students for very serious misbehavior.

The nature of the misbehavior warranting exclusion may vary, as is revealed in a study of a number of court decisions on this subject. The three cases that follow serve as examples.

Recent judicial thinking has held that not all proscribed behavior has to be spelled out specifically in a student code before one can be punished. A student is entitled, however, to be informed about questionable or "gray areas" of conduct which may lead to exclusion. Such regulations as "flagrant disregard of teachers," "loitering in areas of heavy traffic," and "rowdy behavior in areas of heavy traffic" were specific enough to justify thirty-day suspensions, according to a federal district court in Pennsylvania.[30] The Supreme Court of Connecticut held that a state statute authorizing expulsion of students for "conduct inimical to the best interests of the school" was vague and unenforceable because no standards had been set for implementing it.[31] The permanent expulsion of two girls who deliberately planned and attacked a fellow pupil was upheld. The victim was kicked, beaten, and stabbed in the head with scissors.[32]

Often accompanying the exclusion of a student is the obligation of the school district to provide him with the opportunity for

---

30. Alex v. Allen, 409 F. Supp. 379 (W.D. Pa. 1976).
31. Mitchell v. King, 363 A.2d 68 (Conn. 1975).
32. Fortnam v. Texarkana School Dist., 514 S.W.2d 720 (Ark. 1974).

alternative instruction, if the child and his parent cannot afford to pay for the costs themselves. This position was underscored by the Fifth Circuit in 1974:

> In our increasing technological society getting at least a high school education is almost necessary for survival. Stripping a child of access to educational opportunity is a life sentence to second class citizenship unless the child has the financial ability to migrate to another school system or enter private school.[33]

b. *Procedural Due Process.* Courts have been more active over the last two decades with respect to the procedural rights of students who are to be excluded from school rather than with the authority of the school to exclude them. Although some states have had statutes on their books for many years that guaranteed to students certain elements of procedural due process, the matter was not seriously challenged in courts until the 1960's. *Dixon v. Alabama State Board of Education,* the precedent-making decision, involved a case in higher education where students were expelled or placed on probation for a sit-in at a lunch counter.[34] The students were disciplined without any notice of charges, nor were they granted a hearing. This case established the right of students in a public institution of higher education to notice and a hearing prior to suspension or expulsion, a right protected by the due process clause of the Fourteenth Amendment. Specifically, a student was entitled to (1) the names of witnesses against him, (2) an oral or written report on the facts to which each witness testified, (3) an opportunity to present his defense of the charges against him, and (4) an opportunity to produce oral or written testimony of witnesses in his behalf.

The question of the applicability of *Dixon* to the elementary and secondary school setting was not answered for several years. In the meantime, the Supreme Court of the United States ruled on the procedural due process rights of young people with respect to juvenile court proceedings. That landmark 1967 case, *In re Gault,* established the right of young people to procedural rights under the Fourteenth Amendment prior to being committed to a juvenile

---

33. Lee v. Macon County Bd. of Educ., 490 F.2d 458, 460 (5th Cir. 1974).
34. 294 F.2d 150 (5th Cir. 1961), *cert. denied,* 368 U.S. 930 (1961).

home.[35] The case began with a complaint by a neighbor that Gerald Gault, age fifteen, had made an obscene telephone call to her. Based on that complaint, Gerald was arrested. What followed were a series of steps that the Supreme Court found not to be consistent with the Fourteenth Amendment. No notice was left for Gerald's parents, who were at work and later learned from a neighbor where he was. At the Juvenile Detention Home where Gerald was detained, his parents were informed of a hearing to be held the following day. The arresting officer filed a petition with the Court; the parents saw it after two months had elapsed.

At the initial hearing, the complainant was not present, no one was sworn, no transcript was made, and the only testimony given was by the presiding judge. At the formal hearing approximately one week later, the parents asked that the complainant be present but the request was denied. A conflict developed over who said what. Nonetheless, the judge found Gerald guilty based on his using vulgar, obscene language and for being habitually involved in immoral matters. The latter finding grew out of Gerald's being, at the time, on six months' probation for stealing.

The Supreme Court of the United States decided the case in 1967. It held that a minor in juvenile court was entitled to the following constitutional protection: 1. specific notice of charges against him with time to prepare for a hearing, 2. notification of the right to counsel or, if counsel cannot be afforded, the right to court-appointed counsel, 3. privilege against self-incrimination, and 4. right to confrontation and cross-examination of witnesses. The Court expressed concern for, but did not rule specifically on the constitutional right of appellate review and a transcript of the proceedings.

Gault did not apply specifically to school exclusions, but a number of lower courts began to clarify the procedural due process rights of students in exclusionary hearings. That matter was treated specifically by the Supreme Court in 1975 in *Goss v. Lopez*.[36] It involved the suspension of nine students at several schools in Columbus, Ohio, for a variety of reasons. Under Ohio law, a principal was empowered to suspend a pupil for up to ten

---

35. *In re* Gault, 387 U.S. 1, 87 S. Ct. 1428, 18 L. Ed. 527 (1967).
36. 419 U.S. 565, 95 S. Ct. 729, 42 L. Ed. 2d 725 (1975).

days. He was required to notify the student's parents within twenty-four hours and state the reasons for the suspension. If a pupil or a parent appealed to the board of education, a hearing for the student was then required.

Some of the students denied the misconduct, and the matter was eventually appealed to the Supreme Court. The Court held that in suspensions of less than ten days, a student must be given at least informal notice of the charges against him and the opportunity for some sort of hearing. If he denies the charges, he must be informed of the evidence against him and be given the opportunity to present his side of the story.

The Court did not extend all the standards of *Gault* to a public school exclusionary hearing. It held that a school does not have to allow a student to be represented by counsel, to have witnesses, or to confront and cross-examine witnesses against him.

The Court ruled that a student has an entitlement to a public education, a property right protected by the Fourteenth Amendment. That right can be taken away only by adhering to minimum procedures. In school suspensions, due process is flexible as determined by the nature of the misconduct and the severity of the penalty. The more serious the misconduct and the stricter the penalty, the greater adherence to procedural due process is required. It held that school officials may remove a student from school prior to a suspension if his presence is a danger to persons or property or is disruptive to teaching and learning. The Court did not rule on the elements of due process for suspensions of longer than ten days but observed that more may be needed for students.

One month after *Goss* the Supreme Court handed down another decision that also had some bearing on due process.[37] The case involved the issue of a student's being allowed to sue school board members for damages for a denial of constitutional rights. In this case, the right denied was procedural due process in an expulsion hearing. The Court held that individual school board members could be sued when they denied to students their constitutional rights. On remand to a lower court for a determination of whether due process had been followed in informing students and parents

---

37. Wood v. Strickland, 420 U.S. 308, 95 S. Ct. 992, 43 L. Ed. 2d 214 (1975).

about a hearing, the Eighth Circuit held that the inadequate notice was a violation of procedural due process.[38]

A 1978 decision by the Supreme Court clarified further the above decision. The Court held that, where students have been suspended from school without procedural due process, the students, if not injured, are entitled to recover nominal damages, which the Court set as being $1.00.[39]

That decision grew out of two cases that arose over the suspension of a pupil for allegedly violating a school rule against use of drugs and of another pupil for violation of a rule against males wearing earrings. The two cases were consolidated before the Supreme Court. The Court ruled that before damages are awarded, one must first submit proof that actual injury was caused by a denial of procedural due process.

Another ruling by the Supreme Court in 1978 clarified the rights of students in exclusionary hearings. This case, involving higher education, reaffirmed that academic discipline is the province of scholars, not courts.[40] A student dropped from a medical program for lack of progress in the clinical work was not entitled to due process protection granted to students in exclusions for behavior reasons. The Court recognized that the breaking of school rules was not an issue; rather the discipline hinged on the perceptions of the student's supervisors about her progress in the program. Their judgment was sufficient to support a cause for removal.

In less than two decades, the Supreme Court has handed down several decisions as to what constitutes minimal due process for students. It has required some schools to afford students more rights than they had and to require some schools to do less than they are now doing. Beyond the Supreme Court guides, a local administrator is bound also by state law. Thus, requirements may be compatible with the Fourteenth Amendment and still vary from state to state. They may also vary depending on the circumstances

---

38. Strickland v. Inlow, 519 F.2d 744 (8th Cir. 1975).

39. Carey v. Piphus, 435 U.S. 247, 98 S. Ct. 1042, 55 L. Ed. 2d 252 (1978).

40. Board of Curators of the University of Missouri v. Horowitz, 435 U.S. 78, 98 S. Ct. 256, 54 L. Ed. 2d 171 (1978). For a discussion of the case, see Thomas J. Flygare, *The Horowitz Case: No Hearing Required for Academic Dismissals,* 626-27 PHI DELTA KAPPAN, 59 (May, 1978).

of a given situation. Given those conditions, the following standards generally apply.[41]

1. NOTICE OF CHARGES. It is accepted now that, before a student can be excluded from school, he must first be given notice of the charges against him. The notice may be oral if there is no question or disagreement about the student clearly having been engaged in the misconduct. For the most part, written notice is preferred and should state the specific charges against the student, the school policy or rule that was broken, and the date, time, and place of the hearing. The student should be advised of his rights in the hearing, although a *Miranda* warning need not apply. He should also be advised that he can waive a hearing and have an informal conference with the principal for a disposition of the matter. Although it is not formally required, a copy of the notice should be given to both the student and his parents. Specific state statutes or local board policies may require procedures with respect to the content and delivery of the notice.

2. RIGHT TO A HEARING. Courts have consistently ruled that a court-like atmosphere does not have to govern a disciplinary hearing.[42] A school disciplinary hearing is an administrative hearing, not a trial. Thus, it may be conducted with a degree of informality. It must be conducted, however, with fairness. As a minimum, this requires that a student be given the opportunity to present his case, after he has had sufficient time to prepare for it. Although courts have not spelled out what constitutes sufficient time, presumably from one to five days is adequate. The difference in time would depend on the complexity and severity of the incident.

Most hearings might be held in the principal's office with the student, his parents, and witnesses present.

3. RIGHT TO COUNSEL. Courts are divided on the question as to whether a student can have counsel. It is understood that parents may be present to advise their child; it is less clear that legal counsel are entitled to represent him. Some courts have ruled

---

41. For a more thorough treatment of the elements of procedural due process, *see* ROBERT E. PHAY, THE LAW OF PROCEDURE IN STUDENT SUSPENSIONS AND EXPULSIONS, Topeka: National Organization on Legal Problems of Education, 1977.

42. Madera v. Board of Educ., 267 F. Supp. 356 (S.D.N.Y 1967), 386 F.2d 778 (2d Cir. 1967), *cert. denied,* 390 U.S. 1028 (1967).

that an attorney may be present but he may not engage in an adversary relationship; that is, he may be available to counsel his client but not cross-examine or refute testimony.

There is some legal weight that in an expulsion hearing in which the school board attorney plays a prominent role, a student should also be entitled to have an attorney represent him.

4. WEIGHT OF EVIDENCE. Again, the formal rules of evidence that govern a court trial do not apply in an exclusionary hearing.[43] Prior to suspension of students, a student should have the opportunity to examine the evidence against him, question the individual conducting the hearing, and refute testimony of witnesses. Only when it is ascertained that the charges can be supported by substantial evidence or guilt beyond a reasonable doubt, should one be declared guilty of the charges.[44] That standard eliminates a lesser one of circumstantial evidence or the preponderance of the evidence. It also implies that an administrator may no longer take, as accepted or unquestioned fact, the statement of a person reporting a student for violation of school rules, if the student denies it.

5. CALL OF WITNESSES. Court decisions are not in full agreement with respect to the right of a student to confront, cross-examine, and compel witnesses to appear. In some states, school boards have subpoena power while it is lacking in others. A number of recent court decisions have held that confronting and cross-examining witnesses is fundamental to due process.[45]

6. PRIVILEGE AGAINST SELF-INCRIMINATION. The Fifth Amendment protection against self-incrimination does not apply to school disciplinary proceedings; it applies only to criminal proceedings. The testimony given by a student in a school disciplinary hearing can later be used in a criminal proceeding, although a student may then object to the use of statements made at the school hearing.

Courts have also held that disciplining a student for breaking a school rule by school officials and trying that individual for the

---

43. Boykins v. Fairfield Bd. of Educ., 492 F.2d 697 (5th Cir. 1974), *cert. denied*, 420 U.S. 962 (1975).

44. *In re* Winship, 397 U.S. 358, 90 S. Ct. 1068, 25 L. Ed. 2d 268 (1970).

45. Givens v. Poe, 346 F. Supp. 202 (W.D.N.C. 1972); Smith v. Miller, 514 P.2d 377 (Kan. 1973).

same offense in a court case does not constitute double jeopardy, a concept which applies only to criminal proceedings.

7. RIGHT TO A TRANSCRIPT. Courts are not in agreement as to whether a student, as a matter of right, is entitled to a transcript of the proceedings.[46] It would seem proper to supply him with one, the cost to be borne by him.

8. RIGHT TO APPEAL. A number of states provide some mechanism for a student to appeal an adverse exclusionary decision. Typically, it may go through the Department of Education or directly into the courts. Increasingly, students have resorted to federal rather than state courts and sought an exclusionary reversal on the basis of a denial of due process under the Fourteenth Amendment.

In recent years the procedural due process rights accorded students in school disciplinary hearings have undergone clarification. This clarification has resulted essentially in placing restrictions on administrative and school board authority before a student can be suspended or expelled. Unquestionably, students have due process rights, and the nature and extent of these rights vary with the circumstances. The key elements that have guided judicial decision-making have been fairness and reasonableness. Where both have been applied, school officials have usually been upheld. Where they have not been applied, students have usually won.

§ 10.4. Search and Seizure.

a. *The Constitutional Issue.* One of the recent areas involving the control of student behavior has been the matter of search and seizure. School administrators have been called upon to search students and their property, principally for harboring or dealing in drugs. These searches have prompted the question of the applicability of the Fourth Amendment to the United States Constitution to the school setting. That amendment provides:

> The right of the people to be secure in their persons, houses, papers, and effects, against unreasonable searches and seizures, shall not be violated, and no

---

46. Buttny v. Smiley, 281 F. Supp. 280 (D. Colo. 1968); Pierce v. School Comm., 322 F. Supp. 957 (D. Mass. 1971).

Warrants shall issue, but upon probable cause, supported
by Oath or affirmation, and particularly describing the
place to be searched, and the persons or things to be
seized.

The Amendment does not define what constitutes a legal search
nor does it specify what constitutes an unreasonable one.
Consequently, the courts have been asked to clarify these two
questions. The Amendment guarantees to citizens the right to be
secure against governmental intrusion with respect to their
property and possessions. A citizen is protected to the extent that
limitations are placed upon government in order to insure
unwarranted intrusion by it into a person's property and
possessions. This restriction does not insulate a citizen from any
and all searches; rather he is protected only from unreasonable
searches and seizures. The Amendment requires that three
elements be present in order for a search to be legal: the issuance
of a warrant based upon probable cause, an oath supporting the
necessity of the search, and specific identification of the elements
to be searched.

Initially, the Fourth Amendment restricted the federal
government only. It was not until 1949 that it was made applicable
to the states through the incorporation, by implication, of the
Fourth Amendment, into the Fourteenth.[47]

The Fourth Amendment applies specifically to law enforcement
officials and criminal cases. Less vigorous and exacting standards
apply to school officials when they engage in a search. In order for
a search to be legal, it must be directed toward maintaining a
climate so that the school can function as an educational institution.
Unquestionably, a school official may search a school in the normal
course of his duty, such as insuring the safety of the building from
fire hazards and in insuring that the premises are free of
unsanitary conditions and hazardous materials.

A more serious question arises with respect to the application
of the Fourth Amendment to a school official's search of a student,
his property, and his possessions. To date, most courts have
distinguished between the rigid standards governing search by law
enforcement officials and the standards governing search by

---

47. Wolf v. Colorado, 338 U.S. 25, 69 S. Ct. 1359, 93 L. Ed. 1782 (1949).

school officials. This distinction has been enunciated in clarifying school disciplinary proceedings and criminal indictments. That is, a penalty exacted by a school administrator is less severe than that handed down by a court; consequently an educator is not subject to all the standards of justice that courts must observe.

One of the reasons for the lack of understanding of the Fourth Amendment and its application to juveniles stems from the actual role of the school administrator in a search. As it concerns the seizure of materials, the Amendment is not applicable to private persons. The question then arises as to whether a school official is viewed as being an agent of the state and thus subject to the limitations of the amendment, or whether he is considered as being a private individual, acting *in loco parentis*. Some courts have held that, within the meaning of the Fourth Amendment, school officials are not actually functioning as governmental agents. This interpretation does not mean that the Amendment is entirely inapplicable to students, for it does place limitations on the authority of school officials, namely, to have probable cause for a search.

As a priviate individual, a school official has considerable autonomy in conducting searches and seizures. In doing this, it is expected that he exercise initiative and reasonable judgment in determining if a student is harboring illegal or unsafe materials, has broken a school rule, or is creating problems inimical to the safety and welfare of others. Where there has been reasonable cause to believe that a student meets one of the above conditions, the administrator has been upheld in conducting a search; furthermore, he has been expected to do it as a duty. The legal question has centered around the circumstances under which the search was conducted and the admissibility of evidence growing out of the search.

b. *Consent to Search.* In a number of instances school officials have searched students, their property, and their possessions with or without the person's consent. In some cases a search has been made without the student's knowledge. Where consent has been freely and knowingly given, one cannot later challenge the evidence seized in the search.[48]

---

48. *In re* State in Interest of G. C., 121 N.J. Super. 108, 296 A.2d 102 (1972), citing State v. King, 44 N.J. 346, 209 A.2d 110 (1965); Schaffer v. State, 5 Storey 115, 184

Where consent has not been given, courts have had to determine if the search was valid. Two cases are illustrative. In 1969 a California court held that a search without consent was legal.[49] It recognized that the greater interest accrued society by protecting itself from drug users and possessors than in upholding an individual's rights. In this case, the vice-principal conducted a search of a student's locker after he received information that one could purchase Methedrine pills from her. The search was upheld on the grounds that the administrator was acting as a private individual, preserving order, and functioning *in loco parentis.*

The other case involved the search of a student's person.[50] After receiving information that the boy had marijuana, the principal summoned the student to the office and directed that his pockets be emptied. At first the student refused but later complied. The court held that the principal's conduct was necessary and proper in maintaining order and discipline.

To date, courts have not required that, in the search of lockers, students must first give consent. In the search of a student's person, administrators have usually refrained from actually coming into physical contact with the individual but instead have directed that he empty his pockets or other effects. That strategy, in effect, constitutes student consent.

c. *Probable Cause.* A reasonable school search is one conducted by a superior charged with the responsibility for maintaining discipline and order and security. A student's rights must yield when there is danger of the institution's being undermined as an educational enterprise. Where there is a reasonable belief that one has narcotics in his possession, this constitutes probable cause for a search.

In determining whether or not a particular search is reasonable when conducted by school officials, one must consider two factors: the nature of the place to be searched and the purpose for which the search is conducted.

1. THE NATURE OF THE PLACE. School property is state

A.2d 689 (Del. Super. 1962), *cert. denied,* 374 U.S. 834 (1962); People v. Fahrner, 213 Cal. App. 2d 535, 28 Cal. Rptr. 926 (1963).

49. *In re* Donaldson, 269 Cal. App. 2d 509, 75 Cal. Rptr. 220 (1969).

50. M. by Parents R. and S. v. Board of Educ., 429 F. Supp. 288 (S.D. Ill. 1977).

property whose title rests with the local board of education. Although schools often supply lockers to students, the state retains control of them. One reasonable stipulation restricting the use of a locker is that it must not contain anything in violation of law. "Not only have the school authorities a right to inspect but *this right becomes a duty when suspicion arises that something of an illegal nature may be secreted there.*" [51]

In *State v. Stein,* the court differentiated between school property and other kinds of property. A school locker is not like a house, a car, or a private locker which connote private possession. A student may have exclusive control of his locker as opposed to fellow students, but that possession is not exclusive against the school and its officials. [52]

A different kind of possession relates to the search of an individual and his own property. A student's car has different characteristics of ownership from a student's locker. In *Keene v. Rodgers,* the question arose as to the legality of the search of a student's automobile on campus. [53] The car was draped with flags, and desecration was suspected. On orders from their superordinates, two campus officers searched the vehicle. The owner assisted by unlocking the car without protest. Inside were found frayed flags, a can of beer, and a bag of marijuana, all in violation of the school's code of behavior. The search was deemed to be proper, and this decision extended the jurisdiction of an administrative search from school-owned property to student-owned property on campus.

This principle extends, for the most part, to the search of a student's person. In large measure this has amounted to a student searching himself. When this issue is examined in more detail later in this chapter, some exceptions will be noted.

2. THE PURPOSE OF THE SEARCH. A principal is responsible for the safety and welfare of students in his school. He is expected to protect a student from himself as well as the greater school population. Whenever an administrator has sufficient reason to

---

51. People v. Overton, 301 N.Y.S.2d 479, 249 N.E.2d 366, 367 (1969).

52. State v. Stein, 203 Kan. 638, 456 P.2d 1 (1969), *cert. denied,* 397 U.S. 947 (1970).

53. Keene v. Rodgers, 316 F. Supp. 217 (D. Me. 1970). *See also* Speake v. Grantham, 317 F. Supp. 1253 (S.D. Miss. 1970).

believe that a student may be harboring something illegal or harmful, he has the authority to make the search.

Search by a principal is not without limits. There must be reasonable cause to believe that a student is in possession of something illegal or harmful. This standard will not uphold an administrator engaging in a "fishing expedition" or conducting a search without good reason. When he is acting within the scope of his authority and with good cause, a school administrator does not have to have his search measured legally against that of a police officer.

The standard governing the source of information leading to a search is not as rigid as that which applies to information given a policeman. The source of information need not be corroborated for purposes of reliability.[54]

Probable cause exists when one has knowledge of or information about the existence of illegal or dangerous materials on campus. For example, the following set of facts gave an administrator sufficient cause to search a student: 1. He had information that the student had sold drugs on campus earlier in the day. 2. He had observed bulges in the student's pockets. 3. He had observed a pouch tied to the student's belt. 4. The student had shown the contents of the pouch (money) but not the contents of his pockets. The student initially resisted in a search of his pockets, and all these circumstances provided sufficient cause for the search.[55] Probable cause existed when a student, caught smoking, was ordered to empty his pockets which held marijuana.[56]

In contrast, a New York court agreed that school officials had insufficient cause to engage in a particular search.[57] A teacher had observed a teen-age boy entering a restroom twice within an hour and leaving each time within five to ten seconds. The student had been under observation for six months for possibly dealing in drugs. During this time he had also been seen eating with a student, also under suspicion. In the judgment of the teacher, these circumstances constituted unusual behavior. The teacher then

---

54. *In re* C., 26 Cal. App. 3d 403, 102 Cal. Rptr. 682 (1972); People v. Young, 90 Cal. Rptr. 924, 12 A.3d 878 (1970).

55. *In re* C., *supra.*

56. Nelson v. State, 319 So. 2d 154 (Fla. App. 1975).

57. People v. D., 34 N.Y.2d 483, 315 N.E.2d 466 (1974).

reported the matter to a second teacher, the coordinator of security. The coordinator then reported the matter to the principal who ordered that the boy be brought to the office. Before the boys' dean and the principal, the security officer searched the boy. After finding thirteen glassine envelopes in the boy's wallet, the coordinator then had the boy stripped. A vial containing nine pills was uncovered.

While recognizing that school authorities have broad authority in maintaining discipline, the court resolved the immediate issue by weighing the interest of society against an individual's rights. In this case, the individual's rights were deemed to be paramount. Probable cause did not exist. The limited information had failed to make a sufficient case for the search. The court also deplored the indignity done the student by forcing him to strip by pointing out the possible psychological damage that can be done to a sensitive young person.

Teachers of a fifth grade went too far in conducting a strip search for $3.00 reportedly having been stolen from another student. The court held that the search went too far in subjecting all students to it.[58]

d. *Administrative v. Police Searches.* For a number of decades courts have differentiated between searches by private individuals and those by governmental officials. The Supreme Court ruled nearly six decades ago that the Fourth Amendment was designed to restrain governmental authority and no one else.[59] Searches by governmental officials must comply with considerably stricter standards than those done by persons not acting in a governmental capacity. The general rule has been that evidence obtained in an illegal search and seizure by a private individual is admissible in a criminal proceeding. In marked contrast, evidence taken in an illegal search by law enforcement officials is inadmissible.

Courts have looked to the initiator of the search in determining the degree to which one is bound by the Fourth Amendment. It has been established that school administrators do not need a warrant when acting *in loco parentis*. When they initiate a search but later call on a policeman for assistance, the policeman does not need a

---

58. Bellnier v. Lund, 438 F. Supp. 47 (N.D.N.Y. 1977).
59. Burdeau v. McDowell, 256 U.S. 465 (1921).

warrant. However, if the policeman initiates a search, he needs a warrant, even if school officials cooperate with him.

It has been held that where police are regularly assigned to a school, they are less subject to the requirements of the Fourth Amendment than are those not attached to it. In *Waters v. United States,* the court held that the range of a school's security officer was not as extensive, without a warrant, as that of a school administrator.[60]

The courts are not in full agreement as to whether a school administrator is a government official for purposes of search. The distinction is acute in terms of its application to the school setting, for it dictates the degree of autonomy that an administrator has under or outside the Fourth Amendment.[61]

An administrator acting under the color of a private individual — *in loco parentis* — would be able to admit evidence gathered in a search even if it was held to be illegal. If he were acting under color of the Fourth Amendment — as an agent of the state — evidence seized in an otherwise illegal search would be inadmissible. For the most part, courts have ruled that school administrators are not bound by the Fourth Amendment.

e. *Illegal Searches.* In consistently upholding the searches that school administrators make, courts have clothed principals with considerable discretion. With very slight exceptions, the courts have seen the officials as acting responsibly, based on information they had and in displaying reasonableness in the search itself.

It is possible, however, for a search to go beyond the limits which a court will accept as being reasonable. When that happens, an injured party may properly have recourse against the administrator. More specifically, he may sue under the Civil Rights Act of 1871, Section 1983, referred to in Chapter Four. Under this act several junior high school students brought action against school officials, Chester City, and city police for what they charged

---

60. Waters v. United States, 311 A.2d 835 (1973).

61. *See,* for example, People v. Stewart, 63 Misc. 2d 601, 313 N.Y.S.2d 253 (1970); Moore v. Student Affairs of Troy State Univ., 284 F. Supp. 725 (N.D. Ala. 1968); Piazzola v. Watkins, 316 F. Supp. 624 (M.D. Ala. 1970). Contrast with State v. Baccino, 282 A.2d 869 (Del. Super. 1971); People v. Jackson, 65 Misc. 2d 909, 319 N.Y.S.2d 731 (1971); State v. Young, 234 Ga. 488, 216 S.E.2d 568 (1975), *cert. denied,* 423 U.S. 1039 (1975).

as being an illegal search.[62] After a child complained of a ring having been stolen, the principal and assistant principal initiated a search of eight girls. They were unsuccessful and proceeded to call police. When the police were unsuccessful in questioning the girls, they brought in a police matron who subjected the girls to a strip search. The search did not uncover the ring.

The court could not determine to what degree the school administrators were possibly liable for the search, for although they had initiated it, they relinquished the assignment to police. What was not clear was whether the school officials had made threats to the girls which forced them to succumb to the searches. Similarly, suit against the city chief of police and the superintendent of schools was not dropped, for it had not been determined whether these two persons had had knowledge of the incident and failed to take action to prevent it. The court held that the nature of the act rather than the status of individuals governed the action taken under color of law.

What the court did hold was that the search had exceeded the bounds of necessity. Although the court did not say so, presumably a stolen ring is not so serious a problem as the use of narcotics on campus. A more likely reason was the nature of the search itself. The students were submitted to an indignity not commensurate with the gravity of the problem.

Before the case could be resolved on remand, an out-of-court settlement was made. Each of the girls was awarded $800.00 in damages, to be paid, in part from the city, county, and school district.

In one of the more recent cases involving Louisiana law only, the state's Supreme Court held that a student is afforded the same Fourth Amendment rights as adults when a search results in a criminal prosecution.[63] Unlike earlier cases, the court here ruled that a student does not shed his Fourth Amendment rights when he enters the school campus. The case grew out of a teacher searching a boy's oversized wallet locked in safekeeping while the student was engaged in physical education. The teacher had

---

62. Potts v. Wright, 357 F. Supp. 215 (E.D. Pa. 1973).

63. State v. Mora, 307 So. 2d 317 (La. 1975), *vacated and remanded,* 423 U.S. 809 (1975); 330 So. 2d 900 (La. 1976).

suspected that the student had narcotics based on his having turned his back while filling the storage bag with his wallet, furtive actions, and difficulty in placing his wallet in the bag. Subsequent examination of the wallet revealed narcotics.

In a 1976 Illinois case, a court held that the search of junior high school students was illegal.[64] Similarly, policemen who had joined in the search on the basis of a request by the principal, were also held in violation of the students' constitutional rights. The court ruled that probable cause did not exist; no drugs were found in the search.

Courts have been consistent in upholding administrators in their search of lockers and student vehicles on campus. It is recognized that neither should harbor something harmful or illegal. Courts are not in complete agreement about the search of a student's person. It is acceptable for a student to search himself but having him undress completely or to his underwear exceeds the bounds of necessity and prudence.

Searches have been upheld where probable cause existed. The circumstances of each case determine if probable cause applied. The benefit of the doubt is given to the administrator. However, in the few cases where he is viewed as functioning as an agent of the state, he is held to requirements of the Fourth Amendment.

---

64. Picha v. Wielgos, 410 F. Supp. 1214 (N.D. Ill. 1976).

Chapter Eleven

EXPRESSION

§ 11.0. Introduction.

Throughout the early history of public education in this nation, students usually played a submissive role within their schools. With few exceptions, the general rule was that students did not express themselves in ways deemed "unacceptable" by their administrators and teachers. Typically, students dressed in particular ways prescribed by a school dress code, spoke out in class only when encouraged to do so by their teachers, and usually abstained from placing any items in school publications which had not received prior approval of the school administration or their faculty sponsor.

Beginning in the 1960's, however, the scene began to change. At first, the college campus served as a base for launching a new breed of more activist students, determined to express their beliefs on current political and social issues, and to express their individuality as persons.[1] Gradually, this activist spirit and behavior began to filter down to high schools and even to elementary schools across this country. A new era of student expression was born, resulting in an avalanche of litigation challenging school policies and rules governing student expression.

---

1. *See,* for example, Dixon v. Alabama State Bd. of Educ., 294 F.2d 150 (5th Cir. 1961), *cert. denied,* 368 U.S. 930 (1961).

§ 11.1. Expression Defined.

According to *Black's Law Dictionary,* to express is to make something known (in words) distinctly and explicitly so as not to be left to inference or implication.[2] Generally, individuals in our society express themselves in a variety of ways. Some of these ways are: the written word, pictures and drawings, gestures, symbols, and the spoken word. Given a particular situation, one or a combination of these means might prove more effective than the others in making an individual's feelings, beliefs, or wishes known to others.

The First Amendment to the United States Constitution contains the following language:

> Congress shall make no law ... abridging the freedom of speech, or of the press; or the right of the people peaceably to assemble, and to petition the government for a redress of grievances.[3]

Nowhere in the above statement is the word "expression" used — nor does that word, itself, appear elsewhere in the body of the Constitution. Thus, over the years, mainly through the process of selective incorporation, the federal courts have acted to create the substantive right to freedom of expression.

In the era of the 1960's, federal courts expanded the First Amendment's free speech clause. In addition to covering such matters as students speaking out on campus, also included were such matters as student attire (dress), students wearing symbolic armbands, buttons, and badges, and student hairstyles. All such actions by students came under the purview of the constitutional protection of free speech.[4] Add to that the application of the free press, assembly, and redress for grievances guarantees (also made applicable to public school systems through the Fourteenth Amendment), and it is obvious that student expression in schools underwent radical change. It must be stated at the outset, however, that expression available to students in public schools has

---

2. BLACK'S LAW DICTIONARY 691 (4th ed. 1968).

3. Passed by Congress, September 25, 1789; ratified December 15, 1791.

4. For an excellent article on point, *see* C. Smith, *The Constitutional Parameters of Student Protest,* 1 J. OF LAW AND ED. 39 (January, 1972).

never been judged as absolute, nor has it been equated to freedom of expression available to adults in the community.

§ 11.2. Student Appearance as Expression.

Until recent years, most public school systems in this nation maintained strict rules and regulations concerning student appearance while in the school and in attendance at school functions. Generally, these rules and regulations were the responsibility of building principals to enforce, and were justified as necessary to protect the school's learning environment from disruptive reactions of the majority of students to nonconventional modes of dress and attire worn by other students. Additionally, some school boards and administrators justified codes governing student appearance as necessary to inculcate proper moral, spiritual, and civic values in public school students.

In the past, courts of law were reluctant to substitute their judgments for those of school officials in matters of student appearance. *Pugsley v. Sellmeyer* (1923),[5] offers a good example of this early attitude.

The Clay County, Arkansas, school board had a policy that read: "The wearing of transparent hosiery, low-necked dresses or any style of clothing tending toward immodesty in dress, or the use of face paint or cosmetics, is prohibited." [6] Pearl Pugsley, then 18 years old, who knew of the school policy, came to school one day with talcum powder on her face. A teacher told Pearl to wash her face and to not come to school again with powder on. Pearl disobeyed the mandate, refused to comply with the school policy, and showed up again wearing face powder, whereupon she was denied admission to school. Pearl's father brought suit challenging the reasonableness of the school policy.

Convinced that the school board policy was reasonably calculated to promote school discipline, the Supreme Court of Arkansas denied Pugsley's appeal for remedy. What is more, the Arkansas Supreme Court was convinced that Pearl Pugsley should demonstrate obedience and respect for duly constituted authority,

---

5. 158 Ark. 247, 250 S.W. 538 (Ark. 1923). For another early case on point, *see,* Stromberg v. French, 143 So. 2d 629 (Ala. 1931).

6. *Pugsley, Id.* at 538.

"an essential lesson to qualify one for the duties of citizenship. . . ." [7]

The judicial attitude of noninterference expressed in *Pugsley* was, with few exceptions, generally held by subsequent courts through the late 1960's. For example, in *Leonard v. School Committee*,[8] a 1965 case involving a student hair length regulation, the Supreme Judicial Court of Massachusetts held that school officials had the right to order a student to get his hair cut. The student's parents had claimed in court that school officials could not bar their son from attending classes solely because his hair was grown well over his ears. The hair appearance of a student, they argued, is in no way connected to the successful operation of a public school.

In holding for the school system, the Massachusetts court was convinced that family privacy must give way to reasonable school regulations calculated to protect the rights of other students, teachers, administrators, and the community. And, because of this, the high court would not substitute its judgment for that of the school committee, unless it can be shown that the committee acted arbitrarily or capriciously.

Ferrell v. Dallas Independent School District (1968),[9] offers another example of judicial noninterference in school regulations proscribing student appearance. In *Ferrell,* three male students were denied enrollment in a Dallas, Texas, high school because of their "Beatle-type" hair cuts. Members of a musical group, the students claimed that their hair style was a necessity to their role as musicians and was acceptable as judged by standards within their field of entertainment.

The principal of the high school required that the three boys have their hair trimmed before they could be admitted to his school. He was of the opinion that the length and style of the boys' hair, unless cut, would be so distractive as to cause a disturbance in school.

Taking their case ultimately to the United States Court of Appeals for the Fifth Circuit, the boys argued that the school regulation was not only unlawful under the constitution and

---

7. *Id.* at 539.
8. Leonard v. School Comm. of Attleboro, 212 N.E.2d 468 (Mass. 1965).
9. 392 F.2d 697 (5th Cir. 1968).

statutes of their state, but was also violative of the Fourteenth Amendment to the United States Constitution. The substance of their claim was that they were being discriminated against because of their hair length.

Upholding the school regulation and the principal's ultimatum, the Fifth Circuit Court opined that the Constitution does not establish an abolute right to free expression and that this right can be infringed upon by the state where a compelling reason exists to do so. In *Ferrell*, the compelling reason for the hair regulation and the principal's haircut order was obvious; namely, the maintenance of an effective and efficient school.

a. *Tinker v. Des Moines.* Beginning in the late 1960's, court attitudes regarding student appearance began to change. Two important cases marking the emergence of a new judicial standard are: *Burnside v. Byars* (1966),[10] and the landmark case from the United States Supreme Court, *Tinker v. Des Moines* (1969).[11]

In *Burnside,* students in an all-Negro high school in Mississippi sought injunctive relief against the enforcement of a school regulation forbidding the wearing of freedom buttons in school. Their principal mandated that they could not wear the buttons in school. He based his order on two reasons. First, because the buttons (which read: "One Man One Vote," "SNCC") did not have any bearing on their education. Second, the wearing of the buttons would "cause commotion" in the school.

Losing their case before the trial court, the students appealed to the United States Court of Appeals for the Fifth Circuit. In their appeal the students argued that wearing the buttons was an exercise of free speech, protected by the First Amendment of the United States Constitution. The appellate court agreed with them and reversed the trial court with directions to invalidate the rule.

Convinced that children in public schools do have a First Amendment right to express ideas (a substantive right), the Fifth Circuit Court was of the opinion that school authorities must therefore show a compelling reason for violating that right. And,

---

10. 363 F.2d 744 (5th Cir. 1966). It should be noted that the same court, on the same day, reached the opposite result when presented with different facts in a similar case, Blackwell v. Issaquena, 363 F.2d 749 (5th Cir. 1966).

11. 393 U.S. 503, 89 S. Ct. 733, 21 L. Ed. 2d 731 (1969).

since it could not be shown by school authorities that the wearing of the buttons had actually and materially disrupted the school, the principal's prohibition and ultimate action were unreasonable.

In 1969, the United States Supreme Court heard *Tinker v. Des Moines,* an Iowa case involving student appearance, in the form of symbolic expression. This time, however, the matter involved students wearing black armbands to protest the Vietnam war.

A group of adults and parents had decided to publicize their objections to the war in Vietnam and their support of a truce by wearing black armbands during the holiday season and by fasting on December 16 (1965), and New Year's Eve. Hearing of the plan, the principals of the Des Moines schools met and adopted a policy that any student wearing an armband to school would be asked to remove it, and if he refused he would be suspended until he returned without the armband.

Aware of the regulation, John Tinker, Mary Beth Tinker, and Christopher Eckhardt wore black armbands to school and were sent home until they would come back without their armbands. They did not return to school until after the planned period of protest had expired.

Claiming civil rights deprivations under 42 U.S.C. Section 1983, the students (through their fathers) sought nominal damages and injunctive relief in a United States District Court. Holding that the action of the school authorities was reasonable in order to prevent disturbance, the district court dismissed the complaint.[12] On appeal, the United States Court of Appeals for the Eighth Circuit affirmed the lower court decision.[13]

The United States Supreme Court rendered a decision in *Tinker,* on February 24, 1969. The high court reversed the lower courts and remanded the case. In the opinion of this nation's court, "... undifferentiated fear or apprehension of disturbance is not enough to overcome the right to freedom of expression." [14] The school regulation in question, said Mr. Justice Fortas, violates the constitutional rights of students if it cannot be justified "by a showing that the students' activities would materially and

---

12. *See* 258 F. Supp. 971 (D. Iowa 1966).

13. 383 F.2d 988 (8th Cir. 1967) (1968).

14. 393 U.S. 503, 507.

substantially disrupt the work and discipline of the school." [15] Thus, the *Tinker test* of "material and substantial disruption" came into being and became the major tool for judicial analysis when working to settle student expression litigation.

The impact of the *Tinker test* was far-reaching. Cases continued to come before the courts (federal and state), involving issues of student expression.

A 1974 decision from the Supreme Court of Virginia offers an example of the *Tinker test* being applied. The case, *Pleasants v. Commonwealth,*[16] involved the Hanover County, Virginia, public school system.

The defendants and thirty-four other students were arrested, charged with unlawful trespass, and ultimately convicted in County Court, for their activities while engaged in a protest on the grounds of Patrick Henry High School. The protestors were demanding that the principal immediately readmit to school some recently suspended students. The principal refused to meet the demand and the protest became progressively noisier and more disruptive.

The students appealed their conviction to the Supreme Court of Virginia, presenting two arguments. First, as bona fide students at Patrick Henry High School they had a right to be on school grounds, during the school day, absent the violation of some written regulation of the school board. Second, they argued that their protest on school grounds was constitutionally protected by the First Amendment, citing the *Tinker* decision as controlling.

Regarding their first point, the Virginia Supreme Court was of the opinion that the school principal acts as a duly authorized agent of the school board. As such, he is charged with the duty of maintaining order and discipline in the school. In doing so, said the court,

> ... he was vested with the inherent power to revoke, for good cause, the right of any student to remain on school property when that student alone or in concert with others, disrupted regular school activities or the maintenance of good order and discipline.[17]

---

15. *Id.* at 740.
16. 203 S.E.2d 114 (Va. 1974).
17. *Id.* at 116.

That the principal is duty bound to take reasonable measures to restore order, was the opinion of the court.

Appellants' reliance on *Tinker* was likewise not acceptable to the Virginia Supreme Court. After reiterating the importance of First Amendment rights of students in school the court focused on the facts presented in *Pleasants.* Certainly, said the Virginia court, students can freely express themselves. They may not, however, "... do so in a manner which would materially and substantially interfere with discipline and good order in the operation of the school or with the rights of others." Such behavior, it concluded, is not immunized by the guarantee of free speech.[18]

b. *Student Appearance Post-Tinker.* Not too long after the *Tinker* decision came down, a United States District Court in Connecticut was faced with dress code challenge in *Crossen v. Fatsi.*[19] The code at issue required that all students be neatly dressed and groomed, maintain standards of modesty and good taste conducive to an educational atmosphere, and refrain from wearing "extreme" styles of clothing and grooming.[20]

The plaintiff-pupil claimed that his beard and mustache were not prohibited under the code, because he did not consider it to be an "extreme style or fashion." And, among other things, his appearance was a matter of privacy and personal expression, protected by the United States Constitution, Ninth and Fourteenth Amendments. At no time, however, did plaintiff claim that his appearance was an exercise of free expression or symbolic speech.

In holding the school dress code unconstitutional the district court made several important determinations, each of which furnishes workable guidelines for school boards and administrators. The court first considered the wording of the regulation, then the purpose of its existence.

The wording of the school code in question, said the court, is too vague and overbroad. "It leaves to the arbitrary whim of the principal, what in fact constitutes extreme fashion or style in the

---

18. *Id.* at 116-117. Justice Harmon quotes directly from *Tinker* at 393 U.S. 503 (1969).

19. 309 F. Supp. 114 (D.C. Conn. 1970).

20. *Id.* at 115-116.

matter of personal grooming. . . ." [21] Thus, the existing rule is "too imprecise to be enforceable. . . ." [22]

Regarding the purpose of the rule, the court resorted to *Tinker*-type language. A code, said the court, ". . . must clearly define the standards and it should be reasonably designed to avoid the disruption of the classroom atmosphere and decorum, prevent disturbances among students, avoid the distraction of other pupils or interference with the educational process of the school." [23] In the instant case the above condition did not exist.

The school district was thus enjoined from suspending or disciplining plaintiff-student, using the existing dress code. Additionally, the student's record was to be expunged of any notations referring to the diciplinary incident.[24]

Massie v. Henry (1972)[25] is another case in point and involved some male high school students in Haywood County, North Carolina. In *Massie,* plaintiff-students had worn their hair and or sideburns at a length in direct violation of a school rule (recommended by a student-faculty-parent committee and adopted by the high school principal). A district court found for the school system, declared the regulation justified, and found that none of plaintiffs' constitutional rights had been denied.[26]

In rendering a decision to reverse the district court, the United States Court of Appeals for the Fourth Circuit was convinced by three factors. First, there was no evidence shown that anyone's health was impaired by the length of the students' hair. Second, no sufficient proof was shown of any "disruptive effect" caused by the plaintiffs' actions. Third, school officials insisting on conformity of students for conformity's sake alone, without having any more compelling reason, was not enough to substantiate the grooming code.

In sum, the Fourth Circuit Court was of the opinion that school officials bear the burden of establishing the necessity of infringing upon a student's freedom. There must be sufficient proof, said the

---

21. *Id.* at 117.
22. *Id.* at 118.
23. *Id.*
24. *Id.* at 119.
25. 455 F.2d 779 (4th Cir. 1972).
26. District Court decision unreported.

Court, that the school action (school rule and its enforcement) outweighs the protection of student rights. As a district court said in deciding a 1973 Massachusetts dress code case, school authorities must show a countervailing interest sufficient to justify intrusion into an area of constitutionally protected right.[27] Absent a clear showing of a connection between the compelling reason or reasons for a dress code and the code itself will cause the code to fail in court.[28]

§ 11.3. Student Publications as Expression.

While federal and state courts have been faced with numerous cases involving student appearance (dress, hair, and other symbolic expression), so too have cases been brought challenging school rules and procedures governing student publications. These "freedom of the press-type cases" have involved both school sponsored and non-school sponsored publications.

a. *School-Sponsored Publications.* Schools officials have legal responsibility for all school sponsored publications. Generally, school authorities may be held accountable for what is said or otherwise depicted in school publications. Thus, school boards and school administrators usually exercise more control over school publications than they do over non-school sponsored publications. As Reutter and Hamilton have stated,

> Publications paid for with school funds or produced as a part of the curriculum of a school are subject to more controls than are papers produced by students off premises. . . . However, the fact that a newspaper is financed by the school does not give the school authorities either the duty or the right to determine content per se.[29]

---

27. Bishop v. Cermenaro, 355 F. Supp. 1269 (D.C. Mass. 1973). For a recent decision upholding a student grooming code (regulating hair style) *see* Royer v. Board of Educ., 365 N.E.2d 889 (Ohio 1977). *See also,* Mercer v. Board of Trustees, 538 S.W.2d 201 (Tex. 1976).

28. Independent School Dist. No. 8 v. Swanson, 553 P.2d 496 (Okla. 1976).

29. REUTTER, JR., AND HAMILTON, THE LAW OF PUBLIC EDUCATION, 554 (2d ed. New York, N.Y.: The Foundation Press, 1976). It should also be said that school officials may not use the power to "cut off funding" to a school publication as a tool of censorship. *See* Joyner v. Whiting, 341 F. Supp. 1244 (M.D.N.C. 1972). *See also* Mississippi Gay Alliance v. Goudelock, 536 F.2d 1073 (5th Cir. 1976), where it

The authors' last point referring to determinations of *content*, has, in recent years, become a very sensitive and litigious issue.

Requiring public school students to submit written material to school authorities for their review, prior to publication in a school sponsored periodical, is not necessarily unreasonable or unconstitutional, per se. Several factors must be taken into consideration before such a determination can be made. For example, one must first identify the presence of or lack of a compelling reason stated by school officials for having a "prior submission" policy. Second, one must ask if students and faculty know of the existence of such a policy, and whether the policy has ever been explained to all students and faculty. A third issue to probe concerns the purpose of the school publication itself. Another area to probe is the language of the school policy. Is the policy definitive and clear in the types of material that are prohibited, or is the policy too broad and vague? Finally, are there procedural safeguards built into the implementation of the prior-submission policy?

Gambino v. Fairfax County School Board [30] is a 1977 decision of the United States Court of Appeals for the Fourth Circuit, and involves the contents of portions of an article submitted for publication, entitled "Sexually Active Students Fail to Use Contraceptives," in *The Farm News,* a newspaper published in the Hayfield Secondary School (a public school in Fairfax County, Virginia).

The article in question was submitted to the school principal for prior review and possible publication in the school paper, a procedure followed (by prior agreement) when material was thought to be potentially controversial. After reviewing the material, the school principal ordered that the students not publish the article as written. The principal considered the portions of the article dealing with information on contraceptives to be in violation of School Board notice 6130, in effect at the time, which prohibited

---

was held that even though a university student newspaper was supported in part by student fees collected by the state university, the First Amendment was applicable only if school officials had also exercised direct control over student publication of material. Financial support alone is not enough to establish "state action." At 1074-1075.

30. 429 F. Supp. 731 (E.D. Va. 1977), *aff'd,* 564 F.2d 157 (4th Cir. 1977).

the schools from offering sex education until a decision had been reached on a proposed program. She said, however, that the rest of the article (containing results obtained from a canvass of Hayfield student attitudes toward birth control), could be published. The students insisted on printing the whole article, as written. The U.S. District Court (Eastern District of Virginia) held for the students, and enjoined the school authorities from prohibiting publication of the entire article in the school newspaper.

On appeal, the school board's major contentions were:

> (1) The first amendment does not apply to *The Farm News* because it is an in-house organ of the school system, funded and sponsored by the Board, and therefore cannot be viewed as a public forum; (2) the school's students are a captive audience because the newspaper is solicited for and distributed during school hours, and students cannot avoid exposure to the controversial article — therefore the public forum doctrine does not apply; and (3) even if the newspaper itself is subject to the first amendment protection, the article is not protected because its publication would undermine a valid school policy which prohibits the teaching of birth control as a part of the curriculum.[31]

In affirming the lower court's decision the Fourth Circuit Court reiterated the district court's opinion that the Fairfax County School Board's general policy toward student publications caused *The Farm News* to be a newspaper established as a "public forum for student expression," thus it came under the First Amendment's protection. What is more, students are not a captive audience simply because they are compelled to attend school. Finally, since the school newspaper was established as a "public forum" and not as an "official school publication," it cannot be viewed as a part of the curriculum. Thus, "the general power of the Board to regulate course content does not apply."[32]

Trachtman v. Anker[33] is another 1977 decision involving prior disapproval by school officials of publication of a sex survey in a student publication. This controversy began when a staff member

---

31. 564 F.2d. 157.
32. *Id.* at 158.
33. 426 F. Supp. 198 (S.D.N.Y. 1977), *aff'd,* 563 F.2d 512 (2nd Cir. 1977).

on *The Styvesant Voice,* a student publication at Styvesant High School, in New York City, submitted a plan to the school's principal, to survey the sexual attitudes of students and publish the results in the *Voice.* The principal denied the request. On appeal to the Chancellor of the New York City Schools and to the school board, the students were subsequently advised that they could not conduct the survey.[34]

Taking their case into federal district court, plaintiff students claimed that the school authorities' actions in prohibiting the distribution of the questionnaire and preventing publication of the results violated the First Amendment. Upon hearing the evidence, the district court judge was convinced that distribution of the questionnaire and information might prove "psychologically harmful" to thirteen and fourteen year old students (ninth and tenth grade) who were "emotionally immature"; therefore, permission to distribute the questionnaire to them could be denied consistent with the First Amendment.[35] However, school authorities could not take such actions when said survey and information was to be made available to "older students." Thus, the psychological and educational benefits to be gained from distribution of the questionnaire to this group of students (eleventh and twelfth grade) and the publishing of the results in the "Voice" for this same group to read could not be prohibited.[36]

On appeal, the case was remanded back to the district court with instruction to dismiss the complaint. According to the United States Court of Appeals for the Second Circuit, "... The First Amendment right to express one's views does not include the right to importune others to respond to questions when there is reason to believe that such importuning may result in harmful consequences." [37] School officials need only show a reasonable basis to justify restraints on secondary school publications, distributed on school property. Reason to believe that "harmful consequences might result to students" offers such a reasonable basis for action and meets the "forecast" requirements set forth in *Tinker.*

---

34. 563 F.2d 512, 514-15.
35. *Id.* at 515.
36. *Id.*
37. *Id.* at 519-20. Supreme Court *review denied,* 435 U.S. 925 (1978).

b. *Non-school Publications.* Courts have consistently held that school authorities have the power to reasonably regulate the time, place, and manner of distribution of nonschool publications on school property, during the school day. School officials have had legal difficulties, however, with prohibitive actions regarding the control of content of nonschool publications.[38]

Even though student publications may be nonschool in origin, school officials still bear the burden of showing compelling reasons for interfering with student First Amendment rights. Usually, rules and regulations for controlling nonschool publications on school grounds built upon the need to protect the school's educational environment from disruption will withstand judicial scrutiny, when put to the test.[39]

Where school officials have reasonable rules and regulations setting requirements for time, place, and manner of distribution of nonschool publications, students are expected to comply with those requirements. Direct disrespect for and disobedience of these reasonable requirements may result in disciplinary actions being taken against the student violators.[40]

In drafting reasonable time, place, and manner prohibitions, school officials must keep in mind that "expression" is involved. Therefore, the statements must be narrowly tailored to further the school system's compelling interest for having the regulations.[41]

School officials must be cautious when establishing rules requiring administrative review and approval of contents of nonschool publicatons prior to their possible distribution on school grounds. In recent years, courts have been reluctant to give unlimited authority to school officials for deciding on the acceptability of materials contained in nonschool publications.[42]

There have been several cases wherein school officials have attempted to forbid the distribution of nonschool materials because they found the contents to be libelous, vulgar, obscene, repulsive,

---

38. 16 A.L.R. (Fed) 189.

39. *Id.* at 196. *See,* for example, Eisner v. Stamford Bd. of Educ., 440 F.2d 803 (2nd Cir. 1971).

40. *See,* for example, Schwartz v. Schuker, 298 F. Supp. 238 (E.D.N.Y. 1969), and Graham v. Independent School Dist., 335 F. Supp. 1164 (S.D. Tex. 1970).

41. McCall v. State, 354 So. 2d 869 (Fla. 1978).

42. Fujishima v. Bd. of Educ., 460 F.2d 1355 (7th Cir. 1972).

or otherwise objectionable. A review of the court decisions on point reveals that the judges themselves cannot agree on the degree of specificity needed to define such terms, and to thus sustain the administrative actions taken.[43] There is general agreement, however, that students must be made aware of a school system's definitions of such terms as obscene, prior to the enforcement of the rule.[44]

Also necessary to establish the reasonableness of prior approval policies is the existence of procedural guidelines for implementation in school situations. *Quarterman v. Byrd* (1971) is an important decision emphasizing the need for procedural safeguards to implement school policy.[45]

In *Quarterman,* a tenth grade student at Pine Forest High School, North Carolina, was suspended from school for ten days and placed on probation. He had violated a school rule which prohibited the distribution of any advertisements, pamphlets, printed material, announcements or other paraphernalia without express permission of the school principal.[46]

Two months later, the same student distributed an "underground" paper in which one of the articles concluded with the following statement (in capital letters):

> "WE HAVE TO BE PREPARED TO FIGHT IN THE HALLS IN THE CLASSROOMS, OUT IN THE STREETS BECAUSE THE SCHOOLS BELONG TO THE PEOPLE. IF WE HAVE TO — WE'LL BURN THE BUILDINGS OF OUR SCHOOLS DOWN TO SHOW THESE PIGS THAT WE WANT AN EDUCATION THAT WON'T BRAINWASH US INTO BEING RACIST. AND THAT WE WANT AN EDUCATION THAT WILL TEACH US TO KNOW THE REAL TRUTH ABOUT THINGS WE NEED TO KNOW, SO WE CAN BETTER SERVE THE PEOPLE!!! [47]

He was again suspended from school for ten school days.

---

43. Baker v. Downey City Bd., 307 F. Supp. 517 (C.D. Cal. 1969), Papish v. Board of Curators, 464 F.2d 136 (8th Cir. 1971), Antonelli v. Hammond, 308 F. Supp. 1329 (D. Mass. 1970), and Koppell v. Levine, 347 F. Supp. 456 (E.D.N.Y. 1972).

44. *See* Vought v. Van Buren, 306 F. Supp. 1388 (E.D. Mich. 1969), and Baughman v. Freienmuth, 478 F.2d 1345 (4th Cir. 1973).

45. 453 F.2d 54 (4th Cir. 1971).

46. *Id.* at 55.

47. *Id.* at 55-56.

The United States Court of Appeals for the Fourth Circuit was not called upon to assess the language in the student publication. Rather, the court was called upon to decide the constitutional validity of the regulation for violation of which plaintiff student was disciplined.[48]

Early in the court's opinion it is made clear that "school officials may by appropriate regulation, exercise prior restraint upon publications distributed on school premises. . . ."[49] Specifically, said the court, ". . . where they can 'reasonably forecast substantial disruption of or material interference with school activities' on account of the distribution of such printed material."[50]

Lacking in the school's regulation, however, and thus making the regulation invalid was the absence "of any criteria to be followed by the school authorities in determining whether to grant or deny permission . . ."[51] to distribute certain materials. Procedural safeguards are needed, said the court, "in the form of 'an expeditious review procedure' . . ."[52] to reach the school authorities' decision to prohibit the distribution.

In 1973, the Fourth Circuit Court applying the *Quarterman test* in *Baughman v. Freienmuth,*[53] set forth specific requirements for establishing reasonable prior regulations. In the statement were the following items:

(1) Prior restraints must contain precise criteria sufficiently spelling out what is forbidden so that reasonably intelligent students will know what they may or may not write.

(2) A definition of the term "distribution" and its application to different kinds of material must be included.

---

48. *Id.* at 57. *See also,* Riseman v. School Committee, 439 F.2d 148 (1st Cir. 1971).

49. *Quarterman, supra,* at 58.

50. *Id.,* In Jacobs v. Board of School Comm'rs, the United States Court of Appeals for the Seventh Circuit made it clear that the occasional presence of "earthy" words in a student publication cannot be found to be likely to cause substantial and material disruption of the educational objectives of a school. 349 F. Supp. 605 (S.D. Ind. 1972), 490 F.2d 601 (7th Cir. 1973), at 610. *Cert. denied,* 417 U.S. 928 (1974).

51. *Id.* at 59.

52. *Id.*

53. *Supra,* note 44.

(3) There must be *prompt* approval or disapproval of what is submitted to school officials for their review.
(4) The results of failure to act promptly must be specified.
(5) An adequate and prompt appeals procedure must be included.[54]

Hernandez v. Hanson[55] is a 1977 decision from a United States District Court in Nebraska. In this case, plaintiffs brought a class action challenging the policies and regulations of the Omaha Public School District which required students to obtain prior approval before distributing literature in the schools on behalf of nonschool sponsored organizations. It was board policy that students, staff members, or the school facilities could not be used in any way to advertise or promote the interests of any community or nonschool agency or organization without prior board approval. Certain procedures were spelled out for individuals to use to gain the necessary prior approval, beginning with submitting a written request to the principal of the school.[56] Also included in the procedures were several reasons why a request might be acted upon unfavorably. For example, when the content of the material is commercial in nature, or sectarian, or obscene (which was defined in detail).[57]

At no time did plaintiffs challenge the prerogative of the board to regulate time, place, and manner of distribution. At issue was the board's right to require prior approval of all material.[58]

In deciding the case, District Judge Denney held that there is nothing, per se, unreasonable in requiring prior approval of written distributions by students so long as procedural safeguards are affected. What is more, the board's outright prohibition of literature that is "sectarian in nature" was valid.[59]

District Judge Denney found fault with the school board's policy to screen all literature meant for distribution to "several students"

---

54. *Id.* at 1351. The need for "reasonably clear" screening procedures is also emphasized in Shanley v. Northeast Ind. School Dist., 462 F.2d 960 (5th Cir. 1972).
55. 430 F. Supp. 1154 (D. Neb. 1977).
56. *Id.* at 1157.
57. *Id.* at 1157-1158.
58. *Id.* at 1158.
59. *Id.* at 1155.

and not to "all students," since it was not likely that "disruption" of the school would occur from such limited distributions. He also was of the opinion that prohibiting material just because it was "commercial" in nature was at odds with the First Amendment.[60]

§ 11.4. Freedom of Association and Assembly.

Americans have long cherished the right to gather together and assemble with others in whom they find a common bond. In our society there exist all kinds of clubs, associations, societies, and other such formalized organizations (both public and private) joined by people who share a common interest or cause. Historically, some organizations have been more acceptable to the greater social system than have others, creating numerous court battles fought to establish and clarify what have come to be called the freedom of association and the right to peaceably assemble.

In recent years public schools have become places where formal clubs and associations of students have become a part of the daily life of the school, with some even having a formal designation as co-curricular. From time-to-time, however, other student organizations and groups have come into existence without the expressed sanction of school officials. In these situations the battles for formal recognition within the school's program have been taken into the courts on First and Fourteenth Amendment grounds. As in other matters discussed in this Chapter, the federal courts have been faced with the problem of determining where, in fact, the student's rights to association and assembly begin, and the school's prerogatives to infringe upon these guarantees begin.

a. *Association. Gay Alliance of Students v. Matthews* is a 1976 decision of the United States Court of Appeals for the Fourth Circuit.[61] In the case, student leaders of the Gay Alliance of Students had submitted to Virginia Commonwealth University officials an application for registration as a student organization with all the rights and privileges granted to bona fide student organizations. Their application was ultimately turned down by the Board of Visitors (the university's governing board).

---

60. *Id.*
61. 544 F.2d 162 (4th Cir. 1976).

Even though the Board did not state any reasons for its disapproval action, it was stipulated by the parties that the Board was motivated by the following: (1) recognizing the Alliance as a campus organization would increase opportunities for homosexual contacts, (2) students, who otherwise might not have joined would tend to do so if the group was recognized, and (3) recognition of the Alliance by the university would tend to attract other homosexuals to the university.[62] The district court had found that no cognizable constitutional deprivation was imposed by withholding recognition. However, the district court did order that the university provide the Alliance with access to school facilities, access to the school newspaper, access to school bulletin boards, and many other privileges. On appeal, the Fourth Circuit Court held that the university's refusal to register the association on the same terms as those applied to other student organizations violated the First and Fourteenth Amendments. Said Judge Winter,

> ... The very essence of the first amendment is that each individual makes his own decision as to whether joining an organization would be harmful to him, and whether any countervailing benefits outweigh the potential harm.[63]

If individuals have a right, said Judge Winter, to associate with others in furtherance of their mutual beliefs, that right is furthered where registration of a group by a university encourages such association.

Regarding the existence of student societies, fraternities, associations, and clubs in public secondary schools, the courts have also attempted to ensure the free association of students. However, state legislatures and local school boards have, over the years, demonstrated considerable control over student organizations, both school sponsored and nonschool sponsored (but existing on school grounds), as an exercise of their authority to protect the educational environment from disruption.

Courts of law have been reluctant to interfere with school board authority and have consistently held that student organizations found to be inimical to the good government of the school, to

---

62. *Id.* at 164.
63. 544 F.2d at 166-67.

discipline, and to student morale must be prohibited within the school. Likewise, the judges have stated that student organizations that cause disruption of the learning environment must be prohibited.[64] As the Court of Civil Appeals of Texas said, in deciding a 1968 case in point,

> ... while the last thing we would wish to do is to interfere with the right of freedom of association or the civil rights of students involved, we must maintain an orderly system of administration of our public schools.[65]

b. *Assembly.* The United States Supreme Court has long declared that holding a peaceful public meeting to conduct a lawful discussion is a constitutionally protected right of all citizens.[66] Equally clear, however, is that public gatherings that became less than peaceful or where speakers incite groups to riot are no longer protected and are therefore subject to governmental control and regulation to preserve law and order.[67]

Lawrence University Bicentennial Commission v. City of Appleton,[68] is a 1976 decision of a United States District Court in Wisconsin. In this case an association of college students had applied for permission to rent the Appleton High School East gymnasium for purposes of a public lecture by Angela Davis. Their application was disapproved by the board of education by a vote of 4 to 2. According to the board, their policy stated that school buildings were not to be used for religious or political activities unless the activity is nonpartisan or nondenominational.[69]

Plaintiffs argued that Ms. Davis' lecture was to be nonpartisan and not political in nature. They also contended that the board had, in the past, allowed other groups to assemble in school buildings (for example, the League of Women Voters) where candidates and holders of political office gave speeches.

No evidence was ever presented to the board of education that violence and disruption accompanied any of Ms. Davis' previous

---

64. *See,* for example, Holroyd v. Eibling, 188 N.E.2d 797 (Ohio 1962), and Robinson v. Sacramento, 53 Cal. Rptr. 781 (Cal. 1966).

65. Passel v. Fort Worth, 429 S.W. 2d 917 (Tex. 1968).

66. *See* De Jonge v. Oregon, 299 U.S. 353, 57 S. Ct. 255, 81 L. Ed. 278 (1937).

67. *See* Feiner v. New York, 340 U.S. 315, 71 S. Ct. 303, 95 L. Ed. 295 (1951).

68. 409 F. Supp. 1319 (E.D. Wis. 1976).

69. *Id.* at 1322-23.

lectures. Nor was there any evidence that any violence would occur at the proposed lecture.[70]

In granting plaintiffs' request for a preliminary injunction and ordering that the student association shall be permitted to use the school's facilities for their lecture, Chief Judge Reynolds found fault with the words "political" and "religious" used in the board policy. The distinctions drawn by such words, he said, ". . . are impermissible because they have the effect of regulating speech on the basis of its content, and this state officials may not do." [71]

No additional evidence was presented by the board to show that the students' use of the gym would interfere with any other scheduled activities. Nor was the format of the lecture anything unusual from that of any other groups using the facility.

Judge Reynolds did not remove the prerogatives of school authorities to control the use of school buildings by groups. He did warn, however, that there are limitations on this authority.

> . . . It is true that the state need not open the doors of a school building as a forum and may at any time choose to close them. Once it opens the doors, however, it cannot demand tickets, of admission in the form of convictions and affiliations that it deems acceptable.[72]

In *People v. Witzkowski,*[73] some university students had received permission from school officials to conduct an "antiwar demonstration" in the south lounge of the student union building. Instead of remaining in the authorized area the students moved, on their own, to a lobby area where they seated themselves on the floor blocking the entrance to a room where the Marine Corps was recruiting. When university security ordered them to leave they refused to do so. After repeated warnings protestors were ultimately arrested.[74]

The student demonstrators were convicted of violating an Illinois statute prohibiting interference with public institutions of higher learning. The Appellate Court of Illinois upheld that conviction. In

---

70. *Id.*
71. *Id.* at 1323.
72. *Id.* at 1324-25.
73. 357 N.E.2d 1348 (Ill. 1976).
74. *Id.* at 1350.

the opinion of that Court, the purpose of the statute was to protect the institutions from disruption and not to suppress free expression. And, the student protestors had been given adequate notice and ample time, prior to their arrest, to vacate the university building.[75]

c. *Time and Place Regulations.* In *Grayned v. City of Rockford,*[76] the United States Supreme Court upheld the prerogative of school officials to forbid deliberately noisy or diversionary activities by students that disrupt or are about to disrupt normal school activities. According to the Court, school officials do not offend the First Amendment by fixing times and places for such activity.

In judging the reasonableness of time and place regulations regarding student assembly, four factors will be considered by the courts. First, the nature of the place where prior control of assembly is made applicable will be considered (the school). Second, the special characteristics of the people present in that place will be examined (the students). Third, the normal pattern of activities conducted in the place will be established (education). Finally, the impact of the assembly activity on those normal activities will be assessed (disruption).[77]

§ 11.5. Flag Salute.

Over the years, there have been incidents in public school systems involving students who refuse to participate in a salute to the American flag and in the recitation of the Pledge of Allegiance. In these situations students have expressed their defiance of such exercises (most of which were required either by state law or school board policy), for a variety of reasons.

In the early cases, deprivation of religious freedom was often cited by those who refused to participate in flag salute ceremonies. The Jehovah's Witnesses organization was one group that took exception to the flag salute exercises in public schools.

Minersville v. Gobitis,[78] decided in 1940, was the first flag salute

---

75. *Id.* at 1353.

76. Grayned v. City of Rockford, 408 U.S. 104, 92 S. Ct. 2294, 33 L. Ed. 2d 222 (1972).

77. *Id.*

78. 310 U.S. 586, 60 S. Ct. 1010, 84 L. Ed. 1375 (1940).

case decided by the United States Supreme Court. In that case, involving Jehovah's Witnesses who saw the local school board's requirement that all students participate in the flag salute as an expression of belief and worship contrary to their religion's dictates, this nation's highest court did not consider the requirement of saluting the flag in any way repugnant to the United States Constitution.

Three years later, however, in *West Virginia State Board of Education v. Barnette*,[79] the United States Supreme Court had another chance to review a flag salute case involving Jehovah's Witnesses. This time the West Virginia State Board of Education required that the salute to the flag become a regular part of the day's activities in every public school of the State, with refusal to participate considered an act of insubordination, dealt with accordingly. Students who were expelled from school for their refusals to salute the flag were denied readmission to the school until they complied with the requirement.

The Supreme Court in *Barnette,* held the flag salute requirement an unconstitutional exercise of governmental authority. To the Court's majority such a requirement "invades the sphere of intellect and spirit which it is the purpose of the First Amendment to our Constitution to reserve from all official control." [80]

In the years following *Barnette,* public school districts enacted policies meant both to preserve the requirement that students salute the flag and to protect the right of students who wish not to participate in the exercise. These policies usually allowed students who objected to the exercise to either leave the room or to stand silently while the pledge of alleginace was said. There have been court cases brought by students challenging such policies.

Generally, recent courts have held that school boards cannot require students to salute the flag. What is more, school authorities cannot require that students, who refuse to participate in the salute to the flag, either leave the place where the exercise is held or stand silently during the exercise. So long as the student who refuses to participate is quiet, and is nondisruptive of the exercise itself or

79. 319 U.S. 624, 63 S. Ct. 1178, 87 L. Ed. 1628 (1943).
80. *Id.*

of the rights of those participating in the exercise, he or she cannot be chastised or in some other way punished.[81]

§ 11.6. Summary.

While student expression remains a sensitive area of school law, the possibility of large numbers of situations reaching the courts is now greatly reduced. Beginning with *Tinker,* the United States Supreme Court developed a manageable judicial standard applied by subsequent courts as they adjudicate student expression cases.

Out of the litigious 1960's came the legal mandate that public school students shall not be deprived of their First Amendment protections while in attendance at school, unless school authorities can show a compelling reason for infringing upon those guarantees. Clearly, student expression that materially and substantially interferes with or disrupts the school's educational environment is not immunized from disciplinary action.

In exercising any form of control over student expression (dress, symbolic expression, oral expression, publications, association, or assembly), contemporary school officials must, in addition to establishing a compelling reason, establish fair procedures for implementing their control action. And, students must know of these procedures before they are applied to their particular matter.

Finally, school authorities are not at liberty to censure student expression solely because they consider the mode of attire or contents of the publication or speech distasteful. The courts require that matters of style preference and taste not be primary motivating factors in making decisions involving the First Amendment.

---

81. *See,* for example, Holden v. Board of Educ., 216 A.2d 387 (N.J. 1966); Frain v. Baron, 307 F. Supp. 27 (E.D.N.Y. 1969); and Goetz v. Ansell, 477 F.2d 636 (2nd Cir. 1973).

Chapter Twelve

RELIGION

§ 12.0. Introduction.

The framers of the federal Constitution included two clauses in the First Amendment that treat religion: free exercise and establishment of religion. The free exercise clause means that a person may believe what he wishes. He may believe in his God or no God, and government will not interfere with that belief. Government may, however, restrict the practice of one's belief if it harms or abuses the rights of others.

The establishment clause means that government is neutral in matters of religion. It does not favor one religion over another, many religions over some, or all religions over none. It does not promote one religious activity over another nor does it compel participation in a religious activity. What many people do not understand is that the United States is not a government of religion; rather, it is a nation of essentially religious people.

In spite of government's professed neutrality in religion, the fact remains that it has not been, nor can it be, completely separated from religion. If it were, policemen and firemen employed by the state or its agents would not answer an emergency call from a parochial school or church. Government does respond to such a call, not in terms of aiding religion but under the umbrella of its police power in which it looks after the health, safety, and welfare of all its citizens.

When this country was in its colonial and early constitutional periods, its schools were largely nonpublic, and their mission was largely theocratic. The aim of many of them was preparing young men for the ministry and all students for personal salvation. However, as states began to organize public schools, the question arose as to the church-state relationship in education. The issue was not as hotly debated then as now, for communities were essentially homogenous and compulsory attendance was not universal.

When there were early challenges to government and to religion or religious practices in the schools, they were based on violations of state constitutions and state statutes. It was not until this century that the federal Constitution was cited in contesting religious practices in schools. Initially, these cases were premised on the Fourteenth Amendment, for it restricted state action, unlike the Bill of Rights, which restricted the federal government. Over a period of years, however, through a number of Supreme Court decisions, the Justices have used clauses in the Bill of Rights to act as a restriction on states as well. This is known as the incorporation doctrine. The free exercise clause was incorporated in 1940 [1] and the establishment clause in 1947.[2]

The incorporation doctrine has also made it easier for people to bring suit against government in matters of religion and education. As a result, in the last four decades people have brought an increasing number of suits against school districts based on the religion clauses.

Another reason for an increase of suits involving religion and education has been an increase in the religious heterogeneity of school communities. Justice Clark pointed out in 1963 that there were 83 sects in this country having over 50,000 members.[3] As of 1977 that number was 95, and there were 110 others having a membership from 1,000 — 50,000.[4]

1. Cantwell v. Connecticut, 310 U.S. 296, 60 S. Ct. 900, 84 L. Ed. 1213 (1940).

2. Everson v. Board of Educ., 330 U.S. 1, 67 S. Ct. 504, 91 L. Ed. 711 (1947).

3. School Dist. of Abington Township v. Schempp, 374 U.S. 203, 83 S. Ct. 1560, 10 L. Ed. 2d 844 (1963).

4. INFORMATION PLEASE ALMANAC 1977, 356-62 (New York: Information Please Publishing Inc., 1977).

This chapter will focus on the major issues involving religion in the public schools. To a limited degree, older state court decisions will be reviewed. For the most part, emphasis will be on decisions of the Supreme Court of the United States with lesser emphasis on recent representative state court decisions.

§ 12.1. Finance of Religious Activities.

a. *Textbooks.* The first real test of the constitutionality of using tax funds in support of education in nonpublic schools culminated in a decision by the Supreme Court of the United States.[5] The action was cited as a violation of the Fourteenth Amendment, since the First Amendment had not yet been made applicable to state action. The litigation arose when the state of Louisiana passed a statute that provided for free textbooks for children in nonpublic schools, the cost to come from public tax funds. The practical effect of the legislation was to help those children enrolled in Roman Catholic schools.

Chief Justice Hughes rendered the decision of the Supreme Court. It refuted the argument that the state was taking public property for private use. The Court reasoned that the child and his parents, not the church, reaped the benefits of the legislation, consequently this action did not relieve the parochial schools of any obligations. Further, the state also benefited since it had an interest in the education of all students.

The Court stated its rationale as follows:

> One may scan the acts in vain to ascertain where any money is appropriated for the purchase of school books for the use of any church, private, sectarian, or even public school. The appropriations were made for the specific purpose of purchasing school books for the use of the school children of the state, free of cost to them.[6]

It was from this decision that the term, "child benefit theory" originated. That term has been used to designate the use of public money, directly or indirectly, in support of a child in attendance at a nonpublic school. The legal reasoning is that a distinction can be

---

5. Cochran v. Louisiana State Bd. of Educ., 281 U.S. 370, 50 S. Ct. 335, 74 L. Ed. 1157 (1930).

6. *Id.* at 374.

made between a child and his school as the beneficiary of state funds. Where it can be shown that the child, not the school, benefits, it is sometimes acceptable. However, if the school is the primary beneficiary, the action will not be upheld. It is this theory upon which a justification has been made for use of tax funds in support of parochial education. Court rulings have differed on the subject.

The *Cochran v. Louisiana State Board of Education* decision has spawned a number of court decisions involving not only the textbook issue but also a variety of welfare legislation as a challenge to the child benefit theory. The Supreme Court has ruled on the specific issue of the legality of a state supplying books for nonpublic school students on three occasions since *Cochran.* Each time it has upheld the practice. The second ruling involved a practice of the state of New York which, in a 1975 amendment to a statute, required the state to loan textbooks at no cost to children enrolled in grades 7-12 in both public and nonpublic schools. The Supreme Court held that the statute neither advanced nor inhibited religion.[7] The books were furnished to children, not to schools. Public school authorities selected them, and the state retained ownership of them.

In a decision treated more fully later in this chapter, the Court upheld the loan of textbooks to nonpublic school children in Pennsylvania.[8] In a 1977 decision out of Ohio, the Court dealt with a variety of issues, the loan of textbooks being only one. It ruled that a state may lend textbooks to parochial school children.[9]

State courts have also ruled on the constitutionality of using tax funds for textbooks for children in parochial schools. More often than not, they have taken a position contrary to the nation's Supreme Court and ruled against the legality of such legislation. These cases have been based on the narrow issue of whether the statute was in violation of the state's constitution and did not consider whether it contravened the federal Constitution. In Oregon the Supreme Court held in 1961 that the child benefit

---

7. Bd. of Educ. of Central School Dist. No. 1 v. Allen, 392 U.S. 236, 88 S. Ct. 1923, 20 L. Ed. 2d 1060 (1968).

8. Meek v. Pittinger, 421 U.S. 349, 95 S. Ct. 1753, 44 L. Ed. 2d 217; *reh. denied,* 422 U.S. 1049 (1975).

9. Wolman v. Walter, 433 U.S. 229, 97 S. Ct. 2593, 53 L. Ed. 2d 714 (1977).

theory could conceivably be modified to include any kind of expenditure for the benefit of the child.[10] It ruled that the concept should be modified; consequently a statute providing for free textbooks to nonpublic school pupils was held to be in violation of the state's constitution.

The Missouri Supreme Court held in 1974 that it was counter to the state's constitution to require school boards to loan textbooks to teachers and pupils in parochial schools.[11] It was also unconstitutional to provide texts to children in private schools. It ruled that when a sect establishes a religious school to promote its tenets, a sectarian purpose is evident. Further, individuals can have and do promote a sectarian purpose.

In *Gaffney v. State Board of Education,* the Supreme Court of Nebraska ruled against a textbook loan statute.[12] It was held to be in violation of the state's constitution which forbade any aid or appropriation to any educational institution not exclusively owned by the state.

The Illinois Supreme Court ruled in 1973 that a textbook loan program to nonpublic school students was unconstitutional.[13] Under the legislation, parents could request specific books from a list maintained by the Superintendent of Public Instruction. These books were to be loaned to parents of nonpublic school students who requested them, provided the district loaned them to public school students. The court held that parents were not entitled to the books as a matter of course, neither had the state a duty to provide them. The court ruled that legislation unconstitutional on the ground that the taxpayers of the local school district pay for the texts of public school students while the state pays for the texts for nonpublic school students.

In contrast to the above five state court decisions outlawing texts for parochial school students at public expense, a decision by the Supreme Court of Rhode Island in 1968 upheld such action.[14] That court ruled that the state statute providing for texts for

---

10. Dickman v. School Dist., 232 Ore. 238, 366 P.2d 533 (1961).
11. Paster v. Tussey, 512 S.W.2d 97 (Mo. 1974).
12. 192 Neb. 238, 220 N.W.2d 550 (1974).
13. People *ex rel.* Klinger v. Howlett, 56 Ill. 2d 1, 305 N.E.2d 129 (1973).
14. Bowerman v. O'Connor, 247 A.2d 82 (R.I. 1968).

children in nonpublic schools was not in violation of either the state
or federal constitutions.

b. *Transportation.* The second area of aid to children in
nonpublic schools to get in the federal courts involved
transportation. Although this subject has prompted litigation since
1912, the first major federal court decision occurred in 1947.[15] It
grew out of a statute in New Jersey that authorized local school
districts to make rules and contract for bus transportation. Ewing
Township authorized reimbursements to parents of children
attending both public and parochial schools. This statute was
challenged as being in violation of the First and Fourteenth
Amendments.

In a 5-4 ruling, the Supreme Court of the United States held that
no denomination could be excluded from the benefits of public
welfare legislation because of their faith or lack of it. Writing for
the majority, Justice Black based the Court's decision on the
establishment clause of the First Amendment. He gave his
definition of that clause:

> The "establishment of religion" clause of the First
> Amendment means at least this: Neither a state nor the
> Federal Government can set up a church. Neither can
> pass laws which aid one religion, aid all religions, or
> prefer one religion over another. Neither can force nor
> influence a person to go to or to remain away from
> church against his will or force him to profess a belief
> or disbelief in any religion. No person can be punished
> for entertaining or professing religious beliefs or
> disbeliefs, for church attendance or non-attendance. No
> tax in any amount, large or small, can be levied to support
> any religious activities or institutions, whatever they
> may be called, or whatever form they may adopt to teach
> or practice religion. Neither a state nor the Federal
> Government can, openly or secretly, participate in the
> affairs of any religious organizations or groups and vice
> versa. In the words of Jefferson, the clause against
> establishment of religion by law was intended to erect a
> "wall of separation between church and state." [16]

The majority held that, against that standard, the establishment
clause had not been violated. The bus legislation was viewed as

---

15. Everson, *supra* note 2.
16. *Id.* at 15.

amounting to a welfare measure in seeing that children arrive to and from school safely. In doing this, the Court held that there was no violation of the federal Constitution. The issue of a violation of the state's constitution was not before the Court. It is significant to note that the decision did not require that transportation be furnished; it held only that a state may provide it.

The Supreme Court refused to hear a federal court decision out of Missouri and thereby upheld the lower court's decision which ruled that a state is not required to furnish transportation to nonpublic school students.[17] More recently, in the *Wolman v. Walter* decision of 1977, the Court held that it was unconstitutional for the state to finance field trips for parochial school students.[18] Like *Everson,* the Court ruled 5-4 on this specific issue. The rationale of this holding was that field trips could presumably be financed for children to go to religious centers or to engage in religious study.

Two other lower federal court decisions also invalidated legislation for transporation for parochial school students. A federal district court in Iowa held that the school district option of providing transportation outside the school district lines advances religious activity and is thus unconstitutional.[19] The federal district court in Rhode Island ruled as unconstitutional a state statute which provided transportation costs for parochial school students.[20]

State court rulings have tended to disallow the use of tax funds in support of pupil transportation to nonpublic schools. The controlling case, decided before *Everson,* was *Judd v. Board of Education,* a 1938 decision out of New York.[21] Here, the court rejected the child benefit theory. It took the position that free transportation for children in parochial and private schools encouraged attendance at those schools. Over three decades later

---

17. Leukemeyer v. Kaufmann, 364 F. Supp. 376 (W.D. Mo. 1973), *cert. denied,* 419 U.S. 888 (1974).

18. Wolman, *supra* note 9.

19. Americans United for Separation of Church and State v. Benton, 413 F. Supp. 955 (S.D. Iowa 1976).

20. Members Jamestown School Comm. v. Schmidt, 427 F. Supp. 1338 (D. R.I. 1977).

21. 278 N.Y. 200, 15 N.E.2d 576 (1938).

an appellate court in New York extended *Judd* when it disallowed field trip transportation for parochial students.[22]

The child benefit theory as applied to transportation was also rejected by the Alaska Supreme Court in 1961.[23] It voided a statute authorizing transportation by holding that the constitution prohibited the appropriation of public money for the support or benefit of any sectarian, denominational, or private school. To hold otherwise would be for the state to give a direct benefit to the schools excluded by the constitution. The Supreme Court rejected it again in 1968 as it applied to transportation of children in private schools.[24]

Two transportation decisions have been rendered by Wisconsin courts. The Supreme Court held in 1968 that if transportation were provided for some children, it would have to be provided to all equally.[25] The issue was whether it was mandatory to bus students to a parochial school. Eight years later, the second decision held that, because a parochial school was situated 130 feet beyond a designated limit meant that transportation was not required.[26] The statute had allowed for transportation of parochial school students five miles beyond the public school district boundaries.

Two state courts have specifically upheld the payment of transportation to nonpublic school students. A Massachusetts court ruled in 1955 that elementary school children in both public and nonpublic schools must be given free transportation.[27] The Illinois Supreme Court upheld a statute requiring local school boards to provide the same transportation for nonpublic school pupils as it did for public school pupils.[28]

This issue is still not resolved as can be seen by the court opinions above. Based on the preponderance of court rulings, federal courts have tended to uphold transportation of nonpublic school students on the ground that it is not in violation of the federal Constitution. State courts have tended to negate statutes on the ground that it

22. Cook v. Griffin, 364 N.Y.S.2d 632 (App. Div. 1975).
23. Matthews v. Quinton, 362 P.2d 932 (Alas. 1961).
24. Spears v. Honda, 449 P.2d 130 (Alas. 1968).
25. Cartwright v. Sharpe, 40 Wis. 2d 494, 162 N.W.2d 5 (1968).
26. Young v. Board of Educ., 74 Wis. 2d 144, 246 N.W.2d 230 (1976).
27. Quinn v. School Comm., 332 Mass. 410, 125 N.E.2d 410 (1955).
28. Board of Educ. v. Bakalis, 54 Ill. 2d 448, 299 N.E.2d 737 (1973).

violates the state's constitution. Thus, a state statute may be legal, according to the federal Constitution and illegal within the jurisdiction of the state's constitution.

c. *Teachers' Salaries.* The use of public tax funds to pay for salaries of teachers in nonpublic schools has not resulted in the amount of litigation as have the two previous issues. This plan was novel in that it did not aid students directly but expanded the concept of child benefit to teachers. This question has reached the Supreme Court of the United States where decisions were handed down in 1971 and 1973. The litigation involved cases out of Rhode Island and Pennsylvania. In each instance the Court declared as unconstitutional the payment of teachers' salaries from tax funds.[29]

Rhode Island's statute authorized the expenditure of state funds to supplement salaries of elementary school teachers in nonpublic schools. These supplements, not to exceed 15 percent of a teacher's current salary, were to be paid directly to the teachers. Other terms of the legislation were that a parochial school teacher's salary, including the supplement, could not exceed that of a public school teacher. The teacher had to be certified by the state and had to teach courses and use materials that were found in the public schools.

Pennsylvania's act authorized the Secretary of Education to purchase specified secular services from nonpublic schools. Among other services, the state would reimburse a nonpublic school for teachers' salaries. This case was combined with the one from Rhode Island for a hearing.

The Supreme Court relied initially on a two-part test, devised in 1963, in determining whether the legislation was legal: 1. Does the act have a secular legislative purpose? 2. Does the primary effect of the act either advance or inhibit religion? The Court then added a third test: 3. Does the act excessively entangle government and religion? The Court concluded that the program did not meet this test under the three guidelines it propounded: the character and purposes of the institutions that are benefited, the nature of the

---

29. Lemon v. Kurtzman; Early v. DiCensio, 403 U.S. 602, 91 S. Ct. 2105, 29 L. Ed. 2d 745, *reh. denied,* 404 U.S. 876 (1971).

aid the state provides, and the resulting relationship between government and the religious authority.

Kuser states that excessive entanglement exists when "a religious institution is required to yield to governmental supervision, regulation, or inspection in exchange for a state-provided benefit, usually financial assistance in some form. These controls are required to assure the use of the benefits provided for secular purposes, not for sectarian purposes in any form." [30]

The Court distinguished how books differ from teacher salaries in terms of child benefit:

> Unlike a book, a teacher cannot be inspected once so as to determine the extent and intent of his or her personal beliefs and subjective acceptance of the limitations imposed by the First Amendment. These prophylactic contracts will involve excessive and enduring entanglement between state and church. [31]

In a decision two years later, the Court ruled that reimbursement due the nonpublic schools prior to the *Lemon I* ruling of 1971 were to be paid. However, no funds were to be transmitted to the schools for services after that ruling. [32]

d. *Tuition.* Following the Supreme Court's decision in *Lemon I*, the Pennsylvania legislature enacted the Parent Reimbursement Act. It was designed to overcome the constitutional infirmity of *Lemon* by aiding parents rather than teachers. It provided for an annual tuition reimbursement to parents of children enrolled in nonpublic schools. It amounted to $75.00 for each elementary school pupil and $150.00 for each secondary school pupil.

The Supreme Court disallowed the plan. [33] The majority saw the state as promoting rather than being neutral in religion. For the majority, Justice Powell noted that the establishment clause does not allow for novel forms of aid.

The *P.E.A.R.L.* decision, also in 1973, involved the legality of

---

30. Edwin Charles Kuser, "Public Education and the First Amendment under the Burger Court" 69 (unpublished doctoral dissertation, Temple University, 1977).

31. Lemon, *supra* at 619.

32. Lemon v. Kurtzman, 411 U.S. 192, 93 S. Ct. 1463, 36 L. Ed. 2d 151 (1973).

33. Sloan v. Lemon, 413 U.S. 825, 93 S. Ct. 2982, 37 L. Ed. 2d 939, *reh. denied,* 414 U.S. 881 (1973).

three provisions of the legislature of New York, two of them treating tuition.[34] One provision was for a cash reimbursement of $50.00 per elementary school child and $100.00 per secondary school child to parents of low income. The second provision was for tax relief for parents who did not otherwise qualify for tuition payments. Parents could deduct a specified amount per child, depending on their taxable income. The Court ruled that the plan was unconstitutional in that it aided religious education. Again, the Court used the three-part test of *Lemon I.* It then concluded that the aid was indirect — to parents rather than to schools — but that did not lessen the fact that it promoted religion.

A state court decision from Illinois in 1973 also invalidated a tuition grant to parents for children attending nonpublic schools.[35] The grant was designed to equalize the per pupil amount contributed by the state to a local school district and was limited to parents whose income was less than $3,000 per year. The state's highest court ruled that this amounted to an establishment of religion.

e. *Maintenance.* The only significant case to date treating the legality of direct grants from tax funds for maintenance and repair services in public schools is *P.E.A.R.L.,* a 1973 decision by the Supreme Court of the United States.[36] The grants were designed to serve schools whose children were from low income areas. An allocation of $30 to $40 per pupil for a building more than 25 years old could not exceed 50 percent of the average per pupil cost of similar services in public schools. The Court held that the plan was unconstitutional in that it advanced religion. There was no safeguard in the statute to prevent schools from using the grant money for facilities furthering religious purposes.

f. *Special Services.* Yet another issue of the use of tax funds in support of parochial schools has been that of financing specialized kinds of services. These services have involved a variety of programs. The Supreme Court has upheld some and overturned others.

---

34. Committee for Public Education and Religious Liberty v. Nyquist, 413 U.S. 756, 93 S. Ct. 2955, 37 L. Ed. 2d 948 (1973). This decision will hereafter be referred to as P.E.A.R.L.

35. Klinger, *supra* note 13.

36. P.E.A.R.L., *supra* note 34.

In *Levitt,* the Court ruled that New York's reimbursement to nonpublic schools for costs involved in testing, records, and reports constituted an impermissible aid to religion.[37] Of the $28 million originally earmarked for this program, most of it went for the administration of teacher-made tests. Since the Court had no assurance that the tests were free of religious instruction, the Court invalidated the plan.

Two years later the Court invalidated two acts of the Pennsylvania legislature.[38] One act provided for auxiliary services for nonpublic school pupils in their schools. These services included counseling, testing and psychological services, speech and hearing therapy, and teaching services for exceptional, remedial, and educationally disadvantaged students. These services were provided by public school teachers employed by the intermediate unit. The Court held that they constituted an excessive entanglement in that there existed a potentiality for fostering religion. It would have required continual surveillance to insure that religion was not involved in the activities. The second act which provided for aid for teaching materials and audiovisual equipment was also invalidated in that it had the primary effect of advancing religion.

In *Wolman,* decided in 1977, the Court ruled specifically on the legality of six kinds of services to nonpublic school pupils in Ohio.[39] Two of those services, field trips and books, have already been treated in earlier sections of this chapter. In its ruling the Court treated each issue separately and looked to the link between the use of public funds and its direct or indirect fostering of religion.

Issue 1. The Court held that states may finance therapeutic, remedial, and guidance counseling services for parochial school children so long as they are not offered at the parochial school. The fact that these services had been offered in parochial schools had invalidated the Pennsylvania plan. The Court recognized that providing these services at neutral sites does not advance religion nor create an excessive entanglement.

Issue 2. States may provide certain diagnostic services —

37. Levitt v. P.E.A.R.L., 413 U.S. 472, 93 S. Ct. 2814, 37 L. Ed. 2d 736 (1973).

38. *Meek, supra* note 8.

39. *Wolman, supra* note 9.

speech and hearing — at parochial schools. These are viewed as being general health services and are unlike some kinds of teaching and counseling which could be tied in more closely with religion.

Issue 3. States may provide parochial schools with standardized tests and test scoring if that service is made available to public schools. Since these tests are prepared and scored commercially, that fact saved them. Local parochial teachers were not involved, unlike the New York plan. The Court saw that the state has an interest in the quality of instruction at both public and parochial schools, and standardized tests give some indication of that quality.

Issue 4. States may not lend wall charts and slide projectors for use in parochial schools. Here, the Court could not separate the secular from the sectarian function of such materials.

Of the six issues, only two Justices, Stewart and Blackmun, voted in the majority on all questions. A total of 16 dissents were recorded, an indication of the lack of agreement of the Justices.

The Illinios case, treated in the previous section, also involved the issue of the validity of state grants for auxiliary services. They included health, guidance, counseling, psychological, remedial, and therapeutic services for children in nonpublic schools. The Court recognized that the health services were secular, but the legislation did not treat all students alike. It reasoned that the state paid for the costs for parochial school students while the taxpayers paid for the costs of public school students. The Court held that the other kinds of services were susceptible to sectarian activities. Consequently, both kinds of services were ruled unconstitutional.[40]

§ 12.2. Activities Involving Religion.

a. *Prayer and Bible Reading.* The practice of Bible reading and having prayers in the public schools has been challenged in lower courts for decades. In a majority of nine cases decided from 1884-1962, the courts upheld the practice of saying prayers. Even more cases were litigated in state courts on the issue of Bible reading, most of them occurring from 1880-1930, and the courts divided on its constitutionality. It was not until the 1950's that these issues got into the federal courts and the 1960's that the

40. *Klinger, supra* note 13.

Supreme Court ruled on their legality, beginning with *Engel v. Vitale.*[41] That case grew out of a recommendation of the Board of Regents of New York State that the following prayer be recited at the opening of the school day:

Almighty God, we acknowledge our dependence upon Thee, and we beg Thy blessings upon us, our parents, our teachers and our country.[42]

Parents objected to the prayer and brought suit. The Supreme Court ruled in 1962 that the state had no business in carrying on any program of government-sponsored prayer. For precedent, it cited history: the persecution of individuals in European countries and subsequent coercion of colonists to subscribe to a given religious model. The Constitution was written to prevent this from occurring, the Court stated through Justice Black, and it was designed so that government would be neutral in matters of religion.

Whereas, in the narrowest sense, *Engel* treated a specific prayer written by a state, it did not deal with the larger question of the legality of other kinds of prayers. That question was decided the following year in *School District of Abington Township v. Schempp.*[43] The case involved the legality of both prayer and Bible reading as devotional exercises at the opening of the school day. The decision was a jointure of two cases, one out of Pennsylvania, the other out of Baltimore. The Pennsylvania case was a challenge to the state statute requiring ten verses of scripture, without comment. Reciting the Lord's Prayer was optional but taken for granted. There was no provision for children not wishing to participate.

The Maryland case was a challenge to the Baltimore ordinance requiring a chapter of the Bible and the Lord's Prayer daily. At first there was no excusal privilege; later one was made.

---

41. Engel v. Vitale, 370 U.S. 421, 82 S. Ct. 1281, 8 L. Ed. 2d 601 (1962).

42. *The Regents Statement on Moral and Spiritual Training in the Schools,* THE UNIVERSITY OF THE STATE OF NEW YORK BULLETIN TO THE SCHOOLS, 94 XXXVIII (December, 1951).

43. *Schempp, supra* note 3.

The two criteria the Supreme Court used in determining the legality of the practice were also used in subsequent rulings:

> [W]hat are the purpose and the primary effect of the enactment? If either is the advancement or inhibition of religion then the enactment exceeds the scope of legislative power as circumscribed by the Constitution.[44]

The Court ruled that the exercises were religious ceremonies and the fact that they took a very small amount of time was irrelevant. "The breach of neutrality that is today a trickling stream may all too soon become a raging torrent and, in the words of Madison, 'it is proper to take alarm at the first experiment on our liberties.' " [45]

The Court made it clear that it was outlawing a religious practice but it was not forbidding the study of religion. Objective study of religion as history or literature or the study of comparative religions would be acceptable.

One year after *Schempp* the Supreme Court was presented with a variety of issues involving religion in the schools. The case was remanded in light of the *Schempp* holding. At its second consideration, the Court ruled that devotional Bible reading and the recitation of prayers were unconstitutional.[46] The Justices dismissed the appeal on the other issues which included observance of religious celebrations, singing religious songs, displaying religious symbols, holding baccalaureate services, and conducting a religious census.

In an opinion by the Second Circuit in 1965, voluntary prayers for kindergarten students were invalidated.[47] Although many parents wanted the prayers, the principal objected. The students had been reciting the following prayer in the morning:

> God is Great, God is Good and we
> Thank Him for our Food, Amen!

---

44. *Id.* at 222.

45. *Id.* at 225.

46. Chamberlin v. Dade County Bd. of Pub. Instr., 377 U.S. 402, 84 S. Ct. 1272, 12 L. Ed. 2d 407 (1964).

47. Stein v. Oshinsky, 348 F.2d 999 (2nd Cir. 1965), *cert. denied,* 382 U.S. 957 (1965).

In the afternoon, students had been reciting the following prayer:

> Thank You for the World so Sweet,
> Thank You for the Food we Eat,
> Thank You for the Birds that Sing —
> Thank You, God, for Everything.

The court held that there is no constitutional duty for a state to permit public prayer in state-owned buildings.

In spite of the Supreme Court decisions on prayer and Bible reading, the practice has not ended. It has continued in many school systems, sometimes in open defiance of the Courts' rulings or in other places in subtle ways. Some of these practices have also been challenged. A federal district court ruled in 1971 that Alabama's statute requiring daily Bible reading violated the establishment clause, and all public schools in the state were ordered to stop the exercise.[48] The Fifth Circuit disallowed a statute commanding the inculcation of Christian virtues in schools.[49] The practical effect of the command was that Bible verses were read over the public address system and Gideon Bibles were distributed. The court held that these exercises advanced or inhibited religion. It had been held twenty-four years earlier that the distribution of Gideon Bibles to children in public schools was a violation of the Constitution in that it favored one religion over another.[50]

Courts have also looked askance at ingenious efforts to use public schools for activities forbidden by the *Schempp* holding. The Third Circuit prohibited a school district in Pennsylvania from permitting voluntary Bible readings and nondenominational mass prayers in school.[51] In rejecting the argument that the prayers were neutral and that the activity was voluntary, the court held neither matter really changed the legality of the activity.

A court also upheld a school board in refusing to allow high school students to use the school premises for voluntary group meetings.[52] Initially, students met before school and offered group prayers. The meetings were begun without the knowledge or

---

48. Alabama Civil Liberties Union v. Wallace, 371 F. Supp. 966 (M.D. Ala. 1971).

49. Meltzer v. Board of Pub. Instr., 548 F.2d 559 (5th Cir. 1977).

50. Tudor v. Board of Educ., 100 A.2d 857 (N.J. 1953), *cert. denied,* 348 U.S. 816 (1954).

51. Mangold v. Albert Gallatin School Dist., 438 F.2d 1194 (3rd Cir. 1971).

52. Hunt v. Board of Educ., 321 F. Supp. 1263 (S.D. W. Va. 1971).

permission of the faculty and administration. No one sponsored the group. After he learned of these meetings, the principal advised the students that their action violated public policy. The court upheld the principal and ruled that disallowing the practice would not deny the students any of their constitutional rights. The court did not wish to sanction an ingenious effort of students to countermand *Schempp,* and it cited a concurring opinion by Justice Frankfurter:

> Separation means separation, not something else. Jefferson's metaphor in describing the relation between Church and State speaks of a 'wall of separation,' not a fine line easily overstepped.[53]

b. *Meditation.* Since courts have made it clear that public schools cannot be used as vehicles for sponsoring prayer and Bible reading as part of devotional exercises, some states and school systems have sought to accommodate individuals and groups advocating some kind of reflective thought at the opening of the school day. The plans have varied but have been similar in that they provide for an individual to engage in prayer and/or meditation as he wishes. The full impact of these kinds of legislation and policies is yet to be examined fully by the courts, but so far they have been looked upon favorably, provided the state's role is clearly neutral. That test was not met in a New Jersey case when a court disallowed a plan whereby students went to the gymnasium at the opening of school, listened to remarks of the Congressional Chaplain as recorded in the *Congressional Record,* and meditated silently on any subject they wished. The court ruled that since the "remarks" were actually the prayer of the Chaplain, the school was sponsoring a religious service.[54]

A different situation occurred in a Massachusetts case. There, the court held that a statute requiring a period of silence at the opening of school is not in violation of the First Amendment.[55] The statute, with its 1973 amendment, provided for meditation or prayer, as the individual wished, although neither was actually

---

53. Illinois *ex rel.* McCollum v. Board of Educ. of School Dist. No. 71, Champaign County, Ill., 333 U.S. 203, 68 S. Ct. 461, 92 L. Ed. 2d 649 (1948).

54. State Bd. of Educ. v. Board of Educ., 108 N.J. Super. 564, 262 A.2d 21 (1970).

55. Gaines v. Anderson, 421 F. Supp. 337 (D. Mass. 1976).

required. The court ruled that the exercise neither advanced nor inhibited religion and there was no coercion for students to participate. "A state statute which mandates a moment of silence in a public school setting is not *per se* an invalid exercise of police power. All that the statute requires students to do is be silent." [56]

In an advisory opinion by the Supreme Court of New Hampshire, the justices agreed that a statute authorizing silent meditation was legal.[57]

c. *Graduation Exercises.* Since the prayer and Bible reading decisions by the Supreme Court, some individuals have challenged the tradition of having religious activities at secondary school graduation exercises. Two cases have treated the matter of having an invocation and a benediction. Both were decided in 1974, and both held that the prayers could be said. In a case out of Pennsylvania, a court ruled that no substantial federal question was presented and there was no evidence that religion was advanced.[58] The ceremony was held to be more of a public ritual than anything else.

In the other case out of Virginia, the court held that any infringement of the establishment clause was minimal.[59] Like the previous case, the judge ruled that the service was ceremonial, not educational or religious. There was no calculated indoctrination in the prayers. "The event, in short, is so fleeting that no significant transfer of government prestige can be anticipated." [60]

The Supreme Court refused to rule on the legality of baccalaureate programs in the *Chamberlin v. Dade County Board of Public Instruction* decision in 1964.[61]

A different question was raised in a 1974 case when parents challenged the legality of holding a graduation exercise in a Roman Catholic church. They took the position that their children could not attend without violating their conscience. The school board's defense was that the ceremonies were the responsibility of the

---

56. *Id.* at 342.

57. Opinion of the Justices, 307 A.2d 558 (N.H. 1973).

58. Weist v. Mt. Lebanon School Dist., 320 A.2d 363 (Pa. 1974), *cert. denied,* 419 U.S. 967 (1974).

59. Grossberg v. Deusevio, 380 F. Supp. 285 (E.D. Va. 1974).

60. *Id.* at 289.

61. *Chamberlin, supra,* note 46.

seniors who determined where they would be held and who the speakers would be. It also added that attendance was voluntary. The court decided that the board could not delegate those kinds of decisions to students. It also held that it was cruel to force some students not to participate because of their religious beliefs.[62]

§ 12.3. Study of Religion.

a. *At School.* After the Supreme Court incorporated the religion clauses of the First Amendment into the Fourteenth Amendment as a protection for citizens from state government, individuals began to challenge long-standing practices involving religious study in schools. They objected to public schools allowing their facilities to be used for study of religion in general and the Bible in particular. The landmark case that clarified the state-church relationship on this question was *McCollum,* decided in 1948.[63] The Supreme Court invalidated a plan whereby a local Council on Religious Education provided for religious instruction for students from the three major faiths in the community: Catholics, Jews, and Protestants. The Council selected and paid for teachers who went into the schools once a week and taught students whose parents requested the course. The denominations were kept separate and nonparticipants studied in another part of the building.

An avowed atheist challenged this practice, and the Supreme Court ruled 8-1 in her favor. The Court saw that tax-supported property was being used to support religious instruction and the state's compulsory education law assisted with the program of religious instruction.

The *McCollum* case did not address the issue of allowing students to leave public schools for religious study, a matter to be treated in the next section. It merely held that teaching of religion within a public school during the day violated the First Amendment.

A case with a similar factual situation was decided in Virginia in 1970. Teachers from a private organization came into the Martinsville elementary schools during school hours to provide

---

62. Lemke v. Black, 376 F. Supp. 87 (E.D. Wis. 1974).

63. McCollum, *supra*, note 53.

religious instruction for children of parents requesting it. The district court held that this created an establishment of religion.[64] It reasoned that if the class were taught within constitutional limits, every student should be required to attend; if the study were necessary for the education of one child, it should be necessary for all.

In a 1977 decision, a California court held that a student Bible club could not meet on school campus during the day.[65] The club's stated purpose was for students to know God better by prayerfully studying the Bible. Its membership was open to those genuinely interested in the club's purpose. The court held that this activity constituted a breach of the establishment clause.

b. *Outside School.* Four years after *McCollum*, the Supreme Court, *in Zoarch v. Clauson*,[66] ruled on the legality of dismissing students from public schools during the day for study at religious centers. The Court upheld this plan, pointing out that public schools were not being used to promote religion; it merely involved cooperation with religious authorities. The cooperation amounted to an adjustment of pupil schedules and keeping attendance records. The fact that the activities were not held at public schools distinguished it from the *McCollum* decision.

Two lower courts upheld dismissal plans similar to the one above. The Wisconsin Supreme Court upheld a state statute allowing a school board to dismiss children, with parental approval, for religious instruction.[67] The court was satisfied that the plan met its three-part test: 1. *Location.* The teaching was done at churches, not in public schools. 2. *Use of funds.* The only expenditure of public funds involved public school teachers checking monthly attendance reports supplied by the religious instructors, a very minimal cost. 3. *Participation.* Looking at the overall operation of the program, the court was satisfied that the school was not involved in promoting religion.

The Fourth Circuit held in 1975 that a school's scheduling of

---

64. Vaughn v. Reed, 313 F. Supp. 431 (W.D. Va. 1970).

65. Johnson v. Huntington Beach Union H. S. Dist., 137 Cal. Rptr. 43 (Cal. App. 1977).

66. Zorach v. Clauson, 343 U.S. 306, 72 S. Ct. 679, 96 L. Ed. 954 (1952).

67. State *ex rel.* Holt v. Thompson, 66 Wis. 2d 659, 225 N.W.2d 678 (1975).

classes to accommodate pupils interested in religious training sessions was insufficient to create an endorsement of the program.[68] In doing so, it overruled the district court. The circuit court recognized that the key test had an indirect rather than a primary effect on the program. Like *Zorach,* the court saw the program as involving an element of cooperation whereby the students were released to a trailer parked near the school.

A cooperative plan between public and parochial schools involving religious instruction was invalidated by an Oregon court in 1973.[69] This case was based on the state's constitution. The plan consisted of two parts. Seventh and eighth grade children attended public school for four periods and parochial school for three periods. Fifth and sixth grade children were released for four thirty-minute periods per week for religious instruction. The court's main objection to the program was that the students in the two public schools were selected solely from students from the religious school. Thus, religious affiliation was the prerequisite for attendance at the public schools. What the court saw was a public school really being operated within the context of a parochial school. In effect, the state was paying for the salaries of teachers who taught only parochial school students.

§ 12.4. Religion in the General Curriculum.

A state may unquestionably require that specified courses be taken by all students. A state possesses this authority in the interest that it has for all students to become good citizens. A local school board may also require subjects, but that authority is more limited than the state's, particularly when parents object. The right to select courses for children coexists with both school and parent. Some parents have objected to required or elective courses and learning activities in that they clash with their religious beliefs. It is their contention that the school is sponsoring religion in offering the courses and experiences. Issues such as teaching evolution and saluting the flag are treated elsewhere in this book.

Two cases have involved a challenge to activities in required physical education courses as being in conflict with one's religious

---

68. Smith v. Smith, 523 F.2d 121 (4th Cir. 1975).
69. Fisher v. Clackamus City School Dist., 507 P.2d 839 (Ore. App. 1973).

beliefs. In a case from the 1920's a parent objected to dancing as being a required part of physical education. The court held that a student could not be required to take dancing if the parents objected to its being in violation of their freedom of religion.[70]

In a required physical education course, a student refused to wear a prescribed uniform and to engage in certain exercises. She believed that the gym shorts were immodest and the exercises were sinful. The parents refused to allow the girl to participate, even though school authorities made certain adjustments for her, including not wearing the uniform and waiving certain exercises. The court ruled that she was required to take the course, she was not required to wear the uniform, and she could be excused from exercises deemed immodest or sinful.[71]

In 1974 the federal district court in New Hampshire ruled that the state's interest in providing students with a proper education outweighed the rights of parents.[72] The issue arose over parents objecting to students watching movies and television, play acting, and singing or dancing to worldly music. Until 1971, the school board had accommodated the parents' wishes, but the board then nullified its policy as a result of discipline problems, for the excusal involved approximately 20 percent of the students. The parents had also sought exemption from music and health courses for their children. The court saw that to excuse the children from all classes they objected to would cripple their education.

A court held that children of the Jehovah's Witnesses faith could not be required to stand and participate in the singing of the National Anthem.[73] Although the court saw the anthem as being a patriotic rather than a religious exercise, it held that students could legitimately be excused from singing it, based on their religious beliefs.

Parents have also objected to the choice of books that schools use. As a general principle, their right to select them is more limited than their decision as to their child enrolling in a course. In 1975, in a highly publicized situation in West Virginia, a federal district court held that the use of controversial textbooks does not violate

---

70. Hardwick v. Board of School Trustees, 54 Cal.App. 696, 205 P. 49 (1921).
71. Mitchell v. McCall, 273 Ala. 604, 143 So. 2d 629 (1962).
72. Davis v. Page, 385 F. Supp. 395 (D.N.H. 1974).
73. Sheldon v. Fannin, 221 F. Supp. 766 (D. Ariz. 1963).

the constitutional principle of separation of church and state.[74] Parents in Kanawha County had objected to the books, stating that they discouraged Christian principles and good citizenship. The court conceded that some materials in the texts were offensive to the parents' religious beliefs; however, the school board had not abused its authority of selecting the texts. The court recognized that the First Amendment "does not guarantee that nothing about religion will be taught in the schools." [75]

Parents objected to secondary schools having *Oliver Twist* and *The Merchant of Venice* because they viewed them as being offensive to their Jewish faith in that the characters were portrayed as being bigoted. The court held that the books could be used.

> Except where the book has been maliciously written for the apparent purpose of promoting and fomenting a bigoted and intolerant hatred against a particular racial or religious group, public interest in a free and democratic society does not warrant or encourage the suppression of any book at the whim of any unduly sensitive person or group of persons merely because a character described in such book as belonging to a particular race or religion is portrayed in a derogatory or offensive manner. The necessity for the suppression of such a book must clearly depend upon the intent and motive which has actuated the author in making such a portrayal.[76]

---

74. Williams v. Board of Educ., 388 F. Supp. 93 (S.D. W. Va. 1975).
75. *Id.* at 96.
76. Rosenberg v. Board of Educ., 196 Misc. 542, 92 N.Y.S.2d 344, 346 (1949).

Chapter Thirteen

RECORDS

§ 13.0. Introduction.

Not too long ago the extent of school system record-keeping on student personnel (in addition to the academic transcript of grades earned), was limited to matters of student name, address, date and place of birth, dates of attendance, major and minor fields of study, and awards received. Student cumulative records contained grades earned in addition to what is now called directory information.[1]

Today, student records have become dossiers within which the directory information and academic record are but two portions of the whole. In addition to keeping records on attendance, grades, and other academic data, schools usually record comments and descriptive evaluations of student personality, student discipline, student interests, and student attitudes. Also, home and family data concerning economic status and occupational status are often included, as well as information relative to family and student employment, and home environment.

Student records (folders) in contemporary school systems are often kept in several locations within a school and contain information involving almost every aspect of a student's life. Thus, it is not always easy to establish what record in which location is

---

1. Portions of this chapter were presented at the Annual Conference on Legal Issues in Education, Virginia Polytechnic Institute & State University, Blacksburg, Va., 1975.

the student's *official* school record. More will be said concerning this problem in subsequent sections of this chapter.

Legal problems associated with student records, and currently encountered by professionals in public school systems, fall into two interrelated categories. First, there are problems which stem from complaints that school officials have permitted *unauthorized* third parties access to student confidential information; these complaints often claim violations of student and family privacy. Second, there are complaints (growing in number) charging that the information contained in a student's personnel record is not only unwarranted, but is false and irrelevant; these complaints usually involve charges of defamation. In both instances school officials must take immediate steps to eliminate conditions that might result in litigation.

§ 13.1. Access to Student Records and Privacy Protection.

The word *privacy* is not used in the United States Constitution; yet, in our society it is one of our most cherished and sensitive rights. The right to privacy comes through the interpretation of a combination of other rights enumerated in the United States Constitution. In the benchmark case on point, *Griswold v. Connecticut,*[2] Mr. Justice Douglas, in voicing the majority opinion for the Court, developed the place of privacy as a right in the Constitution. In doing so he cited specific Amendments among which were the Fourth, Fifth, and Ninth. More specifically, Douglas relied upon the high court's earlier decision in *Mapp v. Ohio,* wherein the Fourth Amendment was interpreted as creating "a right to privacy, no less important than any other right carefully and particularly reserved to the people." [3]

In 1973, a United States District Court in Pennsylvania heard a case involving the Norristown school system. In that case, *Merriken v. Cressman,*[4] a mother brought action on behalf of her junior high school aged son seeking an injunction with regard to

---

2. 151 Conn. 544, 200 A.2d 479, *rev'd,* 381 U.S. 479 (1965).

3. 367 U.S. 643 (1965), at 656. Mr. Justice Goldberg, in a concurring opinion in *Griswold,* added that he fully agreed that "the right of privacy is a fundamental personal right, emanating from the totality of the constitutional scheme under which we live." Griswold, *supra,* at 494.

4. 364 F. Supp. 913 (E.D. Pa. 1973).

the proposed introduction of a drug abuse program (Critical Period of Intervention Program), designed to identify potential drug abusers and prepare necessary interventions. Plaintiffs maintained that said program was "an involuntary invasion of constitutionally protected rights. . . ." [5] And, as a result, violated their right to privacy.

In ruling for the plaintiffs, District Judge David first established that the "fact that the students are juveniles does not in any way invalidate their right to assert their constitutional right to privacy." [6] Then, he focused on the critical point for school officials to consider as he emphasized the need to strike a balance between "the right of an individual to privacy and the right of the Government to invade that privacy for the sake of public interest. . . ." [7]

There have been several causes upheld by courts for school officials to invade student privacy. For example, as a judge in the Juvenile and Domestic Relations Court of Union County, New Jersey, said in deciding a 1972 case:

> The privacy rights of public school students must give way to the overriding governmental interest in investigating reasonable suspicions of illegal drug use by such students even though there is an admitted intrusion into constitutionally protected rights — rights that are not less precarious because they are possessed by juveniles. [8]

In other words, school officials must establish a compelling reason that outweighs the student's right to privacy.

One other factor should be noted at this point. Courts recognize the *family's* right to privacy as much stronger than is the right of individual student privacy. [9] Therefore, school policies, programs,

---

5. *Id.* at 917.

6. *Id.* at 918.

7. *Id.* at 921. *See also, In re* State in Interest of C., 296 A.2d 102 (N.J. 1972).

8. *In re* State in Interest of G.C., 121 N.J. Super. 108, 296 A.2d 102 (1972). In La Porte v. Escabana Area Pub. Schools, 51 Mich. App. 305, 214 N.W.2d 840 (1974), the Court of Appeals of Michigan upheld a school board regulation requiring all student and faculty to carry identification cards, and held that such was not an invasion of privacy.

9. *Constitutional Law — Right to Privacy — Personality Test Used by School Officials to Identify Potential Drug Abusers Without Informed Consent of Parents*

and procedures must also be cautious not to threaten the privacy of a family. Herein lies the crux of the problems associated with *access* to students records. Thus, school authorities have both ethical and legal responsibilities to strike a *balance* between the school system's need to know more about its students, and the student and his family's right to privacy.[10] This would be a simple matter if it were not for one crucial factor — namely, the desire of others, outside the school, to gain access to the school's wealth of student information.

a. *Third Party Access.* According to Killian, "[t]he basic problem involved in the maintenance of student records is the fact that improper release of their contents may result in personal liability for defamation of the student or the invasion of his civil rights." [11] The emphasis in his statement must be placed on the phrase "improper release."

Suffice it to say, school systems are constantly receiving requests from parents, college recruiters, prospective employers, the local police, federal agencies, credit bureaus, students and a host of others who want to see, and often demand to see, student records. Serious *legal* and *ethical* questions are posed to school administrators and guidance personnel each time someone enters school asking for student information. Most of the *legal* and *ethical* questions raised are very complex and, as such, there is no simple answer to any one of them.

The problem of access to student records has been and still is a fertile area for litigation. In recent years, studies by organizations like the Russell Sage Foundation,[12] by other professional organizations, and by private individuals have shed light on the fact that outside agencies (police, employers, credit bureaus, etc.) often have access to student records with relative ease as compared to the parents of the children involved. In 1971, a New York Court made the point that a confidential relationship

---

Violates Students' and Parents' Right of Privacy, 27 VAND. LAW REV. 372, 380 (March, 1974).

10. *See Merriken v. Cressman, supra,* note 3.

11. J.D. Killian, *The Law, the Counselor, and Student Records,* 48 PER. AND GUID. J. 423 (1970).

12. Guidelines for the Collection, Maintenance and Dissemination of Pupil Records, Russell Sage Foundation (1970).

exists between school authorities and students and as such school officials have liability for intentional or negligent divulgence of information about a student to unauthorized third parties.[13]

Statutes and policy regulations governing access to student records must be examined on a state-by-state basis if one is to completely comprehend the formal steps taken to remedy possible violations of family and student privacy. Some states have been more restrictive than others.

Michigan (1961), Indiana (1965), Wisconsin (1968), and North Dakota (1969), led the way in passing laws restricting access to student records and protecting the confidentiality of student information by eliminating unauthorized scrutiny. A good example of a state where proper legal steps were taken along these lines is Delaware, in 1970. The following quotation is taken from that year's Delaware Code:

> All personnel records of pupils in all public schools in Delaware and in all private schools in Delaware, including but not limited to, test scores, marks given according to a school grading system, psychological or medical reports, reports related to discipline, personal and anecdotal reports, reports by guidance counselors, are deemed to be confidential and not to be disclosed or the contents thereof released to non-school personnel. . . .[14]

The Delaware statute did provide for certain exceptions. Records would be furnished upon request to a federal, state, county, or municipal governmental agency under court order. Also records would be furnished, upon the signed request of a student fourteen years old or older, to a college, university, or employer. And, most important, was the provision that parents be given access to information concerning their own children (specifically academic data, health data, and information on behavior).

More recently, Arizona and Wisconsin enacted statutes to further insure the confidentiality of student personnel records in an attempt to protect student and family privacy in those states. In May of 1974, the Governor of Arizona signed into law a provision entitled "Permissible Use of Pupil Records." That provision limited

---

13. Blair v. Union Free School Dist., 324 N.Y.S.2d 322 (1971).
14. DEL. CODE ANN., Tit. 14, § 4114 (1970).

access to records and student information to parents or other legal guardians, to professional staff of the school district wherein the pupil is enrolled, and the pupil after he had reached age eighteen. Other schools, institutions, or agencies could gain access to pupil records only through written instruction of the parent or guardian, and upon approval of the local school board.[15] In Wisconsin, in 1974, a bill was also signed into law containing similar restrictions and protections.[16]

In Virginia, the *Virginia Freedom of Information Act* protects scholastic records by exempting them from being open to public inspection and copying by citizens of the State. Only the person who is the subject of that record shall have access to the record.[17] Additionally, the Virginia Legislature, in 1976, added a specific section [18] to the School Code covering scholastic records. According to this new provision:

> **§ 22-275.26. Limitations on access to records. —** No teacher, principal or employee of any public school nor any school board member shall permit access to any written records concerning any particular pupil enrolled in the school in any class to any person except under judicial process unless the person is one the following:
>
> 1. Either parent or a guardian of such pupil or such pupil; provided, however, that local school boards may require that such pupil, if he be less than eighteen years of age, as a condition precedent to access to such records, furnish written consent of his or her parent or guardian for such access. Such parent, guardian or pupil shall have access to all written records relating to such pupil maintained by the school except as otherwise provided by law, and need only appear in person during regular hours of the school day and request to see such records. No written material concerning such pupil shall be edited or withheld except as otherwise provided by law, and the parent, guardian or pupil shall be entitled to read such material personally.
>
> 2. A person designated, in writing, by such pupil if he is eighteen years of age or older, or by either parent or

---

15. ARIZ. REV. STAT., § 15-152 (1974).

16. WIS. STAT. ANN., § 118.125 (1974).

17. VA. CODE ANN., § 21-342 (1974). *See also,* Opinion of the Attorney General of Virginia, May 22, 1974.

18. *Id.* § 22-275.26 (1976).

a guardian of such pupil if he is less than eighteen years of age.

3. The principal, or someone designated by him, of a school where the pupil attends, has attended, or intends to enroll.

4. The current teachers of such pupil.

5. A State or local law-enforcement officer, including a probation officer, parole officer or administrator, or a member of a parole board, seeking information in the course of his duties.

6. The Superintendent of Public Instruction, or a member of his staff, or the division superintendent of schools where the pupil attends, has attended, or intends to enroll, or a member of his staff.

7. An officer or employee of a county or city agency responsible for protective services to children, as to a pupil referred to that agency as a minor requiring investigation or supervision by that agency.

The restrictions imposed by this section are not intended to interfere with the giving of information by school personnel concerning participation in athletics and other school activities, the winning of scholastic or other honors and awards, and other like information. Notwithstanding the restrictions imposed by this section, a division superintendent of schools may, in his discretion, provide information to the staff of a college, university, or educational research and development organization or laboratory if such information is necessary to a research project or study conducted, sponsored, or approved by the college, university, or educational research and development organization or laboratory and if no pupil will be identified by name in the information submitted for research.

Notwithstanding the restrictions imposed by this section, the names and addresses of pupils, the record of a pupil's daily attendance, the pupil's scholastic record in the form of grades received in school subjects, the names of a pupil's parents or guardian, a pupil's date and place of birth, and the names and addresses of other schools a pupil has attended may be released to an officer or employee of the United States seeking this information in the course of his duties, when a pupil is a veteran of military service with the United States, or an orphan or dependent of such veteran, or an alien. (1975, c. 639; 1976, c. 682.)

Thus, it can be said that steps have been taken and are being taken within the various states to insure against unauthorized access to student information by outside individuals and agencies. Evident in these statutory developments is an establishment and a protection of the legal rights of parents and students to gain legal access to school records affecting them.

b. *Parent Access.* The right of a parent to see the school record of his or her child has been a long, uphill battle which is not over yet. However, as steps were being taken in state legislatures, so too has there been precedent established in case law. Through such early cases as *Van Allen v. McCleary,*[19] parents were being granted a common-law right to see the record of their child. However, precedent was also established in early case law, through such cases as *Marquesano v. Board of Education,*[20] that parents, like other individuals and agencies, must establish a "sufficient interest" in their child's record to gain access to that record.[21]

c. *Public Law 93-380: The Buckley Amendment.* In 1974, President Ford signed Public Law 93-380. In that law, which deals mainly with federal financing of educational projects and programs, is a subsection entitled "Protection of the Rights and Privacy of Parents and Students." [22] It is quite clear that this subsection (called the Buckley Amendment because of its patron, Senator James Buckley of New York), mandates that federal funds will not be made available to any state or local educational agency, any community college, or school which prevents parents from seeing the *complete* educational record of their child, and which allows unauthorized third parties to examine those records.

---

19. 211 N.Y.S.2d 501 (1961).

20. 191 N.Y.S.2d 713 (1959). *See also,* Dachs v. Board of Educ., 277 N.Y.S.2d 449 (1967).

21. There are other situations within which student records may be legitimately used. For example, they may be used in courts and other legal proceedings, in guidance conferences, and by school administrators who might be informing a substitute teacher about potential discipline problems in their classes. *See, e.g.,* Johnson v. Board of Educ., 220 N.Y.S.2d 362 (1961); Madera v. Board of Educ., 267 F. Supp. 356, 386 F.2d 778 (2d Cir. 1967); and Ferraro v. Board of Educ., 212 N.Y.S.2d 615, *aff'd,* 221 N.Y.S.2d 279 (1961), in that order.

22. Education Amendments of 1974, Part C., General Education Provisions Act, Title V. § 513, at 88-91. For a concise review of the new law, *see* Joan Brannon, *Access to Student Records: Family Educational Rights and Privacy Act of 1974,* 4 SCHOOL L. BULL. 1 (October, 1974).

What is more, parents have the right to challenge, in a hearing, the accuracy, truth, and relevance of data contained in that record.[23] The crucial point now, however, is to define "educational record." Is a teacher's grade book a student record? Are notes on students, kept in a principal's personal file, considered a student record? Can such records be kept free from parent and student scrutiny? These are just a few unclear areas of possible litigation.

Significantly, that same law requires that no portion of a student's record may be released to any outside agency or person without prior, *written consent* of the parent, or the student where he/she has reached eighteen years of age or is in attendance at an institution of higher learning. And, that the written authorization form be kept in the student's file for the parents and/or student to see. Significantly, however, teachers and administrators in the school attended by a student, who establish a "legitimate interest," may gain access to student information without prior consent of parents.[24]

New federal protections of student and family privacy, coupled with emerging state statutes, and built upon the precedents of early case law, serve to protect the confidentiality of student records by forbidding scrutiny by unauthorized outside persons and agencies. Ironically, in closing access to student records by unauthorized outsiders, and in legally establishing parental and student rights to examination of complete student records, a new era of litigation opened. Now, instead of legal fights to gain access, the information that is contained in the student dossier, once seen by student or parents, might be the grounds for *defamation* claims or even civil rights claims.

§ 13.2. Contents of Student Records and the Law of Defamation.

Legally, professional personnel in schools owe students a standard of care which is much greater than they realize. Not only

---

23. *Id.* at 89. The Act requires school systems to adopt and publicize procedures regarding access.

24. *Id.* "Parental consent letters must be sufficiently informative and complete to constitute an exercise of 'informed consent' on the part of the parents." *Constitutional Law . . . , supra,* note 10, at 378. *See also, Meeks v. Cressman, supra,* 920-22. Students may waive their own rights to access, but cannot be required to do so.

is a student to be protected from any *foreseeable harm* to his physical being, so too is he to be protected from any foreseeable harm to his mental being, and to his *reputation* and *good name.*

Simply stated, defamation can be defined as, "Any words tending to harm a person's reputation so as to lower him in the estimation of the community or to deter people from associating with him. . . ." [25] In essence, this area of law grants us protection of our liberty by helping maintain freedom of movement among other people, and freedom to pursue life, happiness, and prosperity.

Inherent in the concept of *defamation* is the notion that one's reputation and character be free from injury caused by *false* and *malicious* statements communicated by one individual about another individual to a third party. Herein reside the twin torts of *libel* (usually communicated by writing or printing), and *slander* (usually communicated by word of mouth).[26]

The legal concept of defamation applies to school systems and to issues of student records if, in an examination of the complete record of a student by that student or his parent, statements and comments included in that record can be interpreted as either *false, unwarranted,* and possibly *malicious* — with injurious results to the student and his civil right of liberty to freely pursue his education in school (a possible violation of Fourteenth Amendment guarantees).

Despite the increased statutory protection of student records by *limiting access* and by the forbidding of scrutiny to unauthorized third parties, school records are still open to inspection by professional personnel within schools — administrators, supervisors, counselors, and teachers. Therefore, statements in the record communicate various impressions of students (their behavior and their potential), with the possibility of prejudging student behavior and potential with injurious results. Cause of action might be established by plaintiff parents in a tort claim, and possibly in a constitutional claim wherein violations of the Fourteenth Amendment are at issue (violations of liberty, in particular).

---

25. *Killian, supra,* n. 14, at 427. *See also,* Black's Law Dictionary 505 (Rev. 4th Ed. 1968).

26. BLACK'S LAW DICTIONARY at 1060-61; and at 1559.

a. *School Professional Personnel and Defamation.* The major protection available to all professional personnel in schools, to eliminate possible involvement in suits by students and parents claiming defamation, was stated most succinctly in the transcript of a "Symposium on Libel and Slander in Illinois," published more than a decade ago in the *Chicago-Kent Law Review.* The report said, "In almost all jurisdictions a defendant in a civil action for defamation, is excused from liability if he can prove the truth of his ... statements." [27]

It behooves the administrator, teacher, school social worker, and other professionals to think carefully about what they say about students in the student's record. If questioned, school personnel must be able to show that their evaluations of students were: 1. not the results of hearsay, 2. true, 3. placed in the record with good motives, and 4. relevant to the educational development of the child — no matter how critical the comments.

Certain precautions might well be taken by school professional personnel. Some suggestions are:

(1)   Be certain that all statements made about a student and all evaluations of students are made by individuals within whose professional prerogatives it is to make such statements and evaluations. For example, classroom teachers should not write comments evaluating the medical condition of a child including any possible psychiatric disabilities.[28]

(2)   Good faith requires that one always separate *fact* from *fiction* before making a statement about a student.

(3)   Document the source of each comment and evaluation.

(4)   Be certain to refrain from making any statements about students that are "value judgment" statements — filled with subjectivity.

(5)   Always be able to demonstrate the direct connection between the statement or evaluation and the school's function — the educational development of the student in question.

(6)   If there is any doubt about the need to record a

---

27. 43 CHI-KENT LAW REV. 83 (1966).

28. In Depperman v. University of Ky., 371 F. Supp. 73 (E.D. Ky. 1974) it was held that comments on student "emotional fitness" might be *actionable.*

particular piece of information in a student's record (among the items not required to be kept) don't include the data.

There is one final suggestion to consider. Professionals in schools must constantly remind themselves that they have moral, ethical, and professional responsibilities to do all in their power to *help* students develop educationally. Therefore, anything they say or write about a student must stem from that purpose, and from no other.

b. *School Counselors and Defamation.* Several avenues of protection are open to school counselors. These avenues greatly reduce their vulnerability to *defamation-type* claims.

Currently, in some states (*e.g.,* Virginia), school counselors are eligible for state *licensure* equal to that of other similar professionals (*e.g.,* psychologists). There are several advantages to receiving state licensure. Among these are:

(1) Increased legal status and acceptance as professionals,
(2) Clients in schools (students and their parents) will be protected as statutory privilege of communication will be eventually extended to counselors in schools — now limited to licensed psychologists in schools, and
(3) Standards for entry into school counseling will be upgraded, thus the profession would assume stricter control over practice with a result of more ethical conduct in practice. Thus, there will be less chance of irresponsible statements made in evaluating [29] students.

The granting of testimonial privilege is viewed as another major advantage of licensure for counselors in education, much the same as it is granted to licensed psychologists who work in schools.

---

29. The American Personnel and Guidance Association recently published a position paper outlining the pros and cons of professional licensure. Thomas J. Sweeney, *Licensure in the Helping Professions,* APGA (May, 1974). Also, there have been numerous articles written in professional journals suggesting the possibility of counselors in education even receiving courtroom "testimonial privilege" as is currently granted licensed psychologists. *See,* for example, *Testimonial Privileges and the Student-Counselor Relationship in Secondary Schools,* 56 IOWA L. REV. 1323, 1329 (June, 1971).

Among the states where testimonial privilege exists, is Iowa. In the 1974 *Acts and Resolutions of the Iowa Legislature,* the Iowa Code was amended to read as follows:

> No qualified guidance counselor . . . who obtains information by reason of his employment as a qualified school guidance counselor shall be allowed, in giving testimony, to disclose any confidential communications properly entrusted to him by a pupil or his parent or guardian in his capacity as a qualified school guidance counselor and necessary and proper to enable him to perform his duties as a qualified school guidance counselor.[30]

The effect of licensure, and statutory privilege, serves to protect counselors in schools in legal matters, and to protect the student and his family in matters of confidence and privacy. However, this alternative does not extend any protections to administrators, supervisors, or teachers (who are also asked to enter anecdotal comments and evaluations), from suits charging defamation of character or from Section 1983-type suits for violations of student's civil rights.

§ 13.3. Purging, Expunging, and Destroying Records.

Over the years, several questions have been raised regarding the *removal* of information from a student's record and the total destruction of the record itself. A corollary question might be: Once a piece of information becomes a part of a student's school record, who decides what can be removed from that record?

Until recently, the ultimate responsibility in matters of student information, collected and kept by the school, fell upon the building principal. Principals, along with guidance personnel where they existed, were often designated by the board and/or superintendent to be the "official custodians" of the school's student records, wherever the records were kept within the school building. The

---

30. IOWA CODE, § 622.10 (amendment approved May 27, 1974). *See also,* the school codes of Maine, North Carolina, North Dakota and Oregon. For a comprehensive article dealing with the *total* question of *privileges* in the federal courts in light of considerations of *individual privacy, see* T.G. Krattenmaker, *Testimonial Privileges in Federal Courts: An Alternative to the Proposed Federal Rules of Evidence,* 62 GEO. LAW REV. 61 (1973).

final determination for what was or was not kept in the student folder was the principal's.

Currently, record-keeping responsibility and procedures usually differ from school system to school system. The similarity in all, however, is that.someone professional, within each school building, must be designated as the official custodian of student records. And, this person will decide all matters associated with those records (inclusion of information, release of information, purging of records, expungement of records, and destruction of information and records.)

a. *Purging and Expunging.* Student records must be subjected to continuous examination and scrutiny by authorized school officials in search of outdated, irrelevant, and inaccurate data. As established in previous sections of this chapter, parents (and students where law allows) must also be given opportunities (on their request) to *purge* (clear, correct) their child's school record.

Today's public school systems would be remiss and vulnerable to litigation if they did not have, in place, policy and procedures covering the act of purging student records. In some situations, statutes mandate steps to be taken in this process.

To purge or expunge something from the record is to completely remove, strike, or erase the item from that record. Purging the record wipes the record clear of something no longer considered necessary to that record. Some purging of records is school-system initiated, as a part of a regular process of up-dating. Over the years, however, some individuals have taken school systems into court seeking forced expungement as a part of the remedy sought.[31]

In *Einhorn v. Maus*,[32] some public high school students in Springfield Township, Pennsylvania, conducted a peaceful demonstration during the school's graduation ceremony. It seems that they had distributed literature and wore armbands demanding that education in their school district be "humanized." The participating students were disciplined for their actions.

The disciplined students brought suit in federal district court

---

31. In Jacobs v. Benedict, 35 Ohio Misc. 92, 301 N.E.2d 723 (1973).
32. 300 F. Supp. 1171 (E.D. Pa. 1969).

seeking a preliminary injunction to prevent school officials from: 1. placing notations on their school records, referring specifically to the demonstration and ultimate disciplinary action, and 2. communicating information regarding that matter to college admissions officers, where said students made application.

In denying students' motion for the injunction, the district court made the following statement:

> School officials have the right and, we think, a duty to record and to communicate true factual information about their students to institutions of higher learning, for the purpose of giving to the latter an accurate and complete picture of applicants for admission.[33]

Additionally, students could not show either immediate threat or actual irreparable harm to themselves because of the school's actions.

Hatter v. Los Angeles City High School District (1971),[34] involved high school students who had been disciplined for opposing the school's annual chocolate drive for raising money to support various student activities. The students urged a "student boycott" of all chocolate sales, as a means of protesting the high school's dress code. One student was suspended for the duration of the drive, for passing out *leaflets* urging the boycott, across the street from the school. A second student was reprimanded and threatened with suspension for wearing a tag on her dress, while in school, urging students to boycott the chocolate sale.

Plaintiff students brought a class action suit under 42 U.S.C. Section 1983, alleging infringement of their constitutional rights of free speech and due process. In addition to injunctive relief regarding further interference by school officials in their constitutionally protected rights, plaintiffs sought a court order requiring school officials to "expunge from school records all mention of the disciplinary action taken against them. . ."[35]

The United States District Court hearing their complaint denied relief and dismissed the action.[36] The United States Court of

---

33. *Id.*
34. 452 F.2d 673 (9th Cir. 1971).
35. *Id.* at 674.
36. 310 F. Supp. 1309 (C.D. Cal. 1970).

Appeals for the Ninth Circuit reversed the district court's dismissal and remanded the matter with directions to vacate that order and to conduct further proceedings.[37] Thus, the specific request for expungement of the students' records was not acted upon.

A more recent case (1973), from a court of common pleas of Ohio (Hamilton County), also involved a request by a plaintiff junior high school student for (among other things), an expungement of his school record following a disciplinary episode. In *Jacobs v. Benedict,*[38] school authorities removed a student from his position as president of the student council, removed him as a member of the honor society, prevented his further participation in extracurricular activities, and reduced his grades because of his failure to comply with school rules on grooming (prohibiting mustaches, regulating hair length, and dimensions of sideburns).

Holding for the student, and in declaring the school rules unlawful, the Ohio court directed reinstatement of the student to the positions from which he had been removed, and ordered reinstatement of eligibility to extracurricular activities. Additionally, the court held that the student was entitled "to expungement and deletion of point reduction in grades and detrimental notations on his school record. . . ." [39]

b. *Destroying Records.* Little has been said in case law regarding the authority to destroy student records, and state statutes are often silent on such matters as the length of time that student records must be kept by school systems. Thus, policy and practice in such matters have been left to local school boards.

Despite the differences in policy and practice existing from school system to school system, most have followed the recommendations of such groups as the Russell Sage Foundation. Generally, the entire student record is kept for a period of five years following the student's graduation. Then, after that only the *academic* record (grades, awards, test scores, rank in class, etc.), plus dates of attendance are kept (often on microfilm). *Non academic* records (*e.g.,* discipline matters) are often destroyed.

Generally, the authority to decide what to keep and what not to

37. 9th Cir. *supra,* at 675.
38. *Jacobs v. Benedict, supra,* at n. 31.
39. *Id.* at 724.

keep is a board decision. The actual task of destroying records is one for the administration, and not one for teachers.

§ 13.4. Summary.

Student records in public school systems are public records and as such should not be kept in secret. At the same time, however, school records should not be open to unauthorized and unwarranted scrutiny. More importantly, the privacy of each student and his or her family must be constantly protected.

It is an established fact of law that student records in public school systems are open to inspection by parents and other legal guardians. Additionally, federal law and state law provide (within certain age limitations) the same access to students who are the subjects of a given record.

Student records are to be kept free from irrelevant, erroneous, and false information that might have a damaging effect on students and their families. Thus, a constant process of purging must be implemented to protect against such happenings.

Contemporary public school systems must maintain carefully planned procedures for keeping, reevaluating, and using student records. In this way only will the vulnerability to court suit be reduced.

Table of Cases

Chamberlin v. Dade County Bd. of Pub. Instr., 377 U.S. 402, 84 S. Ct. 1272, 12 L. Ed. 2d 407 (1964), § 12.2.

Chambers v. Board of Educ., 397 N.Y.S.2d 436 (1977), § 7.0.

Chance v. Board of Examiners, 330 F. Supp. 203 (S.D.N.Y. 1971), 534 F.2d 993 (2nd Cir. 1976), § 7.6.

Chapman v. Board of Educ., 394 N.Y.S.2d 52 (App. Div. 1977), § 7.0.

Chilton v. Cook County School Dist. No. 207, Maine Township, 26 Ill. App. 3d 459, 325 N.E.2d 666 (1975), § 4.6.

City of Beloit by Beloit School Bd. v. Wisconsin Empl. Rel. Comm'n and Beloit Educ. Ass'n, 242 N.W.2d 231 (Wis. 1976), § 5.1.

City of Madison Joint School Dist. No. 8 v. Wisconsin Empl. Rel. Comm'n, 429 U.S. 167, 97 S. Ct. 421, 50 L. Ed. 2d 376 (1976), §§ 5.1, 8.2.

City of New York v. DeLury, 23 N.Y.2d 175, 295 N.Y.S.2d 901, 243 N.E.2d 128 (1968), § 5.3.

Clifton Teachers' Ass'n Inc. v. Board of Educ., 136 N.J. Super. 336, 346 A.2d 107 (1975).

Cochran v. Louisiana State Bd. of Educ., 281 U.S. 370, 50 S. Ct. 335, 74 L. Ed. 1157 (1930), § 12.1.

Coe v. Bogart, 519 F.2d 10 (6th Cir. 1975), § 7.2.

Coffman v. Kuehler, 409 F. Supp. 546 (N.D. Tex. 1976), § 10.1.

Collins v. Janey, 147 Tenn. 477, 249 S.W. 801 (1923), § 3.3.

Collinsville Community Unit School Dist. No. 10 v. White, 5 Ill. App. 3d 500, 283 N.E.2d 718 (1972), § 3.3.

Committee for Public Education and Religious Liberty v. Nyquist, 413 U.S. 756, 93 S. Ct. 2955, 37 L. Ed. 2d 948 (1973), § 12.1.

Commonwealth *ex rel.* Matthews v. Coatney, 396 S.W.2d 72 (Ky. 1965), § 3.4.

Commonwealth *ex rel.* Waychoff v. Tekavec, 456 Pa. 521, 319 A.2d 1 (1974), § 3.4.

Connell v. Higginbotham, 403 U.S. 207, 91 S. Ct. 1772, 29 L. Ed. 2d 418 (1971), § 8.2.

Conte v. Board of Educ., 397 N.Y.S.2d 471 (App. Div. 1977), § 5.1.

Conte v. School Committee of Methuen, 356 N.E.2d 261 (Mass. 1976), § 7.2.

Cook v. Griffin, 364 N.Y.S.2d 632 (App. Div. 1975), § 12.1.

Grayned v. City of Rockford, 408 U.S. 104, 92 S. Ct. 2294, 33 L. Ed. 2d 222 (1972), § 11.4.

Green v. County School Bd., 391 U.S. 430, 88 S. Ct. 1689, 20 L. Ed. 2d 716 (1968), § 9.4.

Griffin v. County School Bd., 377 U.S. 218, 84 S. Ct. 1226, 12 L. Ed. 2d 256 (1964), § 9.4.

Griggs v. Duke Power Co., 401 U.S. 424, 91 S. Ct. 849, 28 L. Ed. 2d 158 (1971), § 7.6.

Griswold v. Connecticut, 200 A.2d 479, 381 U.S. 479, 85 S. Ct. 1678, 14 L. Ed. 2d 510 (1965), *rev'd,* 381 U.S. 479 (1965), § 13.1.

Grossberg v. Deusevio, 380 F. Supp. 285 (E.D. Va. 1974), § 12.2.

Guerrieri v. Tyson, 24 A.2d 468 (Pa. 1942), § 4.6.

Gulesian v. Dade County School Bd., 281 So. 2d 325 (Fla. 1973), § 6.1.

Hagerstrom v. Clay City, 343 N.E.2d 249 (Ill. 1976), § 7.4.

Hanover v. Northrup, 325 F. Supp. 170 (D. Conn. 1970), § 8.1.

Hardwick v. Board of School Trustees, 54 Cal. App. 696, 205 P. 49 (1921), §§ 9.0, 12.4.

Hargrave v. Kirk, 313 F. Supp. 944 (M.D. Fla. 1970), *judgment vacated, sub. nom.,* Askew v. Hargrave, 401 U.S. 476 (1971), § 6.5.

Harrod v. Board of Educ., 500 S.W.2d 1 (Mo. 1973), § 8.1.

Hart v. School Bd., 340 So. 2d 121 (Fla. 1976), § 7.4.

Hatter v. Los Angeles City H. S. Dist., 452 F.2d 673 (9th Cir. 1971), *rev'g,* 310 F. Supp. 1309 (C.D. Cal. 1970), § 13.3.

Hefner v. Board of Educ., 335 N.E.2d 600 (Ill. App. 1975), § 5.1.

Hembree v. Jefferson City Bd. of Educ., 337 So.2d 9 (Ala. 1976), § 7.3.

Hernandez v. Hanson, 430 F. Supp. 1154 (D. Neb. 1977), § 11.3.

Hernandez v. Houston Ind. School Dist., 558 S.W.2d 121 (Tex. 1977), § 6.5.

Hobson v. Hansen, 269 F. Supp. 401 (D.C.D.C. 1967), § 9.4.

Hogenson v. Williams, 542 S.W.2d 456 (Tex. App. 1976), § 10.1.

Holden v. Board of Educ., 216 A.2d 387 (N.J. 1966), § 11.5.

Hollister v. North, 50 Ill. App. 3d 56, 365 N.E.2d 258 (1977), § 3.4.

Holroyd v. Eibling, 188 N.E.2d 797 (Ohio 1962), § 11.4.

Horton v. Meskill, 172 Conn. 615, 376 A.2d 359 (Conn. 1977), § 6.5.

M. by Parents R. and S. v. Board of Educ., 429 F. Supp. 288 (S.D. Ill. 1977), § 10.4.

Madera v. Board of Educ., 267 F. Supp. 356 (S.D.N.Y. 1967), 386 F.2d 778 (2nd Cir. 1967), §§ 10.3, 13.1.

Maier v. Beeser, 341 N.Y.S.2d 411 (N.Y. 1972), § 9.2.

Mailloux v. Kiley, 448 F.2d 1242 (1st Cir. 1971), § 8.1.

Mancha v. Field Museum of Natural History, 5 Ill. App. 3d 699, 283 N.E.2d 899 (1972), § 4.6.

Mangold v. Albert Gallatin School Dist., 438 F.2d 1194 (3rd Cir. 1971), § 12.2.

Mapp v. Ohio, 367 U.S. 643, 81 S. Ct. 1684, 6 L. Ed. 2d 1081 (1965), § 13.1.

Marquesano v. Board of Educ., 191 N.Y.S.2d 713 (1959), § 13.1.

Marsh v. Birmingham Bd. of Education, 349 So. 2d 34 (Ala. 1977), § 7.3.

Martin v. Dayton School Dist., 536 P.2d 169 (Wash. 1975), § 7.5.

Martin v. Kearney, 124 Cal. Rptr. 281 (Cal. App. 1975), § 4.1.

Maryland v. Lindquist, 278 A.2d 263 (Md. 1971), § 8.1.

Massie v. Henry, — F. Supp. — (W.D.N.C. 1971), § 11.2.

Massie v. Henry, 455 F.2d 779 (4th Cir. 1972), § 11.2.

Matter of Baum, 382 N.Y.S.2d 672 (1976), § 9.1.

Matter of Franz, 378 N.Y.S.2d 317 (1976), § 9.1.

Matter of Lewisburg Area Educ. Ass'n, 371 A.2d 568 (Pa. Cmwlth. 1977), § 5.4.

Matter of Wagner, 383 N.Y.S.2d 849 (N.Y. 1976), § 9.4.

Matthews v. Quinton, 362 P.2d 932 (Alas. 1961), § 12.1.

McCall v. State, 354 So. 2d 869 (Fla. 1968), § 11.3.

McCarthy v. Philadelphia Civil Service Comm'n, 424 U.S. 645, 96 S. Ct. 1154, 47 L. Ed. 2d 366 (1976), § 8.2.

McInnis v. Shapiro, 293 F. Supp. 327 (N.D. Ill. 1968), aff'd mem., sub. nom., McInnis v. Ogilvie, 393 U.S. 322 (1969), § 6.5.

McLaughlin v. Tilendis, 398 F.2d 287 (7th Cir. 1968), § 5.3.

McLaurin v. Oklahoma State Regents, 339 U.S. 637, 70 S. Ct. 139, 94 L. Ed. 1149 (1950), § 9.4.

McLeod v. State, 122 So. 2d 737 (Miss. 1929), § 9.4.

Medeiros v. Kijosaki, 478 P.2d 314 (Hawaii 1970), § 8.1.

Meek v. Pittinger, 421 U.S. 349, 95 S. Ct. 1753, 44 L. Ed. 2d 217, reh. denied, 422 U.S. 1049 (1975), § 12.1.

Moore v. Student Affairs of Troy State Univ., 284 F. Supp. 725 (M.D. Ala. 1968), § 10.4.

Moore v. Tangipahoa Parish School Bd., 421 F.2d 1407 (5th Cir. 1969), § 9.4.

Morelli v. Board of Educ., 42 Ill. App. 3d 722, 358 N.E.2d 1364 (Ill. 1976), §§ 7.4, 7.5.

Morgan v. Kerrigan, 530 F.2d 401 (1st Cir. 1976), § 9.4.

Morris v. Board of Educ., 401 F. Supp. 188 (D. Del. 1975), § 5.1.

Morris v. School Dist., 144 A.2d 737 (Pa. 1958), § 4.3.

Morrison v. Hamilton County School Bd., 494 S.W.2d 770 (Tenn. 1973), *cert. denied,* 414 U.S. 1044, § 7.4.

Mower v. Leicester, 9 Mass. 237 (1812), § 4.3.

Mt. Healthy City School Dist. v. Doyle, 429 U.S. 274, 97 S. Ct. 568, 50 L. Ed. 2d 471 (1977), §§ 7.4, 7.5.

Mullins v. Eveland, 234 S.W.2d 639 (Mo. 1950), § 3.3.

Muskego-Norway Consolidated Schools Joint Dist. No. 9 v. Wisconsin Empl. Rel. Bd., 35 Wis. 2d 540, 151 N.W.2d 617 (1967), § 5.3.

Nance v. Williams, 564 S.W.2d 212 (Ark. 1978), § 6.3.

National Educ. Ass'n v. State of South Carolina, 434 U.S. 1026, 98 S. Ct. 756, 54 L. Ed. 2d 775 (1978), § 7.6.

National Labor Relations Board v. Jones and Laughlin Steel Corp., 301 U.S. 1, 57 S. Ct. 615, 81 L. Ed.893(1937), § 5.0.

Neilan v. Board of Directors of Ind. School Dist. of Sioux City, 200 Iowa 860, 205 N.W. 506 (1925), § 8.1.

Nelson v. Heyne, 491 F.2d 352 (7th Cir. 1974), § 10.1.

Nelson v. State, 319 So. 2d 154 (Fla. App. 1975), § 10.4.

Newark Teachers v. Board of Educ., 373 A.2d 1020 (N.J. Super. 1977), § 5.4.

New Jersey Civil Service Ass'n v. Mayor and City Council of Camden, 343 A.2d 154 (N.J. Super. 1975), § 5.1.

New York City School Bds. Ass'n v. Board of Educ., 383 N.Y.S.2d 208 (App. Div. 1976), § 5.1.

Nigosian v. Weiss, 343 F. Supp. 757 (E.D. Mich. 1971), § 8.2.

Niles v. City of San Rafael, 116 Cal. Rptr. 733 (Cal. App. 1974), § 4.6.

Northampton Area Bd. of Educ. v. Zehner, 360 A.2d 793 (Pa. 1976), § 6.2.

Pennsylvania Labor Rel. Bd. v. State College Area School Dist., 337 A.2d 262 (Pa. 1975), § 5.1.

Pennsylvania Labor Rel. Bd. v. Zelum, 329 A.2d 477 (Pa. 1974), § 5.2.

People v. Ball, 58 Ill. 2d 36, 317 N.E.2d 54 (1974), § 10.1.

People v. Becker, 112 Cal. App. 2d 324, 246 P.2d 103 (1952), § 3.4.

People v. D., 34 N.Y.2d 483, 315 N.E.2d 466 (1974), § 10.4.

People v. De Caro, 17 Ill. App. 3d 553, 308 N.E.2d 196 (1974), § 10.1.

People v. Donner, 302 N.Y. 833, 100 N.E.2d 57 (N.Y. 1951), § 9.1.

People v. Fahrner, 213 Cal. App. 2d 535, 28 Cal. Rptr. 926 (1963), § 10.4.

People v. Jackson, 65 Misc. 2d 909, 319 N.Y.S.2d 731 (1971), § 10.2.

People v. Overton, 301 N.Y.S.2d 479, 249 N.E.2d 366 (1967), § 10.4.

People v. Stewart, 63 Misc. 2d 601, 313 N.Y.S.2d 253 (1970), § 10.4.

People v. Witzkowski, 357 N.E.2d 1348 (Ill. 1976), § 11.4.

People v. Young, 90 Cal. Rptr. 924, 12 A.3d 878 (1970), § 10.4.

People ex rel. Klinger v. Howlett, 56 Ill. 2d 1, 305 N.E.2d 129 (1973), § 12.1.

Perry v. Grenada, 300 F. Supp. 748 (N.D. Miss. 1969), § 9.4.

Perry v. Sindermann, 408 U.S. 593, 92 S. Ct. 2694, 33 L. Ed. 2d 570 (1970), § 7.5.

Peter W. v. San Francisco Unified School Dist., 131 Cal. Rptr. 854 (Cal. App. 1976), § 4.7.

Peters v. Bowman Public School Dist. No. 1, 231 N.W.2d 817 (N.D. 1975), § 3.3.

Philadelphia Fed'n of Teachers, Local No. 3, AFL-CIO v. Board of Educ., No. 3583 (Ct. Common Pleas, October 4, 1976), § 8.2.

Phillipi v. School Dist. of Springfield, 367 A.2d 1133 (Pa. 1977), § 7.7.

Piazzola v. Watkins, 316 F. Supp. 624 (M.D. Ala. 1970), § 10.4

Picha v. Wielgos, 410 F. Supp. 1214 (N.D. Ill. 1976), § 10.4

Pickering v. Board of Educ., 391 U.S. 563, 88 S. Ct. 1731, 20 L. Ed. 2d 811 (1968), § 8.2.

Pierce v. School Comm., 322 F. Supp. 957 (D. Mass. 1971), § 10.3.

Pierce v. Society of Sisters, 268 U.S. 510, 45 S. Ct. 510, 69 L. Ed. 1070 (1925), §§ 1.5, 9.1.

Pinellas County Classroom Teachers' Association v. Board of Pub. Instr., 214 So. 2d 34 (Fla. 1968), § 5.3.

Speake v. Grantham, 317 F. Supp. 1253 (S.D. Miss. 1970), § 10.4.

Spears v. Honda, 449 P.2d 130 (Alas. 1968), § 12.1.

Spokane Educ. Ass'n v. Barnes, 517 P.2d 1362 (Wash. 1974), § 5.1.

State v. Baccino, 282 A.2d 869 (Del. Super. 1971), § 10.4.

State v. Bailey, 61 N.E. 730 (Ill. 1901), § 9.1.

State v. Beeson, 266 A.2d 175 (N.J. 1970), § 8.1.

State v. Board of School Directors of Milwaukee, 14 Wis. 2d 243, 111 N.W.2d 198 (1961), § 8.1.

State v. Christ, 270 N.W. 376 (Iowa 1936), § 9.4.

State v. King, 44 N.J. 346, 209 A.2d 110 (1965), § 10.4.

State v. La Barge, 357 A.2d 121 (Vt. 1976), § 9.1.

State v. Miday, 140 S.E.2d 325 (N.C. 1965), § 9.2.

State v. Mora, 307 So. 2d 317 (La. 1975); 330 So. 2d 900 (La. 1976), § 10.4.

State v. Priest, 270 So. 2d 173 (La. 1946), § 9.4.

State v. Stein, 203 Kan. 638, 456 P.2d 1 (1969), *cert. denied,* 397 U.S. 947 (1970), § 10.4.

State v. Whisner, 351 N.E.2d 750 (Ohio 1976), § 9.1.

State v. Yoder, 182 N.W.2d 539 (Wis. 1971), *aff'd,* 406 U.S. 205, 92 S. Ct. 1526, 32 L. Ed. 15 (1972), § 9.1.

State v. Young, 234 Ga. 488, 216 S.E.2d 568 (1975), *cert. denied,* 423 U.S. 1039 (1975), § 10.4.

State Bd. of Educ. v. Board of Educ., 108 N.J. Super. 564, 262 A.2d 21 (1970), § 12.2.

State Employees Ass'n of New Hampshire, Inc. v. Mills, 344 A.2d 6 (N.H. 1975), § 5.1.

State *ex rel.* Anderson v. Board of Educ., 233 S.E.2d 703 (W. Va. 1977), § 3.4.

State *ex rel.* Broussard v. Gauthe, 262 La. App. 105, 265 So. 2d 828 (1972).

State *ex rel.* Daoust v. Smith, 371 N.E.2d 536 (Ohio 1977), § 6.1.

State *ex rel.* Edmundson v. Board of Educ., 2 Ohio Misc. 137, 201 N.E.2d 729 (1964), § 3.3.

State *ex rel.* Holt v. Thompson, 66 Wis. 2d 659, 225 N.W.2d 678 (1975), § 12.3.

State of Delaware v. AFSCME, 292 A.2d 362 (Del. 1972), § 5.1.

Stein v. Oshinsky, 348 F.2d 999 (2nd Cir. 1965), *cert. denied,* 382 U.S. 957 (1965), § 12.2.

United States v. Hinds County School Bd., 433 F.2d 602 (5th Cir. 1970), § 9.4.

United States v. Nansemond County School Bd., 351 F. Supp. 196 (1972), *rev'd,* 492 F.2d 919 (4th Cir. 1974), § 7.7.

United States v. Sunflower County School Dist., 430 F.2d 839 (5th Cir. 1970), § 9.4.

United States v. Texas Educ. Agency, 532 F.2d 380 (5th Cir. 1976), § 9.4.

Valent v. New Jersey State Bd. of Educ., 274 A.2d 832 (N.J. 1971), § 8.1.

Valentine v. Independent School Dist., 191 Iowa 1100, 183 N.W. 434 (1921), § 10.2.

Valter v. Orchard Farm School Dist., 511 S.W.2d 550 (Mo. 1976), § 7.5.

Van Allen v. McCleary, 211 N.Y.S.2d 501 (1961), § 13.1.

Van Buskirk v. Bleiler, 77 Misc. 2d 272, 354 N.Y.S.2d 93 (1974), § 3.2.

Vanderzanden v. Lowell School Dist. No. 71, 369 F. Supp. 67 (D. Ore. 1973), § 4.5.

Van Dusartz v. Hatfield, 334 F. Supp. 870 (D.C. Minn. 1971), § 6.5.

Vaughn v. Reed, 313 F. Supp. 431 (W.D. Va. 1970), § 12.3.

Visotcky v. City Council, 113 N.J. Super. 263, 273 A.2d 597 (1971), § 3.4.

Vorchheimer v. School Dist., 400 F. Supp. 326 (E.D. Pa. 1975), 532 F.2d 619 (5th Cir. 1977), *aff'd,* 430 U.S. 703 (April 1977), § 9.4.

Vought v. Van Buren, 306 F. Supp. 1388 (E.D. Mich. 1969), § 11.3.

Wardwell v. Board of Educ., 529 F.2d 625 (6th Cir. 1976), §§ 7.1 8.2.

Ware v. Estes, 458 F.2d 1360 (5th Cir. 1972), § 10.1.

Washington v. Davis, 426 U.S. 229, 96 S. Ct. 2040, 48 L. Ed. 2d 597 (1976), § 7.6.

Waters v. United States, 311 A.2d 835 (1973), § 10.4.

Waters v. Wisconsin Steel Workers, 502 F.2d 1309 (7th Cir. 1974), § 7.7.

Watkins v. Local 2369, United Steelworkers of America, 516 F.2d 41 (5th Cir. 1975), § 7.7.

Watson v. Cambridge, 32 N.E. 864 (Mass. 1893), § 9.3.

Watts v. Town of Homer, 301 So. 2d 729 (La. App. 1974), § 4.6.

Young v. Board of Educ., 74 Wis. 2d 144, 246 N.W.2d 230 (1976), § 12.1.

Zorach v. Clauson, 343 U.S. 306, 72 S. Ct. 679, 96 L. Ed. 954 (1952), § 12.3.

Zucht v. King, 260 U.S. 174, 43 S. Ct. 24, 67 L. Ed. 2d 194 (1923), § 9.2.

Index

A

343

C

E

L

O

OATHS.
Academic freedom.
Loyalty oaths, §8.2.

OFFICE HOLDING.
Academic freedom.
Campaigning, §8.2.
Local school districts and boards of education.
See LOCAL SCHOOL DISTRICTS AND BOARDS OF EDUCATION.

OFFICE OF EDUCATION.
Commissioner, §1.4.
Established, §1.4.

OPINIONS.
Sources of education law.
Lawyers opinions, §1.1.

P

PARENTS.
Access to student records, §13.1.

PATENTS.
Federal courts.
Jurisdiction, §1.4.

PENALTIES.
Collective negotiations.
Impasse of negotiations, §5.3.

PERIODICALS.
Index to legal periodicals, §2.9.
Tools of legal research, §2.9.

PICKETING.
Collective negotiations.
Impasse of negotiations, §5.3.

PLACEMENT.
Students.
Assignment and placement.
See ADMISSIONS.

POLICE.
Searches, §10.4.

POLITICAL ACTIVITY.
Academic freedom, §8.2.

PRAYER.
Religious activities, §12.2.

PREGNANCY.
Admission to public school, §9.4.

R

S

STATE GOVERNMENT.
Sources of education law, §1.5.

STATUTES.
Control and punishment.
Guidelines, §10.1.
Sources of education law, §1.1.
Tools of legal research, §2.1.

STRIKES.
Collective negotiations.
Impasse of negotiations, §5.3.

SUBJECTS.
Academic freedom.
Teaching of forbidden subjects, §8.1.
Collective negotiations.
Scope of negotiations.
See COLLECTIVE NEGOTIATIONS.

SUPERINTENDENTS.
Employment and job security.
Legal status, §7.2.

SUPERVISION.
Employment and job security.
Legal status of supervisors, §7.2.
Tort liability, §4.6.
Immunity, §4.6.

SUPREME COURT.
United states supreme court.
See UNITED STATES SUPREME COURT.

T

TAXATION.
Finance and taxation.
See FINANCE AND TAXATION.

TENURE.
See EMPLOYMENT AND JOB SECURITY.

TEXTBOOKS.
Religion.
Finance of religious activities, §12.1.

THIRD PARTIES.
Access to student records, §13.1.

TOOLS OF LEGAL RESEARCH.
American digest system, §2.3.
American law reports annotated, §2.7.
Index to legal periodicals, §2.9.
Law libraries, §2.0.
Legal dictionaries, §2.8.
Legal digest, §2.2.
Legal encyclopedias, §2.6.
Martindale-Hubbell.
Law digest, §2.1.